2ND EDITION

The Quick-Reference Guide to Biblical Counseling

DR. TIM CLINTON AND
DR. RON HAWKINS

BakerBooks
a division of Baker Publishing Group
Grand Rapids, Michigan

© 2009, 2024 by Tim Clinton and Ron Hawkins

Published by Baker Books
a division of Baker Publishing Group
Grand Rapids, Michigan
BakerBooks.com

Previously published in 2007 under the title *Biblical Counseling Quick Reference Guide: Personal and Emotional Issues* by AACC Press

Printed in the United States of America

Library of Congress Cataloging-in-Publication Data
Names: Clinton, Timothy E., 1960– author. | Hawkins, Ronald E., author.
Title: The quick-reference guide to biblical counseling / Dr. Tim Clinton and Dr. Ron Hawkins.
Description: Second edition. | Grand Rapids, Michigan : Baker Books, a division of Baker Publishing Group, [2024] | Includes bibliographical references.
Identifiers: LCCN 2024002302 | ISBN 9781540904461 (paper) | ISBN 9781540904508 (cloth) | ISBN 9781493446957 (ebook)
Subjects: LCSH: Counseling—Religious aspects—Christianity—Handbooks, manuals, etc. | Bible—Psychology—Handbooks, manuals, etc. | Pastoral counseling—Handbooks, manuals, etc. | Bible—Use—Handbooks, manuals, etc.
Classification: LCC BR115.C69 C48 2024 | DDC 253.5—dc23/eng/20240209

Some names and identifying details have been changed to protect the privacy of individuals.

Tim Clinton is represented by Thomas J. Winters and Jeffrey C. Dunn of Winters, King & Associates, Inc., Tulsa, Oklahoma.

Cover design by Gayle Raymer

Baker Publishing Group publications use paper produced from sustainable forestry practices and postconsumer waste whenever possible.

24 25 26 27 28 29 30   7 6 5 4 3 2 1

The
Quick-Reference Guide
to Biblical Counseling

Contents

Introduction

Since the early days of the American Association of Christian Counselors (AACC), we have been consistently asked to catalog and provide "quick-reference" materials that can be easily accessed for the variety of issues faced by mental health professionals, pastors, and lay helpers. This updated guide addresses personal and emotional issues from a biblical perspective and is accompanied by the rest of the quick-reference guides as our response to the growing mental health needs of our day. Topics for the quick-reference guides are:

Personal and emotional issues

Addiction and recovery

Marriage and family issues

Issues in human sexuality

Teenager issues

Women's issues

Singles' issues

Money issues

We are delighted to bring to your fingertips *The Quick-Reference Guide to Biblical Counseling* and trust that God will use it to bring His hope and life to millions of believers throughout America and the world, to whom the continually growing membership in the AACC minister.

Everywhere, we hear stories of people who desperately need God's touch and cry out constantly for His gracious care. The mind-boggling advances in every professional and scientific field have stoked, along with a multibillion-dollar advertising blitz, the false expectation that we can "have it all, and have it all now." This only reinforces the aching "hole in the soul" that so many suffer in the midst of our material abundance and intensifies the stress that we all live under in our 24/7 sociocultural landscape. Does an authentic remedy really exist?

Since you are reading the introduction to this book, you have likely been called to a counseling ministry, anchored in the Bible. A unique feature of this resource is its emphasis on the use of Scripture as an ally in helping the hurting with the resolution of the challenges they are facing. We believe the use of the Bible is not only helpful, but it is the foundation of truth from which our helping proceeds, and the inspired guidebook from which we derive the principles for understanding, assessing, and treating others. Any perspectives and resources needed for and used in counseling—whether they come from psychology, other sciences, classical and church history—should be logical extensions of the Scriptures and evaluated in the light of their truth-value according to the Bible.[1] You have been called and are likely trained to some degree to deliver care and consolation to the many broken-down and brokenhearted souls living in your church and community. You will find this book and this entire series most helpful if you have been called to remind others that "the LORD is close to the brokenhearted; he rescues those whose spirits are crushed" (Ps. 34:18 NLT). He has chosen you as a vessel for delivery of His special grace; you have both the privilege and the responsibility to deliver that care in the most excellent and ethical way possible.

There are a number of critical attributes that you need to exhibit toward others if you are called to intervene in someone's most needy of times—if you are called to "bear one another's burdens" in a way that will "fulfill the law of Christ" (Gal. 6:2). The first characteristic is something you have as a result of God's Spirit working in you and transforming your heart and mind—something that this book cannot give you but can only enhance if you already have it. This is a spirit of authentic kindness—the kindness that draws others to you automatically because they sense that you really do care.

This also reveals a compassionate empathy that can deeply relate to others because you too have walked a path of suffering and pain and yet have not turned bitter or cynical. Instead, you have learned to trust God in everything—especially in those things of life that you would not choose to suffer. You have found God to be faithful to you and yours, and you know Him (which is distinct from *merely knowing about Him*) to be loving and wise and strong and kind. You have truly come to know that "God is our merciful Father and the source of all comfort. He comforts us in all our troubles so that we can comfort others. When they are troubled, we will be able to give them the same comfort God has given us" (2 Cor. 1:3–4 NLT). And if you consistently deliver this comfort and care with integrity, you are a trustworthy servant in whom God delights and blesses.

Added to the twin characteristics of authenticity and empathy are the twin requirements of knowledge and skill—something this book can help deliver to you more directly. The knowledge base of biblical and theological studies, combined with the behavioral and social sciences, is advancing far faster than anyone can keep up with in the twenty-first century. Therefore, we have culled from this burgeoning data the most critical and relevant facts and contextual clues that you should know for each of the forty topics that make up the content of this and all the books to follow. Finally, the eight-step outline we follow in every section will shape your thinking and mold your process so as to increase your skill as a counselor, in whatever role you do such work.

THE THREE LEGS OF HELPING MINISTRY

We have written these books to apply to every leg of our three-legged stool metaphor. We advance the idea that the helping ministry of the church is made up of *pastors*, who serve in a central case-managing role, as the client nearly always returns to the role of parishioner; of *professional Christian counselors*, often who serve many churches in a given geographic area; and of *lay helpers*, who have been trained and serve in the church in individual or group leadership roles.

People serving at all three levels must develop both the character and servant qualities that reflect the grace and truth of Christ Himself. God has also distributed His gifts liberally throughout the church to perform the various ministry tasks that are central to any healthy church operation. For no matter how skilled or intelligent or caring we are, unless we directly rely on the Spirit of God to work in us to do the ministry of God, it will not bear kingdom fruit. He will bring to us the people He wants us to help, and we must learn to depend on Him to touch others in a supernatural way—so that people exclaim, "God showed up (and miracles happened) in that counseling session today!"

Pastor or Church Staff

If you are a pastor or church staff member, virtually everyone sitting in your pews today has been (or soon will be) touched by addiction, divorce, violence, depression, grief, confusion, loneliness, and a thousand other evidences of living as broken people in a fallen world. This guidebook will help you:

- deliver effective counseling and short-term help to those who will come to you with their issues
- teach others and construct sermons about the leading issues of the day with which people struggle
- provide essential resources and materials for staff and lay leaders in your church to advance their helping and teaching ministries

Mental Health Professional

If you are a mental health professional, licensed or certified in one of the six major clinical disciplines, you are likely already familiar with most of the topics in this book. It will assist you best to:

- review the definitions and assessment questions to use in your initial session with a new client
- understand and incorporate a biblical view of the client's problem
- shape your treatment plans with the best principles and resources available from the AACC
- deliver information to your clients that best helps them get unstuck and move forward more resolutely with the right thinking and focused action of this treatment process

Lay Leader or Minister

If you are a lay leader or minister, this book will help you plan and deliver the best care you can from beginning to end. We recommend that you read through the entire book, highlighting the material most useful to you in either individual or group formats. This guide will best help you to:

- understand and accurately assess the person's problem
- guide discussions and deliver helpful suggestions without assuming too much control or yielding too little influence
- remember key principles in the process of moving from problem to resolution more effectively
- remember the limits of lay ministry and make constructive referral to others who have more training

USING *THE QUICK-REFERENCE GUIDE TO BIBLICAL COUNSELING*

You will notice that we have divided each topic into an outline format that follows the logic of the counseling process. The goal and purpose of each of the eight parts is as follows:

1. **Portraits.** Each topic begins with a few vignettes that tell common stories about people struggling with the issue at hand. We have tried to deliver stories that you will most often encounter with the people you serve.
2. **Definitions and Key Thoughts.** This section begins with a clear definition of the issue in nontechnical language. Then we add a variety of ideas and data points to help you gain a fuller understanding of the issue and how it lives in and harms the people who struggle with it.
3. **Assessment Interview.** This usually begins by suggesting a framework by which to approach assessment and is followed by a series of specific questions to ask to gain a more complete understanding of the client's problem. There may be a section of "rule-out questions" that will help you determine whether referral to a physician or other professional is needed.
4. **Wise Counsel.** This section usually presents one or more key ideas that should serve as an overarching guide to your intervention—wise counsel will help you frame your interventions in a better way. These key insights may be cast in either clinical or pastoral form but they are useful to all three types of helpers we have noted above and will give you an edge in understanding and working with the person(s) in front of you.
5. **Action Steps.** This section—along with wise counsel—will guide you in what to do in your counseling interventions. It allows you to construct a logical map that can guide you and your client from problem identification to resolution in a few measured steps—always client action steps (with specific instructions to counselors noted in italics). For without a good action plan, it is too easy to

leave clients confused and drifting rather than moving in a determined fashion toward some concrete change goals.

6. **Biblical Insights.** Here we provide relevant Bible passages to assist you in your counseling work from beginning to end. Embedding the entire process in a biblical framework and calling on the Lord's power to do many things we cannot do solely in our own strength are essential to doing authentic Christian counseling. You may choose to give your clients these verses as homework for study or memorization or as a guide to spiritual direction, or you may want to use them as guides for the intervention process.

7. **Prayer Starter.** While not appropriate with every client, many Christians want—and even expect—prayer to be an integral part of your helping intervention. You should ask each client for his or her consent to prayer interventions, and every client can and should be prayed for, even if he or she does not join you and you must pray silently, or in pre- or post-session reflection. Prayer is usually the most common spiritual intervention used in Christian counseling, and we prompt a few lines of prayer that can serve, in whole or in part, as effective introductions to taking counseling vertically and inviting God directly into the relationship.

8. **Recommended Resources.** We list here some of the most well-known Christian resources and the best secular resources for additional reading and study. By no means an exhaustive list, it will tune you to other resources that will in turn reference further works that will allow you to go as deep as you want in the study of an issue.

ADDITIONAL RESOURCES

The AACC is a ministry and professional organization of nearly fifty thousand members in the United States and around the world. We are dedicated to providing and delivering the finest resources available to pastors, professional counselors, and lay helpers in whatever role or setting such services are delivered. With our award-winning magazine, *Christian Counseling Today*, we also deliver a comprehensive range of education, training, ethical direction, consulting, books, and conference events to enhance the ministry of Christian counseling worldwide. Visit AACC.net.

The AACC provides additional books, curricula, training, and conferences to equip you fully for the work of helping ministry in whatever form you do it. While some of these are noted in section 8 in every chapter of this book, some additional resources for your growth might also include:

The Care and Counsel Bible by Dr. Tim Clinton and many other leading contributors (Thomas Nelson, 2019)

The Struggle Is Real: How to Care for Mental and Relational Health Needs in the Church by Drs. Tim Clinton and Jared Pingleton and many other leading contributors (West Bow Press, 2019)

Competent Christian Counseling: Foundations and Practice of Compassionate Soul Care by Tim Clinton, George Ohlschlager, and many leading contributors (Water-Brook Press, 2002)

Caring for People God's Way (and *Marriage and Family Counseling* and *Healthy Sexuality*—upcoming books in the same series) by Tim Clinton, Archibald Hart, and George Ohlschlager (Thomas Nelson, 2005)

Light University also provides various church and home-based training courses on:

Caring for People God's Way
Breaking Free
Marriage Works
Healthy Sexuality
Extraordinary Women
Caring for Kids God's Way
Caring for Teens God's Way
Mental Health Coaching
Youth Mental Health Coaching

Please join us at AACC.net or at LightUniversity.com to consider other resources and services produced by the AACC for the growth and betterment of the church and the mental health profession at large.

Abortion

PORTRAITS | 1

- Sarah's life has suddenly changed, and she is now faced with a major decision. She is weeks away from graduating at the top of her class and has received a scholarship to her dream university. She attends every youth event, is a leader in her small group, and is at church every time the doors are open. But as she sees the two lines on her pregnancy test, her mind begins to race about where she should go from here.

- Luke is a college sophomore and has been dating his girlfriend for only a few months. This is Luke's first sexual relationship, and three months later, he finds out that his girlfriend is pregnant. They don't have jobs or money, but they begin to discuss marriage. His girlfriend decides they are too young and that they should not keep the baby, even though he wants to. He feels helpless and out of options.

- *God has already forgiven me; why can't I get over this?* Joanne keeps repeating these words in her head as her pastor preaches a message on abortion on Sanctity of Human Life Sunday. As she glances at her husband and two kids beside her in the pew, all she can think about is the abortion she has kept secret since college and the guilt she continues to carry. *I didn't realize what I did was wrong at the time.*

DEFINITIONS AND KEY THOUGHTS | 2

- The term *abortion* actually refers to any premature expulsion of a human fetus, whether naturally spontaneous, as in a miscarriage, or artificially induced, as in a surgical or chemical abortion. Today the most common usage of the term *abortion* applies to *artificially induced abortion*.

- A young woman with an unplanned pregnancy will need to understand that the "*quick and easy*" choice is neither *quick nor easy* but will carry repercussions for the rest of her life.

- Often a woman chooses to keep the abortion a secret, especially if she is part of a Christian community that she perceives might be judgmental or condemning. Her own family members might not know. Therefore the *grief and loss* surrounding an abortion may remain unprocessed for years.

- Abortion can involve multiple losses. These can include the loss of a child, a relationship, and the future dreams for the child.

> Nearly one in four women in the United States (23.7%) will have an abortion by age 45.[1]

- An abortion is *not only experienced as a loss but also often as a trauma*. Some of the possible side effects are a tendency to reexperience the trauma, such as distressing dreams or flashbacks, and a tendency toward denial and the attempt to avoid all thoughts or feelings associated with the abortion.
- Possible other *side effects* from the trauma of an abortion are emotional numbing, sleep disorders, difficulty concentrating, hypervigilance, depression, guilt, and an inability to forgive oneself.
- Coping alone with the reality of an abortion is isolating and may reinforce a woman's *sense of shame*. Self-destructive behaviors, such as substance abuse, may also be present.
- If someone confides in you that she has had an abortion, realize that in sharing this experience, she has decided to trust you. *Be careful with any verbal or nonverbal behaviors* that might complicate her guilt and shame.
- Men are also *affected* by abortion. They can be *unaware* of the pregnancy, feel *helpless* or *pressured* in the decision-making process, or feel *guilt, shame,* or *grief* during the process of or after the abortion has taken place.

Common Misconceptions and Myths about Abortion[2]

Myth 1: "It's a simple procedure; life will resume on Monday."
Myth 2: "It's not a baby; it's a blob of tissue."
Myth 3: "It's okay; abortion is legal."
Myth 4: "My life will be ruined if I have this baby."
Myth 5: "It's *my* choice, *my* responsibility, *my* decision."
Myth 6: "It's okay to have an abortion if there's something wrong with the baby."
Myth 7: "I am alone; no one cares about me."
Myth 8: "I don't deserve forgiveness; I knew it was wrong."
Myth 9: "I got what I deserved; I did it more than once."
Myth 10: "This won't hurt; the pain will subside."
Myth 11: "It is my only option; he doesn't want the baby."
Myth 12: "It's okay in cases of rape or incest."

> Approximately 60% of people who receive abortions are in their 20s, 25% are in their 30s, and 12% are teens.[3]

3 | ASSESSMENT INTERVIEW

For the Woman or Man Contemplating Abortion

1. How do you know that you are pregnant? Have you had a medical examination? (*These gentle questions about the pregnancy will help the counselee feel comfortable and take responsibility.*)
2. How far along are you in your pregnancy?
3. What are your current life circumstances?
4. What do you expect will be your family's response to your pregnancy?

5. Do you have adequate social support?
6. Who is the baby's father? What kind of relationship do you have with him?
7. Have you considered any other options besides abortion? Have you thought about carrying the baby to term?
8. What do you see happening in your life if you have an abortion? What do you see happening if you make a different choice? (*Often abortion is chosen because no other option looks even possible. Sometimes the decision to have an abortion is made quickly to "solve the problem." Communicate with your counselee that she has some time to make her decision. Help her see that her life will not be "ruined" if she carries her baby to term.*)
9. Do you have any questions about pregnancy and abortion? (*Do not assume that she is fully informed about either.*)

For the Woman or Man Who Had an Abortion in the Past

1. What is currently causing distress in your life?
2. Take me back and tell me what happened. (*Listen for any signs of post-traumatic stress, such as disturbing dreams or triggers that bring back the event. By choosing to begin to tell you her story, she is breaking her silence, which is the beginning of the healing process but also potentially disturbing, as denial of the event is no longer possible.*)
3. What were the main reasons at the time for your making the choice that you did?
4. Do you feel depressed, down, or sad most of the time?
5. Do you have difficulty eating or sleeping?
6. Do you have suicidal thoughts? (*If suicidal tendencies are evident, see the section on Suicide and get other help immediately.*)
7. Are you using drugs or alcohol to deal with the pain?
8. How are you managing life now? What triggers your pain?
9. Do you feel that you have been forgiven by God? Why or why not?
10. Do you feel that you can forgive yourself? Why or why not?

> In 2017, an estimated 862,320 abortions were provided in clinical settings in the United States.[4]

WISE COUNSEL | 4

Be sure to provide the woman contemplating abortion with *adequate practical support* to encourage her to carry her baby to term. Have on hand information about agencies that provide medical care and a home to stay in for pregnant women. Emphasize to her that she is making a decision for both her life and her baby's life. Encourage her to see the longer perspective rather than going to college next semester or keeping her place on a sports team. Address any *behaviors that endanger your counselee's safety*, such as suicidal behavior or substance abuse.

1. Ask God for forgiveness.
2. Accept God's forgiveness.
3. Forgive yourself.

4. Seek professional and pastoral care.

5. Visualize God holding your baby.

6. When God gives grace, serve in some capacity to help pregnant young women.

5 | ACTION STEPS

For the Woman or Man Contemplating Abortion

1. Consider Options

- You may feel that your only option is an abortion. This simply isn't so. Throughout the United States, there are nearly three thousand Pregnancy Resource Centers (PRC) staffed by volunteers who want to give true alternatives and who will lovingly help you.
- Find the nearest PRC in your community.

2. Communicate

- You will need to communicate with other family members about the situation.
- *Assess how to do that (depending on what you know of the family members). You may need to be involved as a third party in such a conversation.*

3. Get Help

- *Encourage the counselee to contact the Pregnancy Resource Center.*

4. Follow Up

- *Be sure to follow up with her by setting another appointment.*
- Although you may regret your pregnancy, you can begin immediately to make some wise choices regarding the future of your baby.

For the Woman or Man Who Had an Abortion in the Past

1. Tell Your Story

- Continue to tell your story through future counseling sessions and journaling.

2. Get Help

- Several organizations and materials exist to facilitate the healing from abortion. (*Know which ones exist in your area for a referral. Some possible organizations are Save the Storks, Susan B. Anthony List, Pregnancy and Life Assistance Network, Heartbeat International, and CARE Net.*)

3. Find Support

- *If there is a confidential grief support group in your area, encourage your counselee to attend.*

> The US abortion rate dropped to 13.5 abortions per 1,000 women aged 15–44 in 2017, the lowest rate recorded since abortion was legalized in 1973. Abortion rates fell in most states and in all four regions of the country.[5]

4. Be Reassured

- *Be sure to communicate both verbally and nonverbally your acceptance of her and God's forgiveness to her.*

Healing from an abortion is a process and certainly cannot be accomplished in one session; however, healing is possible. Reassure your counselee that forgiveness, including an ability to accept God's forgiveness and to forgive herself, is possible through God's grace.

Abortion is not the unforgivable sin.

BIBLICAL INSIGHTS 6

God is our refuge and strength,
A very present help in trouble.
Therefore, we will not fear,
Even though the earth be removed,
And though the mountains be carried into the midst of the sea;
Though its waters roar *and* be troubled,
Though the mountains shake with its swelling . . .

The LORD of hosts *is* with us;
The God of Jacob *is* our refuge.

Psalm 46:1–3, 7

Your eyes saw my substance, being yet unformed.
And in Your book they all were written,
The days fashioned for me,
When *as yet there were* none of them.

Psalm 139:16

Before I formed you in the womb I knew you;
Before you were born I sanctified you;
I ordained you a prophet to the nations.

Jeremiah 1:5

Then Herod, when he saw that he was deceived by the wise men, was exceedingly angry; and he sent forth and put to death all the male children who were in Bethlehem and in all its districts, from two years old and under, according to the time which he had determined from the wise men.

Matthew 2:16

> The new human zygote has a genetic composition that is absolutely unique to itself, different from any other human that has ever existed, including that of its mother (thus disproving the claim that what is involved in abortion is merely "a woman and her body").[6]

> The cardiovascular system is the first major system to function. At about 22 days after conception the child's heart begins to circulate their own blood, unique from that of their mother's, and their heartbeat can be detected on ultrasound.[7]

7 | PRAYER STARTER

Lord, we pray for Your grace and wisdom to overflow into _____'s life. _____ is worried, scared, and needs a word from You . . .

8 | RECOMMENDED RESOURCES

Clinton, Tim. *The Care and Counsel Bible.* Thomas Nelson, 2019.

Florczak-Seeman, Yvonne. *A Time to Speak: A Healing Journal for Post-abortive Women.* Love From Above, 2005.

Johnson, A., with Cindy Lambert. *Unplanned: The Dramatic True Story of a Former Planned Parenthood Leader's Eye-Opening Journey across the Life Line.* Tyndale, 2019.

Sproul, R.C. *Abortion: A Rational Look at an Emotional Issue.* Reformation Trust, 2010.

Websites

AACC's Reproductive Health and Sexual Trauma Division Network (AACC.net)

Choose Grace International (ChooseGrace.com)

Christian Care Connect (Connect.AACC.net)

Concepts of Truth International (InternationalHelpline.org)

Heartbeat International (HeartbeatInternational.org/Worldwide-Directory)

Save the Storks (SaveTheStorks.com)

Addictions

PORTRAITS 1

- Jason has been struggling with viewing pornography since he was a teenager. He starts using an accountability app that shares his online activity with his wife and alerts her to any suspicious activity. Jason has multiple projects and deadlines at work and seems stressed. One morning his wife receives an alert, and her heart sinks.
- When Cheryl hurt her back in a car wreck, her doctor prescribed OxyContin to relieve her intense pain. When the bottle was empty, she asked her doctor for a refill, but instead the doctor recommended over-the-counter painkillers. Cheryl wouldn't take no for an answer, so she made an appointment with another doctor, who prescribed another round of OxyContin. When that doctor refused any more refills, Cheryl found dealers who would sell to her. Now, three years later, Cheryl is on heroin, often cut with fentanyl, and her life is a disaster. She has tried to quit several times, but the withdrawal symptoms are too much to handle.
- Ralph is a senior in college and is known around the campus for how many beers he can drink at fraternity parties. However, recently his friends have noticed something has changed. He's been drunk several times recently, according to friends. You receive a call from his parents when he is arrested for a DUI.

> Use of and addiction to alcohol, nicotine, and illicit drugs cost the US more than $740 billion a year related to health care, crime, and lost productivity.[1]

DEFINITIONS AND KEY THOUGHTS 2

- Addiction is defined as "a chronic, relapsing disorder characterized by compulsive drug seeking, continued use despite harmful consequences, and long-lasting changes in the brain. It is considered both a complex brain disorder and a mental illness."
- Addiction is "the most severe form of a full spectrum of substance use disorders, and is a medical illness caused by repeated misuse of a substance or substances."[2]
- Addiction is a "treatable, chronic disorder that can be managed successfully. Research shows that combining behavioral therapy with medications, if available, is the best way to ensure success for most patients. The combination of medications and behavioral interventions to treat a substance use disorder is known as medication-assisted treatment."[3]

- People with addiction (severe substance use disorder) have an "*intense focus on using a certain substance(s), such as alcohol or drugs, to the point that it takes over their life.*"[4]
- Someone with addiction (severe substance use disorder) will have "*distorted thinking, behavior and body functions.*" Addiction can change the wiring in the brain and can cause people to have "*intense cravings for the substance and make it hard to stop using the substance.*"[5]
- If someone has a substance use disorder, they *usually build up a tolerance to the substance, meaning they need larger amounts to feel the effects.*[6]
- Someone with an addiction will *keep using the substance even when they know it will cause problems.*[7]
- There are a number of effective treatments available, and people can recover from addiction and lead normal, productive lives.[8]

Causes of Addiction

- *Emotional:* Addiction often stems from unaddressed emotional pain, trauma, or a desire to escape reality. Individuals may use substances or behaviors as coping mechanisms to numb emotional distress or fill voids.
  - *Relational:* Addiction can be fueled by relational factors, such as strained family dynamics, isolation, or a lack of meaningful connections. Seeking solace in substances or behaviors may result from unmet emotional needs and a longing for acceptance.
  - *Physical:* Some people feel pressure to improve their focus in school or at work or their abilities in sports. This can play a role in trying or continuing to use substances.[10]
  - *Social:* In this respect, teens are particularly at risk because peer pressure can be very strong. Adolescence is a developmental period during which the presence of risk factors, such as peers who use drugs, may lead to substance use.[11]
  - *Spiritual:* Addiction at its core is rebellion against God. In addition, whether it is drugs, alcohol, or sex, the addiction becomes a false idol to the addict.

> In 2016, drug overdoses killed over 63,000 people in the US, while 88,000 died from excessive alcohol use.[9]

Character of Addiction

- *Unmanageability:* For addicts, their dependency on the substance of the addiction is out of their control.
- *Neurochemical Tolerance:* God designed our bodies to adapt to what is presented. Therefore, addicts experience tolerance—their bodies need increasing amounts of a chemical/behavior to procure the same effect.
- *Progression:* Many addicts begin by simply experimenting—trying out a drug, going to a casino, taking a puff on a cigarette. However, because more is needed over time to achieve an effect, the addict will increase addictive actions in strength or frequency.

- *Feeling Avoidance:* The addiction is used to improve the addict's emotional/psychological state—it is a way of avoiding feelings, such as loneliness, anxiety, anger, and sorrow.
- *Consequences:* Estrangement from God, the manifestation of habitual sin, health issues, and social and interpersonal problems are all consequences common to addiction.

ASSESSMENT INTERVIEW 3

Remember that *a key characteristic of addiction is denial.* The substance use is rarely an issue for the user. Breaking down this denial is part of your job in assessment (if it already seems clear that dependency exists).

When interviewing the user, *focus on asking concrete questions* about circumstances, events, and symptoms. When a question is asked in a nonthreatening and nonjudgmental fashion, the counselee should respond fairly honestly. If speaking with a family member, reframe these questions and ask them about the user.

> Nearly 21 million people are grappling with substance use disorder, with only one in 10 getting treatment for the condition.[12]

Rule Outs

1. Has your use of this substance increased or decreased over the years? (*Tolerance, or the need for increasing amounts of the substance, is a key distinguishing factor between a substance abuse problem and dependency. Answering yes to the following questions about alcohol use indicates dependency as well.*)
2. (*If alcohol is the substance*) Have you ever experienced a time when you did not remember what you did while drinking (you had a blackout)? Have you ever experienced anxiety, panic attacks, shakes, or hallucinations after not drinking for a while?

General Questions

1. Has anyone ever suggested that your use of _____ is a problem? If so, why do you think the person said that?
2. Have you ever been concerned about your use of _____? If so, why?
3. How often do you use this substance and how much at each use?
4. Do you ever try to hide your use from family members or friends?
5. At what age did you first use _____?
6. Have you ever done anything while under the influence of _____ that you later regretted? Have you ever had a conviction or ticket for driving under the influence?
7. Did anyone in your family of origin use a substance in excess while you were growing up? Who?
8. Has your use of _____ ever affected your job or your family? What happened?

9. Have you ever quit using the substance? What happened when you did? How did you feel?
10. Do you want to quit for good?
11. How do you see your life improving if you can quit using _____?

4 WISE COUNSEL

Safety is always the key issue. Try to find out if the user has been driving under the influence or has small children at home who might be endangered. If so, take immediate steps to protect the user and others.

Try to speak with other family members, who are old enough to understand, about how to handle the user's behaviors, in particular driving under the influence. Family members must be taught to say no to rides with the user or to call for help if the user is unable to supervise younger children.

If physical or sexual abuse occurs when the user is under the influence, encourage *family members to leave the home immediately*, going to a relative's home or a shelter for victims of domestic violence and reporting the behavior to appropriate authorities.

If *verbal abuse* is an issue when the user is under the influence, encourage family members to seek counseling, especially counseling or group sessions for family members of addicts.

5 ACTION STEPS

1. Sign a Contract of Accountability

- *Develop a contract with the individual that states they will stop using and get immediate help for their addiction.*

2. Do Not Drive

- *Get rid of the user's car the first time he or she drives under the influence—this sets a clear boundary regarding substance abuse.*
- *To protect family members, the user, and innocent bystanders, you need to convince this person to stop driving or doing anything while under the influence.*
- *The Club and other antitheft devices prohibit driving; sophisticated electronic devices can prevent driving unless a Breathalyzer test is first passed.*
- *Point out that this is for the good of the user and others and that continued usage will cause repercussions in the rest of his or her life, such as not being able to drive to work or other places.*

3. Advise a Thorough Medical Checkup

- *A medical exam will rule out any medical problems caused by use of the substance.*
- *With an addiction such as alcoholism, treatment from a doctor is highly recommended.*

4. Connect to Professional Help

- *Allow a professional in chemical dependency to assess whether the substance use is an addiction. Such assessments are available at community mental health agencies, some hospitals, and community substance abuse centers.*

5. Encourage Family Members to Seek Support

- Your community may have support groups such as Al-Anon, Families Anonymous, or a Christ-centered 12-step recovery program. *You may need to do some research to direct the family to a good program. These programs are based on the Twelve Steps of Alcoholism, the most successful program in the world for treating addiction.*

In the past year, 25.1% of adults aged 18 and over had at least one heavy drinking day (five or more drinks for men and four or more drinks for omen).[14]

BIBLICAL INSIGHTS 6

Woe to those who rise early in the morning,
That they may follow intoxicating drink;
Who continue until night, *till* wine inflames them!

Isaiah 5:11

And I said to her, "You shall stay with me many days; you shall not play the harlot, nor shall you have a man—so, too, *will* I be toward you."

Hosea 3:3

All things are lawful for me, but all things are not helpful. All things are lawful for me, but I will not be brought under the power of any.

1 Corinthians 6:12

In the past month, 13% of persons aged 12 years and over used an illicit drug.[15]

Therefore put to death your members which are on the earth: fornication, uncleanness, passion, evil desire, and covetousness, which is idolatry. Because of these things the wrath of God is coming upon the sons of disobedience.

Colossians 3:5–6

7 PRAYER STARTER

Dear Lord, thank You that _____ has come here today to seek help for an addiction. Please help him [her] be open to considering that this might be a true addiction for which he [she] needs to get practical assistance. Lead us by Your Holy Spirit to the resources that will be most helpful and thank You for Your willingness to forgive addiction . . .

8 RECOMMENDED RESOURCES

Anderson, Neil T., Mike Quarles, and Julia Quarles. *Freedom from Addiction: Breaking the Bondage of Addiction and Finding Freedom in Christ*. Gospel Light, 1996.

Arterburn, Stephen. *Healing Is a Choice: 10 Decisions That Will Transform Your Life and 10 Lies That Can Prevent You from Making Them*. Thomas Nelson, 2007.

Clinton, Tim. *Turn Your Life Around: Breaking Free from Your Past to a New and Better You*. Faith Words, 2006.

Hart, Archibald D. *Healing Life's Hidden Addictions: Overcoming the Closet Compulsions That Waste Your Time and Control Your Life*. Vine Books, 1991.

Jantz, Gregory L. *Healing the Scars of Addiction*. Revell, 2018.

Laaser, Mark. *Healing the Wounds of Sexual Addiction*. Zondervan, 2004.

Websites

American Association of Christian Counselors (AACC.net)

Christian Care Connect (Connect.AACC.net)

Adultery

- Susanne insists that Jeremy go with her to counseling. In their first session, she complains that he has been cold, and that they haven't had sex in over four months. Jeremy insists that things are "fine," and he is just preoccupied at work. Susanne bursts into tears, "But you used to be just as busy, and you still wanted me!" Jeremy refuses to go back to the counselor with Susanne. After a few more months, however, he announces that he wants a divorce. Her attorney discovers that Jeremy has been having an affair.

- Tony knows that he and his wife Jessica have been growing distant from each other. After their youngest child goes away to college, Jessica goes back to work to resume her career. Over time, Jessica begins staying at the office later than before and is never home to have dinner with Tony. One night, a friend of Tony's notices Jessica at a restaurant with someone else, and she isn't wearing her wedding ring. When Tony confronts her about it, Jessica tells him she isn't in love with him anymore and that she has been having an affair with a coworker.

DEFINITIONS AND KEY THOUGHTS 2

- Adultery occurs when someone has a sexual relationship with *someone other than one's spouse*. This relationship may or may not include an emotional connection.

- Adultery may also involve an emotional affair. Less understood, an *emotional affair can be even more threatening* to a marriage than physical adultery. It occurs when the husband or wife turns to someone outside the marriage for primary emotional support. For example, when a couple is experiencing conflict, hostility, or distancing, and the husband or wife turns to a friend of the opposite sex for companionship, support, and sharing of personal information, an emotional affair has begun.

> He heals the brokenhearted And binds up their wounds.
> Psalm 147:3

- Tragically, infidelity in marriage is becoming *increasingly common*. Christians are just as likely to be tempted to marital unfaithfulness as non-Christians. Women are as likely to have an affair as men.

- *Poor communication, unresolved conflict, and/or unrealistic expectations* leading to marital dissatisfaction are common reasons for extramarital affairs. Any perceived need that goes unfulfilled in marriage will seek its expression elsewhere.

- Spouses may become involved in affairs because they are exposed to situations for which they are *unprepared* or *have not set wise boundaries.*
- Many affairs begin so gradually as *well-meaning friendships* that the people involved are unaware of how the relationship is changing until significant behavior occurs.
- At times, many adulterers think they are looking for love when in fact they are seeking to feel better about themselves.
- A person may be unfaithful as an act of *retaliation and anger* against his or her spouse.
- For some, as money and positions of power increase, so does an increasing *sense of entitlement* to life's pleasures. It is therefore not surprising that this can extend to the sexual realm as well.
- Ultimately, adultery is a *self-centered choice,* intentionally ignoring the needs of one's spouse and family and the commandments of God in order to satisfy one's own selfish desires.
- At its root, adultery is about a *lifestyle of deception.*

3 | ASSESSMENT INTERVIEW

For the Faithful Spouse

1. How did you find out about the affair?
2. How long have you known? When did you become aware?
3. What do you feel you need right now in light of this information?
4. What feelings has this stirred up for you? (*It is not uncommon for the person to feel a variety of emotions from resentment to sadness.*)
5. What do you want to do about your relationship with your spouse?
6. Are you willing to work with a professional counselor to explore the wounds that have been created?

You shall not commit adultery.
Exodus 20:14

For the Unfaithful Spouse

1. Have you told your spouse?
2. What prompts you to want to discuss this now?
3. Do you want to restore your marriage? (*It is not uncommon for the offending spouse to feel confused as to what he or she wants to do, especially if the affair was long-standing and/or involved a deep emotional commitment.*)

If the Unfaithful Spouse Wants to Restore the Marriage

1. Are you willing to completely cut off all ties to the third party? (*This is the most significant question. You will be able to tell a lot by how the person replies. Is there hesitation? Does he or she avoid eye contact?*)
2. Do you desire to explore the reasons that perpetuated the affair?

3. Are you aware of what needs you were seeking to have met from this relationship?

4. What do you see are the effects on your spouse as a result of your having an affair?

5. Are you willing to take full responsibility for your actions without placing any blame on your spouse?

6. Are you committed to being accountable for your time and relationships on a daily basis?

7. Are you willing to pursue professional counseling?

WISE COUNSEL 4

Is healing possible after infidelity? Yes! According to Dr. Dave Carder, "*Increasing numbers of couples are braving the path of forgiveness and the restoration of their marriages.*"[1] Before couples can begin the healing process, each spouse must be willing to complete each of the following:

- *understand what caused the infidelity in the marriage.* This requires a long, thoughtful look at the marital pattern that has developed, as well as what each person has contributed to the marital breakdown. As difficult as it is, each spouse must focus on his or her own issues as opposed to criticizing and blaming the other person for the problem of infidelity.[2]

- *rebuild trust in each other* by telling each other the truth and by being accountable to each other. It is vital for each person to keep his or her word. If one spouse promises to do something, he or she needs to follow through and do it. Trust can be rebuilt by using gestures of affection and nonsexual touch to express caring and affirmation.[3]

- *take time for restoring and enriching the marriage.* The restoration process involves identifying and reestablishing what was good about the marriage before the adultery happened. Next, the enriching process involves learning and implementing new skills and behaviors to strengthen the relationship.[4]

> National surveys indicate that 15% of women and 25% of men have experienced intercourse outside of their marriage. And, by including emotional and sexual intimacies without intercourse, these percentages increase by 20%.[5]

If the Counselee Is the Faithful Spouse

There is a normal process of grieving that occurs when someone has been deeply wounded.[6]

- *Shock and Denial.* The "No, not me" stage is when the wounded spouse is unwilling to accept the reality of the spouse's unfaithfulness. He or she may blatantly deny facts presented about the spouse's activities.

- *Anger.* The "Why me?" stage is when the person is aware of being violated and hurt and may express deep resentment and/or rage toward the unfaithful spouse.

- *Bargaining.* In the "If I do this, you'll do that" stage, the person wants to see changes in behavior as an avenue to avoid further pain. For example, he or she says, "If you stay, I'll change," rather than addressing the deeper implications of the infidelity.

- *Depression.* The "It really happened" stage is when the person realizes the full impact of the infidelity on the marriage and mourns the loss of what the relationship once was. The wounded spouse realizes he or she will need to make a decision as to the future of the relationship.
- *Acceptance.* The "This is what happened" stage is when the person has come to terms with all of the implications of the unfaithful spouse's actions and is willing to move forward.

> One of the hardest things in my life was finding out that someone I thought I knew and trusted was lying and keeping secrets from me. Discovering the one you love has been viewing pornography, sexting, or having an affair deals a devastating blow.
>
> Dr. Sheri Keffer

These stages can be experienced rapidly within a few hours, or across days or months, depending on the individual. You need to *evaluate which stage the person is currently experiencing* and gently encourage him or her to work through that stage. *Note:* The stages of grieving may be experienced out of order, several at once, and a person may repeat these stages many times.

Encourage the person to *avoid immediately making any long-term decisions.* It is not uncommon for a hurt spouse to have feelings of wanting to end the marriage because the task of rebuilding the relationship seems as though it would take too much energy.

Separation, especially if the affair has been going on for a long time, *may allow both parties time and emotional space to process feelings* and clarify the situation. The goal of separation is to *begin to build a friendship between the person you're counseling and the unfaithful spouse* and to reestablish trust between them.

Strongly encourage the person to require the unfaithful spouse to have *no further contact* with the third person and to ask the unfaithful spouse to *expose the details of the relationship* so there is no further secrecy.

If the Counselee Is the Unfaithful Spouse

- *Require full disclosure of the steps leading up to the affair,* the details of the relationship, and any information that was kept hidden.
- Remind the person that there will be *a "withdrawal" factor* as he or she breaks off any connection with the third party.
- Inform the person that he or she needs to *reengage emotionally with his or her spouse* by spending as much time as possible with him or her.
- The person will need to begin a lifestyle of *accounting for all of his or her time* to begin to rebuild trust.
- Inform the person that healing *will take time.* Developing new patterns and a commitment to learn about oneself and one's spouse on a deeper level will be involved in the healing process.
- Inform the person that *seeking forgiveness* also involves restoration and a deeper commitment to love and honor his or her spouse than has been previously given.

ACTION STEPS 5

1. Pray

Both spouses: Seek daily time before God in prayer, reading the Scriptures, and asking God for the ability to grow in Christlike attitudes and actions.

2. Have No Contact

The unfaithful spouse: You must have no contact whatsoever with the third party. Like an addiction, the way out is to go cold turkey.

3. Make a Commitment

The unfaithful spouse: You must be willing to make a radical commitment to regain the trust that has been broken.

4. Begin a New Lifestyle

The unfaithful spouse: Commit to a lifestyle of transparency and honesty. Remember, there is no area that is off-limits for inquiry.

5. Forgive

The faithful spouse: Commit to the process of forgiveness. Forgiveness is an "act" and a multilayered journey. You will often need to make daily decisions to release the hurt.

6. Work at Reconciliation

Both spouses: Remember that forgiveness is required but reconciliation is conditional. It is based on true remorse and repentance. While the Bible permits divorce for sexual infidelity, and many couples do stay together and heal, some may never be able to work through the brokenness.

7. Get Wise Counsel

Both spouses: You will need to commit to working with a counselor who can help you evaluate the communication patterns that may have contributed to the affair.

> Marriage and family are important to God, but just as important to him are the individuals within those marriages and families.
>
> Leslie Vernick

6 | BIBLICAL INSIGHTS

Trust in the LORD with all your heart,
And lean not on your own understanding;
In all your ways acknowledge Him,
And He shall direct your paths.

Proverbs 3:5–6

You have heard that it was said to those of old, "You shall not commit adultery."

Matthew 5:27

Therefore, putting away lying, "*Let* each one *of you* speak truth with his neighbor," for we are members of one another. "Be angry, and do not sin": do not let the sun go down on your wrath, nor give place to the devil.

Ephesians 4:25–27

> Whoever commits adultery with a woman lacks understanding; He *who* does so destroys his own soul.
> *Proverbs 6:32*

7 | PRAYER STARTER

Dear Lord, there is much pain here today. Hurt and betrayal are affecting this marriage. You have promised, Lord, that You are close to the brokenhearted and will bind up their wounds. You are the Healer and the Restorer. We ask for Your guidance in this painful situation . . .

8 | RECOMMENDED RESOURCES

Carder, Dave. *Torn Asunder: Recovering from an Extramarital Affair.* Moody, 2008.

Dobson, James. *Love Must Be Tough: New Hope for Marriages in Crisis.* Tyndale, 2007.

TerKeurst, Lysa. *It's Not Supposed to Be This Way: Finding Unexpected Strength When Disappointments Leave You Shattered.* Thomas Nelson, 2018.

Van Norman, Kasey. *Nothing Wasted: God Uses the Stuff You Wouldn't.* Zondervan, 2019.

Websites

American Association of Christian Counselors (AACC.net)

Christian Care Connect (Connect.AACC.net)

Aging

PORTRAITS 1

- Will and Marilyn married late and had kids even later. With their kids entering adolescence, they are confronted with the possibility of becoming caregivers for Marilyn's widowed mother who fell, breaking her hip.
- Sarah has served as a frequent volunteer for years, ever since retiring from the school district. But her health has been failing recently, and she's not sure how much longer she can live alone.
- Edward is a widower and has cancer that has spread to his liver. A church member expresses concern over his living conditions, believing that he is not caring for himself properly.

DEFINITIONS AND KEY THOUGHTS 2

- Aging is a natural process. The rate at which people age varies widely according to many factors, such as family history, emotional attitude, chronic medical conditions, and lifestyle.
- Although the risk of disability and illness increases with age, poor health is not an inevitable consequence of aging. Persons with healthy lifestyles that include regular exercise, balanced diet, and no tobacco use have half the risk for disability as those with less than healthy lifestyles.
- Caring for aging parents can be gratifying, but that depends on a lot of complex issues, such as your own health, whether you are still raising children, your financial resources, and your emotional resilience. Even though being a caregiver is laudable, it is not necessarily the wisest decision if there are other options.
- The "sandwich years" refers to the period of middle age when people are often still raising children and are also caring for their parents. They are "sandwiched" between these two generations, and it can feel like either a vice grip or a well-coordinated dance.
- As people age, their *idiosyncrasies tend to become more pronounced.* Easygoing people may continue to be laid back, but those who were uptight at a younger age may become more anxious or paranoid as they age.
- Persons entering their later years *experience many transitions and endure many losses* such as retirement; moving from parenthood to grandparent-hood;

lessened physical abilities, strength, and energy; the deaths of friends and peers; lowered social status; a tighter financial budget; and the loss of a spouse.

3 ASSESSMENT INTERVIEW

As you talk to the aging person or the family member, remember that *aging and caregiving take many forms.* Try not to project your own values on the person. The older person may value independence far more than you would think is healthy, or the family member might be convinced that anyone older than sixty-five can't be independent. *Listen first*, then gently offer a different opinion if necessary.

Rule Outs

1. If the elderly person is confused, has he or she been ill? Is there a chance of depression, dehydration, other medical problems, or poor nutrition? (*Several medical conditions and depression can mimic the symptoms of dementia, so always be sure that medical problems and depression have been ruled out by professionals before making any assumptions about a person's ability to live independently.*)
2. Is the older person lonely? (*Simple loneliness can prompt a person to reach out for help, sometimes acting needier than he or she truly is.*)

General Questions

1. What level of care do you think you [your loved one] need?
2. What are your [your loved one's] financial resources?
3. What medical issues are there? Are these issues terminal, chronic, permanent but not debilitating, degenerative and progressive? (*Clearly, if a medical condition is temporary, the future plans will be very different than if it is terminal, progressive, or chronic.*)
4. How do you feel emotionally about the possibility of needing to get more care [give care to a loved one]?
5. What family members are available to help?
6. Is the aging person in danger?

    Dangerous conditions would include:

    memory loss that leads to accidental fires, wandering, or destructive behavior

    medical conditions that require constant supervision or that contribute to sudden loss of stability or consciousness

    a residence that is deteriorated, unhealthy, or structurally too demanding (for example, too many stairs)

    an emotional state that could lead to extreme despondency or psychosis ("crazy" thinking such as paranoia)

> In God's view, aging is merely the final phase of an upward climb from earth to heaven.
>
> David Seamands

WISE COUNSEL | 4

When counseling a caregiver, impress on the person the complexity of issues related to aging and the wealth of resources for caregivers and for the elderly.

Encourage the person to *gather all the facts* (from doctors, if possible, other family members, neighbors, and others). The goal is to find out how the aging person has been doing and whether there are critical concerns.

Assess whether there is any possibility of physical or financial elder abuse or neglect.

- *Financial abuse* occurs when friends or family members take financial resources from an older person for their own benefit. This is a particular risk when the older person is confused and no longer controlling his or her own finances.

- *Elder neglect* occurs when a spouse or live-in family member deliberately neglects the needs of the older person for food, clothing, shelter, a clean environment, and protection from extremes of temperature. Sometimes this occurs inadvertently when a previously healthy spouse becomes confused or sick and is no longer able to provide a safe environment for a vulnerable spouse.

- *Elder abuse* is physical violence directed at an older person. This could be a form of domestic violence that has been ongoing for years, but the victim is now over sixty-five. Or it could be abuse of an older person by a caregiver who is a family member or a stranger.

> Twenty percent of people over 55 suffer from a mental disorder, and two-thirds of nursing home residents exhibit mental and behavioral problems. Yet, less than three percent of older adults report seeing a mental health professional for their problems.[1]

ACTION STEPS | 5

For the Older Person

Poor health and the loss of independence are not the inevitable consequences of growing older. To preserve health and independence, older persons should consider the following strategies:

1. Have Medical Screenings

- Screening to detect diseases early, when they are most treatable, saves many lives. *Older adults should be encouraged to participate in the recommended screenings.*

2. Lead a Healthy Lifestyle

- A healthy lifestyle is more influential than one's genes in helping older people avoid the decline traditionally associated with aging.

3. Consider Immunizations

- Flu shots, pneumonia vaccines, and other important immunizations can reduce your risk for hospitalization and death from illness.

4. Take Steps to Prevent Injury

- Falling is the most common cause of injury with older adults. Remove tripping hazards in your home and install handrails or grab bars in key areas, like bathrooms and hallways. These simple measures will significantly reduce your chances of falling.

5. Attend Programs That Teach Self-Management

- Consider finding programs to teach older Americans self-management techniques. These programs help older adults cope with and manage the transitions of their later years.

For Caregivers

1. Rank the Need

- With your elderly loved one rank needs in order of importance. Begin to brainstorm how these needs can be met with minimal upheaval. Most of the time, the choice is not between living alone or moving to a nursing home. There are dozens of options in between, including:

    nonmedical home care for cleaning, meals, or home maintenance

    Meals on Wheels and similar programs for delivery of meals

    help at home during key hours for things like bathing and dressing

    adult daycare during daytime hours for those who have family members with them at other times

    seniors housing complexes (apartment complexes with some extra supports available that are offered at a lower price for older folk who need help)

    shared housing with a younger person (who is not a family member)

    retirement home living (which often relieves an older person of loneliness or the need to make meals, maintain a home, and so on)

    catered/sheltered care or assisted living (situations that provide meals, some medication reminders, transportation to stores, and other support services)

    care in a private group home (where two to six older people might be cared for by a couple who make caregiving their full-time job)

    skilled nursing care

2. Consider the Effects

- Consider the effect of any changes in lifestyle on all family members, not just the older one. A change in location, for example, will affect not just the older person but also any family members who are going to be involved.

- Attempt to keep upheaval to a minimum, especially if your family life is already tense or demanding. (*Adding a family member requiring twenty-four-hour care*

> Each year, millions of older people—those 65 and older—fall. In fact, more than one out of four older people falls each year.[2]

to a household with teenagers or a special-needs child, for example, might not be the best idea.)

3. Consider All Options

- Enumerate all the options and then give all of them much prayerful consideration.
- Enlist several people—both in and outside the family—to pray about the possibilities.

The silver-haired head *is* a crown of glory, *If* it is found in the way of righteousness.
Proverbs 16:31

BIBLICAL INSIGHTS 6

You shall rise before the gray headed and honor the presence of an old man, and fear your God: I *am* the Lord.

Leviticus 19:32

Moses *was* one hundred and twenty years old when he died. His eyes were not dim nor his natural vigor diminished.

Deuteronomy 34:7

And now, behold, the Lord has kept me alive, as He said, these forty-five years, ever since the Lord spoke this word to Moses while Israel wandered in the wilderness; and now, here I am this day, eighty-five years old.

Joshua 14:10

> Lord, make me to know my end,
> And what *is* the measure of my days,
> *That* I may know how frail I *am.*
> Indeed, You have made my days *as* handbreadths,
> And my age *is* as nothing before You;
> Certainly every man at his best state *is* but vapor.

Psalm 39:4–5

> Do not cast me off in the time of old age;
> Do not forsake me when my strength fails.

Psalm 71:9

Depression in older adults may be difficult to recognize because they may show different symptoms than younger people. For some older adults with depression, sadness is not their main symptom. They may have other, less obvious symptoms of depression, or they may not be willing to talk about their feelings.[3]

PRAYER STARTER 7

Dear Lord, thank You for the life of _____ and for my life to this point. Please reveal to me/us through Your Holy Spirit what I/we should do next to meet the needs of _____. Give us wisdom and kindness. Help us to see all the options, and lead us in the direction we should go that will be best for all involved . . .

8 RECOMMENDED RESOURCES

Buchanan, Missy. *Living with Purpose in a Worn-Out Body: Spiritual Encouragement for Older Adults.* Upper Room, 2008.

Ethridge, Grant, and Tammy Ethridge. *Parenting Your Parents: A Practical Guide for Caregivers.* Harvest House, 2019.

Graham, Billy. *Nearing Home: Life, Faith, and Finishing Well.* Thomas Nelson, 2011.

Websites

American Association of Christian Counselors (AACC.net)

Christian Care Connect (Connect.AACC.net)

Anger

PORTRAITS 1

- John and his wife never seem to get along. John refuses to go to counseling, and every time his wife brings it up, he slams the door and leaves.
- Azariah doesn't think her parents understand her. All she wants to do is feel trusted by them. Instead, she yells at them every time they take her phone away.
- Shelly feels constantly under supervision at work. Every time she turns in a project, all her boss does is critique it and tell her to start over. She gets so mad that she wants to yell at him.
- Donnie is only four years old but hates when his older brother Joey steals his favorite airplane toy after he has been playing with it for hours. He throws a tantrum, and his parents only tell him to stop and never ask why he is upset.

DEFINITIONS AND KEY THOUGHTS 2

- Anger is a *God-given powerful emotion* (see Eph. 4:26) with intensity that ranges from being frustrated to severe fury. It can last from a few seconds to a lifetime. Anger itself is not a sin. What we *do* in our anger determines whether we sin.
- Anger is best understood as a *state of readiness*. It is a natural response to a real or perceived injustice, and it produces a powerful alertness that allows us to defend good or attack evil. Even Jesus showed anger (see Mark 3:5).
- Anger is *mentioned more than five hundred times in Scripture*; the only emotion in the Bible more common than anger is love. Anger first appears in Genesis 4:5 and last appears in Revelation 19:15.
- Anger can lead to *healthy or unhealthy/sinful behavior. Careful assertiveness* is a healthy response to anger that involves problem-solving and compassion. *Aggression* is an unhealthy/sinful response to anger that involves hurting or controlling others, revenge, or hatred.
- Anger, when it is an automatic response to a situation, is considered a *primary emotion*. Anger can also be a secondary emotion, meaning it is felt in reaction to another feeling, such as fear, hurt, or sadness.

> Many Christians go through life stymied in their effort to grow and live effectively, because of their failure to acknowledge, accept or understand the God-given emotion of anger. They are unaware of its dynamics or potential benefits.
>
> Gary Oliver

Expressions of Anger

Anger always finds an *expression*. It is often revealed as:

- *a response* to a person, situation, or event; to an imaginary or anticipated event; or to memories of traumatic or enraging situations
- *a response* to a real or perceived injustice or hurt—in the form of frustration, betrayal, deprivation, injustice, exploitation, manipulation, criticism, violence, disapproval, humiliation, intimidation, threats, and so on
- *a response* when a boundary in their life has been crossed

People handle anger by:

Internalization

Sometimes people *repress* the anger, meaning they deny anger's presence. This is unhealthy because even though it may not be observable, the anger is still present—turned inward on the person. Repressed anger can lead to numerous emotional and physical problems including depression, anxiety, hypertension, and ulcers.

Or people may *suppress* their anger, meaning they acknowledge anger and then stuff it. With this approach to coping, they redirect anger-driven energy into unrelated activity. This can be effective, though it neglects addressing the root causes of anger. One risk is that people who suppress may become cynical or passive-aggressive—an indirect form of revenge manifesting as sarcasm, lack of cooperation, gossip, and so on.

Ventilation

Healthy expression of anger entails nonaggressive, gently assertive actions that promote the respect of self and others. This addresses problems in a constructive manner.

Unhealthy/sinful expression involves acting in an aggressive way that hurts others. Whether one yells, uses violence, or withdraws, the motivation involves revenge or "payback." Persons expressing anger this way might say, "At least you know where I'm coming from!" However, they refuse to acknowledge the destructive force of their expression.

Physical Symptoms

Physical symptoms of anger include headaches, ulcers, stomach cramps, high blood pressure, colitis, and heart conditions.

Emotional Symptoms

Emotional symptoms include criticism, sarcasm, gossip, meanness, impatience, being demanding, withholding love, and refusing to forgive.

Levels of Anger

Irritation—a feeling of discomfort

Indignation—a feeling that something must be answered; something wrong must be corrected

Wrath—a strong desire for revenge

Fury—the partial loss of emotional control

Rage—a loss of control involving aggression or an act of violence

Hostility—a persistent form of anger; enmity toward others that becomes rooted in one's personality, which affects one's entire outlook on the world and life

> About two in 10 adults world-wide said they experienced anger (23%).[1]

Causes of Anger

External Causes

Anger can be a response to the harm someone has inflicted (a physical attack, insult, abandonment) or to a circumstance where there is no person at fault (100-degree days, physical illness, highway traffic).

Internal Causes

Anger is sometimes caused exclusively by an individual's misperceptions of reality or destructive thinking about normal life issues ("I should not have to pay taxes!"). Also memories of traumatic past events can be an internal impetus of anger, as can biologically rooted causes from medication, caffeine, or other stimulants; and health issues, such as diabetes or dialysis treatments.

ASSESSMENT INTERVIEW 3

When people seek help for anger, *the problem is often already out of control*. Also such persons may be experiencing shame and perhaps even fear because they do not yet understand how to identify and control their angry feelings. At the onset of counseling, *resist the urge to give advice*. Instead, *calmly hear the client's story*. It is important to *ask the rule-out questions* below to see if the problem is rooted in something other than anger. Then choose appropriate questions from the remaining general questions.

Rule Outs

Depression has often been described as "anger turned inward." Both men and women can express their anger as depression.

1. If 10 is extreme depression, and 1 is no depression, where are you today on a scale of 1 to 10?
2. Do you have any thoughts of hurting yourself? (*If suicidal tendencies are evident, get professional help immediately.*)

Substance abuse is often an accompanying issue.

3. Are you ever under the influence of alcohol or drugs when you experience anger? Do you use alcohol or drugs to avoid feelings of anger?

If you suspect that either depression or substance abuse is present, you should first deal with that underlying problem. Refer to the sections on *Depression* or *Addictions* in this manual. Other underlying issues include ADHD, brain trauma, personality disorders, attachment issues, and physical or sexual abuse.

General Questions

1. What makes you angry?
2. How do you express your anger? Is the way you are expressing your anger working?
3. What is your first memory of feeling out of control when you got angry?
4. Do you ever take any action to redirect your anger to a nonrelated activity?
5. Are you ever able to calm your anger? If so, how?
6. Has anger created any health issues?
7. How did you see anger expressed during childhood?
8. Could there be anger from your past that is affecting you now?
9. What was it like to be on the receiving end of someone else's anger?
10. How is the way you express your anger harming you in your relationships?
11. How often do fights get physical?
12. When you get angry, how safe do you feel? How safe do those around you feel?
13. Do others see anger in you that you do not?
14. Do you have anyone with whom to talk about your anger?
15. Will you consider forgiving the people with whom you are angry?
16. Do you pray to God about your anger?
17. Do you ever allow your anger to escalate?
18. Do you deal with your anger "before the sun goes down" (see Eph. 4:26)?

4 WISE COUNSEL

Share some information about anger with the counselee. In your own words, be sure to convey that being angry is not sinning and that anger needs to be expressed and dealt with in constructive ways.

Offer encouragement since the counselee is willing to address the problem, and stress the importance of beginning immediately to do so given the possible destructive ways that anger can be expressed. The Bible says that we should be "looking carefully lest anyone fall short of the grace of God; lest any root of bitterness springing up cause trouble, and by this many become defiled" (Heb. 12:15).

Explain the importance of following the action steps because those who repress their anger are often depressed, anxious, hostile, or have other psychological and biological problems. Those who express their anger in unhelpful ways will devastate their relationships with others. Anger leads to resentment (resentment is anger with a history), which then turns to bitterness or hostility.

Evaluate the history of anger expressed in the client's life. It is possible that the anger the client feels today is not due to a "trigger" but is instead rooted in anger from his or her past. For example, a client who is angry at his boss for being demanding

> Do not say, "I cannot help having a bad temper." Friend, you must help it. Pray to God to help you overcome it at once, for either you must kill it, or it will kill you. You cannot carry a bad temper into heaven.
>
> Charles Spurgeon

might be thinking, "This man is heartless—the same as my father was." Such anger is misdirected at the boss, who is not heartless.

ACTION STEPS | 5

The goal is not to be "anger free." Instead, it is to teach the counselee how to control his or her response to the present anger—both the emotional and biological arousals that anger may cause.

1. Recognize Triggers and Warning Signs

- Focus on the source of the anger. List the triggers (*in session and as homework*). *Until the client can control the anger, he or she should avoid the triggers as much as possible.*
- Learn to identify anger before it is out of control. How do you feel physically when experiencing anger? Do the following:
  - Identify angry feelings while they are still minor. State out loud, "I'm feeling angry right now."
  - Be aware of the first warning signs of anger, which may be physical changes. Anger promotes a sympathetic nervous system response (a physical state of readiness) and the following biological changes: rising heart rate and blood pressure, amplified alertness, tensed muscles, dilated pupils, GI tract disturbances, clenched fists, flared nostrils, and bulging veins.

He who is slow to anger is better than the mighty, And he who rules his spirit than he who takes a city.
Proverbs 16:32

2. Take a Step Back from the Situation

- Brainstorm ways to respond and not react in your anger:
  - Take a "time-out"; temporarily disengage from the situation if possible (twenty-minute minimum).
  - Perform light exercise until the intensity of anger is manageable.
  - "Write, don't fight"; jot down troubling thoughts. This exercise is personal and writings should be kept private, possibly destroyed, not sent.
- Talk with a trusted friend who is unrelated to the anger-provoking situation. Don't just vent; ask for constructive advice.
- Pray about the anger, asking God to give you insight.
- Learn the value of calming. (*A person in a state of fury is not equipped to deal healthily with an anger-provoking situation. Calming will help him or her let some of his angry feelings subside before expressing anger in a healthy way. Note: Ruminating is the opposite of calming, and makes anger worse by repeating destructive thoughts about an anger-producing event.*)

A fool vents all his feelings, But a wise man holds them back.
Proverbs 29:11

3. Learn to Express Emotions in a Healthy Way

- Brainstorm some ways for the client to express his or her anger in a healthy way:
  Respond (rational action); don't react (emotional retort).
  Maintain a healthy distance until you can speak constructively (see James 1:19).
  Confront to restore, not to destroy.
  Empathize (yelling is a failure to empathize). Speak slowly and quietly (makes yelling difficult).
  Surrender the right for revenge (see Rom. 12:19).
- If anger begins to escalate to wrath or fury, it is not the time to engage in interactions with others. Instead, temporarily redirect your energy to solo activities, or reestablish calm before confronting others.

4. Manage It

- A plan should be made for follow-up, perhaps:
  finding an accountability partner
  going to individual counseling
  joining an anger-management group
  considering medication
- You should actively continue spiritual growth if you are going to effectively manage anger. The Bible says, "The fruit of the Spirit is love, joy, peace, longsuffering, kindness, goodness, faithfulness, gentleness, self-control" (Gal. 5:22–23).
- Remember to:
  surrender—to the Holy Spirit (Gal. 5:16)
  reflect—on the mercy and love God provides (Eph. 2:4)
  pray—admit to God feelings and regrets (Matt. 5:43–45)
  forgive—choose to let go of resentment and bitterness (Eph. 4:31–32)
  avoid—ruminating and revenge (1 Cor. 10:13; 1 Peter 1:13)
  give and receive—mutual respect with those close to you (Eph. 5:22, 25)
  love—even those who anger you (1 Cor. 13)
  remember—what it was like to be on the receiving end of someone else's anger (1 Sam. 19:9–10)
  resolve—the anger issues (Eph. 4:26)
- Underlying issues such as deep emotional wounds that have been identified in counseling need to be considered. Make plans to work on such issues through additional counseling and support groups.
- When we learn to control our anger and forgive those who offend us, we are following the example of Jesus, who forgave each of us. Ephesians 4:31–32 says, "Let all bitterness, wrath, anger, clamor, and evil speaking be put away from you, with all malice. And be kind to one another, tenderhearted, forgiving one another, even as God in Christ forgave you."

BIBLICAL INSIGHTS 6

If you do well, will you not be accepted? And if you do not do well, sin lies at the door. And its desire *is* for you, but you should rule over it.

Genesis 4:7

"Be angry, and do not sin": do not let the sun go down on your wrath, nor give place to the devil.

Ephesians 4:26–27

And I became very angry when I heard their outcry and these words.

Nehemiah 5:6

> Make no friendship with an angry man,
> And with a furious man do not go,
> Lest you learn his ways
> And set a snare for your soul.

Proverbs 22:24–25

Then God said to Jonah, "*Is it* right for you to be angry about the plant?" And he said, "*It is* right for me to be angry, even to death!"

Jonah 4:9

> Hot heads and cold hearts never solved anything.
> Billy Graham

PRAYER STARTER 7

Lord, we all get angry. Anger is a powerful emotion that You have given us, and Your Word teaches us clearly about the constructive and destructive force that anger is. Teach _____ to control and process anger in a healthy way, even when threatened and wronged. Bless him [her], God, that he [she] might have wisdom and can see clearly and not hurt others in his [her] anger . . .

RECOMMENDED RESOURCES 8

Anderson, Neil, and Rich Miller. *Managing Your Anger: Resolve Personal Conflicts, Experience Inner Peace, and Win the Battle for Your Mind.* Harvest House, 2018.

Bevere, Lisa. *Be Angry, But Don't Blow It: Maintaining Your Passion Without Losing Your Cool.* Thomas Nelson, 2019.

Chapman, Gary. *Anger: Taming a Powerful Emotion.* Tyndale, 2015.

Oliver, Gary, and Carrie Oliver. *Mad about Us: Moving from Anger to Intimacy with Your Spouse.* Bethany House, 2007.

Websites
American Association of Christian Counselors (AACC.net)
Christian Care Connect (Connect.AACC.net)

Bitterness

1 | PORTRAITS

- Becky has not been to church in over a year. The leaders in her last church sided against her when she brought them concerns about inappropriate advances by a worship leader. She has tried but cannot seem to get past the bitterness. She thought her church cared for her.

- David's father was killed by a drunk driver when David was a teenager. Life was difficult for David's family after that. The driver was given only a light sentence. David is bitter at the unfairness of life.

- Adam's parents constantly belittled him as he was growing up. Now an adult, he suffers from depression and anxiety and cannot figure out why he can't get over it.

- Laura's husband does not seem interested in meeting any of her emotional needs. He is distant and cold when she tries to talk to him about it. She has given up hoping that he will ever change and sees no reason to continue in the marriage.

- Claire's boss is demanding and extremely critical. He humiliated her in front of her coworkers by judging her work unfairly. Claire can't seem to let it go and fantasizes about plots for revenge.

2 | DEFINITIONS AND KEY THOUGHTS

- Bitterness is an attitude of *extended and intense anger and hostility*. It is often accompanied by resentment and a desire to get even. It is a result of not forgiving an offender and letting the hurt and anger grow until the pain and resentment sour the person's view of life.

- Bitterness is a sin that *destroys life*. Hebrews 12:14–15 warns that bitterness corrupts by its poison. Romans 12:17–19 commands not to seek revenge, but rather let God avenge the wrong.

- Bitterness can *be conquered only by forgiveness*. Ephesians 4:31–32 says to get rid of bitterness by replacing it with forgiveness.

Key Elements of Bitterness

- *Unresolved anger*—Ephesians 4:26 says that we can be angry without sinning. But when anger is unresolved and allowed to ruminate, it turns into bitterness.

- *Inability to grieve*—Relationships that do not live up to expectations and that fail to meet legitimate needs can result in feelings of sadness and loss. When people are unable (or unwilling) to face the reality that their needs are never going to be met by a certain relationship, the result can be bitterness. Taking time to grieve the loss is an important prerequisite to becoming free from bitterness. When people refuse to admit that the relationship will never become what they had hoped, the refusal causes bitterness. "Hope deferred makes the heart sick" (Prov. 13:12).
- *Lack of control*—When other people do not meet a person's needs, he or she can become obsessed with thoughts like, "*If they would just do this . . .*" Give it up! People may never do what someone else desires or expects, and they can't be made to. We can control only ourselves; much bitterness could be avoided if people accepted this truth.

Key Characteristics of Bitterness

resentment

obsessive thoughts of revenge

sarcasm

critical or unkind comments

self-righteousness

conflicts with others

hostility

aggressiveness in relationships

controlling behavior

> Acrid bitterness inevitably seeps into the lives of people who harbor grudges and suppress anger, and bitterness is always a poison. It keeps your pain alive instead of letting you deal with it and get beyond it. Bitterness sentences you to relive the hurt over and over.
>
> Lee Strobel

ASSESSMENT INTERVIEW 3

At first, just listen to the client's story. *Show empathy by listening closely* with appropriate feedback and restating emotions to make sure you understand what the person is saying. Bitterness may not be the presenting problem a client brings to counseling, but *it is often the real problem* underneath. Gently lead the client through the following questions to help him or her come to this realization.

If any of the questions hit a nerve, bring back a memory, or upset the client, *stop the questions and deal with that issue.* Let the person talk about it further; show compassion for the pain he or she is feeling. The goal is to help, and this is the purpose of the questions. It is not necessary to have the client answer all the questions.

Rule Outs

1. On a scale of 1 to 10 with 10 being contentment and joy and 1 being total despair, where are you today?
2. Do you use alcohol or drugs to escape your hurt and bitterness?

3. Do you feel you might hurt yourself or others? (*If you suspect that depression or substance abuse is present, you should deal with that along with the bitterness. Research shows that both issues need to be dealt with for full recovery. Refer to the sections on Addictions and Depression. If you think the person is suicidal, make out a safety contract in which he or she promises not to hurt themself without first calling you. If your client calls you, take him or her to the hospital to be placed in a safe environment and get professional help. See the section on Suicide.*)

General Questions

1. What brought you to counseling today?
2. What things have you already tried to deal with this problem?
3. What do you hope will happen as an outcome of counseling?
4. Let's start by getting some background information that will help me get to know you better. Tell me about the family you grew up in, about your mother, father, sisters, brothers, and anyone else who lived in your home or was an important part of your life. (*Attitudes toward life are molded in the family of origin, so it's important to see who and what shaped your client into the person he or she is today. This will help you understand your client and his or her reactions, and help the client understand themself.*)

   Tell me about your adult life, your job, your marriage, your children, your church. (*Ask these questions one at a time, but the general idea is to get the person talking about his or her life and how this problem has affected it.*)
5. It sounds as though you have been hurt a lot in your life. Do you feel bitter about that? (*The client may not admit to bitterness. Other feelings like anger, frustration, or disappointment may arise. You may have to help them see how these feelings can or have turned to bitterness.*)
6. When did you first notice feelings of bitterness?
7. What events led to those feelings?
8. How has this bitterness affected your quality of life?
9. Can you remember anyone else in your life being bitter?
10. How did it affect that person?
11. What effect did that person's bitterness have on you?
12. What feelings did you have when this person or event first caused offense or made you bitter?
13. Tell me why you were angry and what hurt your feelings. (*Often people feel anger when first offended because they are hurt, but underneath the hurt are expectations and underneath the expectations are needs.*)
14. What expectations did you have from the person who hurt you?
15. What need did you have that the person failed to meet?
16. Do you think that person will ever meet your need? Why or why not?
17. Can you accept that?
18. Can you forgive the person for that? (*If forgiveness is a tough sticking point, refer to the section on Forgiveness and work through it in a separate session.*)
19. What would forgiveness look like?
20. Where else could you get your need met?

Let all bitterness and wrath and anger and clamor and slander be put away from you, along with all malice.

Ephesians 4:31
ESV

WISE COUNSEL | 4

Share some information about what bitterness is. If the client does not realize that the root of his or her problem is bitterness, it will help the person see what is going on in his or her life. Share the results of bitterness and the destruction it causes.

Empathize with your client. Help him or her acknowledge legitimate needs that were not met (usually by a parent or spouse). Validate the loneliness and sadness of not having needs met. *Rephrase what your client is saying* so he or she knows you're hearing the real meaning and that you care about the pain.

Explain the importance of following the action steps to get rid of bitterness. Bitterness is a poison that will destroy the person's relationships with others and hurt his or her relationship with God. When people are bitter, they cannot experience a full and healthy relationship with God. Forgiveness is the only way to get rid of bitterness and restore relationships with God and others.

ACTION STEPS | 5

1. Accept

- Make a list of the persons who have hurt you.
- Next to each name, write what you needed from that person.
- Next to that, write how it made you feel when that person did not meet your need.
- In the last column write whether you think the person will ever be able to meet your need. Be honest.
- Accept your loss and grieve it.

2. Forgive

- Ask God to help you forgive. Forgiveness is letting go of anger and your quest for revenge. Realize that you are powerless to forgive through your own strength, but God does not ask you to do something without giving you His strength and power to do it. (*Refer to the section on Forgiveness.*)
- Ask God to help you feel compassion for your offender. Psalm 78:38 says that God is full of compassion.

3. Break the Chain

- Bitterness often runs through families. When a parent does not meet a child's needs, that child can become bitter and is then unable to meet his or her own child's needs. The chain can continue through several generations.
- Ask God to help you break the chain with your generation. (*You may need to help your client say this prayer.*)

> Overcoming bitterness happens when we gain contentment. This does not mean losing sorrow or saying goodbye to discomfort. Contentment means sacrificing itchy cravings to gain a settled soul.
>
> Joni Eareckson Tada

- (*If the client has a bitter parent, help him or her see the parent as emotionally wounded.*) Just as you would not expect a person in a wheelchair to run a marathon, don't expect someone who is emotionally troubled to meet your needs—that person cannot. Ask God to help you have empathy for him or her.

4. Look Elsewhere

- Find somewhere else to get your needs met. If you are an emotional orphan, God will provide people to meet your needs.
- Be proactive and look for those God has provided to meet your needs.
- Join a women's or men's group or look for a prayer partner.
- If your mother did not meet your need for love and acceptance, find an older woman in the church who would be willing to mentor you. She can give you the love and acceptance your mother never could. Finding a man to mentor you as a father may also meet your need.
- If your husband or wife will not meet your need for friendship and intimacy, look around and see if there is a friend (of the same sex) or family member who is willing to be your friend and kindred spirit. Give of yourself to that person and meet each other's needs.

6 BIBLICAL INSIGHTS

Let all bitterness, wrath, anger, clamor, and evil speaking be put away from you, with all malice. And be kind to one another, tenderhearted, forgiving one another, even as God in Christ forgave you. Therefore be imitators of God as dear children. And walk in love, as Christ also has loved us and given Himself for us, an offering and a sacrifice to God for a sweet-smelling aroma.

Ephesians 4:31–5:2

Then Saul was very angry, and the saying displeased him; and he said, "They have ascribed to David ten thousands, and to me they have ascribed *only* thousands. Now *what* more can he have but the kingdom?" So Saul eyed David from that day forward.

1 Samuel 18:8–9

> Can *anyone* teach God knowledge,
> Since He judges those on high?
> One dies in his full strength,
> Being wholly at ease and secure;
> His pails are full of milk,
> And the marrow of his bones is moist.
> Another man dies in the bitterness of his soul,
> Never having eaten with pleasure.

Job 21:22–25

> Strive for peace with everyone, and for the holiness without which no one will see the Lord. See to it that no one fails to obtain the grace of God; that no "root of bitterness" springs up and causes trouble, and by it many become defiled.
>
> Hebrews 12:14–15 ESV

But I say to you who hear: Love your enemies, do good to those who hate you, bless those who curse you, and pray for those who spitefully use you.

Luke 6:27–28

Repent therefore of this your wickedness, and pray God if perhaps the thought of your heart may be forgiven you. For I see that you are poisoned by bitterness and bound by iniquity.

Acts 8:22–23

Pursue peace with all *people*, and holiness, without which no one will see the Lord: looking carefully lest anyone fall short of the grace of God; lest any root of bitterness springing up cause trouble, and by this many become defiled.

Hebrews 12:14–15

PRAYER STARTER 7

Lord, I thank You that _____ has come in today to talk about this painful situation. I thank You, Lord, that while people often disappoint us, You never do. You have promised to meet all of our needs . . .

RECOMMENDED RESOURCES 8

TerKeurst, Lysa. *Forgiving What You Can't Forget: Discover How to Move On, Make Peace with Painful Memories, and Create a Life That's Beautiful Again*. Thomas Nelson, 2020.
Viars, Stephen. *Overcoming Bitterness: Moving from Life's Greatest Hurts to a Life Filled with Joy*. Baker Books, 2021.
Worthington Jr., Everett. *The Power of Forgiving*. Templeton Press, 2005.

Websites
American Association of Christian Counselors (AACC.net)
Christian Care Connect (Connect.AACC.net)

Burnout

1 │ PORTRAITS

Desire without knowledge is not good, and whoever makes haste with his feet misses his way.

Proverbs 19:2 ESV

- Jane hangs up the phone. The nursing home called again; her mother is refusing to eat. Can Jane please come immediately? When Jane gets into her car, she is surprised by the waves of anger that she feels. It seems as though it is up to her to take care of everything. Lately it's been a blur as she moves from caring for her children and her husband to her students and her mother. It seems that everyone always needs something, and lately she is beginning not to care.
- Tom was barely ever home. The new job, while lucrative, had him on the road much of the week. Travel was exhausting, so even when he was home, he barely had the energy to keep up with his two-year-old.
- Cherri is a good student—maybe too good. She's involved in a score of activities and taking advanced classes. She's starting to have difficulty sleeping, she can't relax, and at times, she can't even focus. She's starting to think that nothing she does is good enough, and so she may not even apply to college.

2 │ DEFINITIONS AND KEY THOUGHTS

- Western culture continues to push the limits, has become increasingly obsessed with the "pursuit of excellence," and burnout has reached *epidemic proportions*, even within the church.
- Burnout is a stressful state characterized by *physical, emotional, and mental exhaustion, chronic fatigue, and lethargy.*
- Someone experiencing burnout may
  feel cynical toward life
  have a strong desire to escape
  experience a false sense of failure
  display emotional distancing, numbing, or apathy
  become hypercritical
  experience negative feelings toward others
  show inappropriate anger or sadness
  succumb to depression
  endure a resulting physical illness
  abuse alcohol or drugs

- Burnout is often experienced by those in the *helping professions*, such as clergy, doctors, teachers, police officers, social workers, and others who work extensively with people. It is thought to result from the excessive demands that others place on their energy, time, and resources.

- Burnout can also be felt by *caregivers of the chronically ill* or by overburdened parents. These people often feel trapped by the demands of others, isolated, and unable to find sufficient time for rest and relief.

ASSESSMENT INTERVIEW 3

1. How are you feeling physically? (*If people are experiencing burnout, chances are they haven't been caring for themselves physically. If your client hasn't had a recent physical, recommend that he or she have one.*)
2. How are you feeling emotionally?
3. How long have you felt like this?
4. When did these feelings start?
5. What prompted you to seek help now?
6. What are the stressors in your life?
7. How large a part does each stressor play in your stress level?
8. What kind of support do you get—both with your responsibilities and for yourself personally?
9. How do you perceive yourself? (*For example, someone who feels that he or she must meet all the needs of an aging parent to be a "good" child is going to experience failure.*)
10. What do you do for fun?
11. Are you able to relax?
12. What do you do when you relax?
13. What are the activities you're currently involved in?
14. How would you prioritize these activities?
15. What can be taken out of your schedule?
16. What can be put into your schedule to help you have downtime and family time?
17. What would keep you from doing that?
18. What is the worst thing that will happen if you say no or pull out of certain responsibilities?
19. What will happen if you do nothing?

> Because what you give your attention to is the person you become. Put another way: the mind is the portal to the soul, and what you fill your mind with will shape the trajectory of your character. In the end, your life is no more than the sum of what you gave your attention to.
> John Mark Comer

WISE COUNSEL 4

Any *physical concerns* and issues should be addressed medically.

Try to help the counselee gain some *immediate short-term relief* from his or her responsibilities.

Try to help your counselee *mobilize family members and friends* to begin sharing more of the load. Ironically, someone who is overburdened needs this help the most and is often least able to ask others to provide it.

There is both a *short-term crisis component* to helping someone who is burned out and a *longer-term component* of helping the person begin to live life in such a way that burnout doesn't recur. When someone is burned out and overstressed, immediate relief is essential—getting adequate sleep and relaxation and exercise. Then as the person begins to recover, helping him or her look at some lifestyle issues that caused burnout will be important to prevent burnout from recurring.

5 | ACTION STEPS

1. Take Control

> In a national survey, 76% of respondents said workplace stress "had a negative impact on their personal relationships," 66% have lost sleep due to work-related stress, and 16% have quit jobs because stress became too overwhelming.[2]

- Don't relinquish control of your schedule to the whim of everyone else.
- Put a concrete plan in place to relieve yourself of some of your responsibilities. Enlist the aid of family members and friends. (*Name this as a crisis and help the counselee see his or her need for others' help and care.*)
- *For the school student:* find the balance between what is essential and what is merely "extra."
- Schedule days more sanely, humanely, and relationally.[1]

2. Say No

- *No* is a very helpful word—and often the overworked don't know how to say it.
- While some things can't be dropped (the student has to do the homework; the businessman has to travel), there may be creative ways to schedule your time that will allow for less stress and more rest.

3. Seek God's Will

- God never guides you into an intolerable scramble of overwork—after all, Jesus didn't live that way.[3]
- Before you say yes to any new activity, pray about it. Even if it's a good activity, now may not be the time.

4. Slow Down

- Consciously slow the pace of your life.[4]
- Take the time you need to replenish your resources.

5. Set Priorities

- You may get less done, but you'll be doing the right things.[5]
- When you think about what really matters, much of your frenzied activity will be seen for what it is.

BIBLICAL INSIGHTS | 6

Then God blessed the seventh day and sanctified it, because in it He rested from all His work which God had created and made.

Genesis 2:3

So the LORD said to Moses: "Gather to Me seventy men of the elders of Israel, whom you know to be the elders of the people and officers over them; bring them to the tabernacle of meeting, that they may stand there with you. Then I will come down and talk with you there. I will take of the Spirit that *is* upon you and will put *the same* upon them; and they shall bear the burden of the people with you, that you may not bear *it* yourself alone."

Numbers 11:16–17

But those who wait on the LORD
Shall renew *their* strength;
They shall mount up with wings like eagles,
They shall run and not be weary,
They shall walk and not faint.

Isaiah 40:31

Come to Me, all *you* who labor and are heavy laden, and I will give you rest. Take My yoke upon you and learn from Me, for I am gentle and lowly in heart, and you will find rest for your souls. For My yoke *is* easy and My burden is light.

Matthew 11:28–30

And He said to them, "Come aside by yourselves to a deserted place and rest a while." For there were many coming and going, and they did not even have time to eat. So they departed to a deserted place in the boat by themselves.

Mark 6:31–32

> Do not be anxious about anything, but in everything by prayer and supplication with thanksgiving let your requests be made known to God.
>
> Philippians 4:6 ESV

PRAYER STARTER | 7

Dear Lord, Your child is tired—exhausted. He [she] wants to do so much for You and feels so much responsibility, yet we know that You never call us to burn out. We pray today that You'll help _____ determine what You would have him [her] do—Your priorities, Your will. Help him [her] discern what can be let go and what should be brought in so that life is in balance . . .

8 | RECOMMENDED RESOURCES

Allen, Jennie. *Nothing to Prove: Why We Can Stop Trying So Hard*. Penguin Random House, 2018.

Comer, John Mark. *The Ruthless Elimination of Hurry: How to Stay Emotionally Healthy and Spiritually Alive in the Chaos of the Modern World*. Penguin Random House, 2019.

Murray, David. *Reset: Living a Grace-Paced Life in a Burnout Culture*. Crossway, 2017.

Simpson, Amy. *Anxious: Choosing Faith in a World of Worry*. IVP Books, 2014.

Websites

American Association of Christian Counselors (AACC.net)

Christian Care Connect (Connect.AACC.net)

Death

PORTRAITS | 1

- Dave is forty-six and enjoying life when he is hit by a car and killed while jogging. His wife comes home from work to a mysteriously empty house—and then a police car pulls into the driveway.
- Millie is recovering from a heart attack in the hospital when another massive attack occurs and her heart stops instantly. Her son finds her dead on the floor of her hospital room.
- Melanie and Robert were so excited to add Rebecca to their family of five, but when the little girl is two, a routine physical shows she has a rare and fatal disease. The couple spends the next year and all their money, including the equity in their home, to get the best care possible for their beloved Rebecca. During that year, there are few hopeful signs, but they never give up. Gradually, they are forced to face the hard fact: little Rebecca is slipping away. When she takes her last breath, Melanie and Robert are crushed. They are angry with God, with each other, with doctors, nurses, and everyone else who had tried to save their little girl's life.

DEFINITIONS AND KEY THOUGHTS | 2

- *Death was not God's original desire* for humanity. God created human beings for life not death. Adam had received the breath of life (see Gen. 2:7). It was not until Adam and Eve sinned that death arrived.[1]
- Death is difficult because it is *loss*—real and painful because a loved one is gone; symbolic because it reminds us of lost innocence, sin, and punishment.[2]
- Death is distasteful and dreaded by humans, though God describes it as a gateway to a glorious new day. *Humans see death as an end* of a journey; God sees it as the beginning of a journey to a better life.[3]
- Responses to death are as *different* as are individuals.
- The bereaved may *ask questions* like, "Why did God take him away?"; "Why did I get mad at her before she left the house?"; "What was I thinking when I let him go without me?"; "What if . . . ?"; "Why . . . ?"
- Sudden death can lead to a *complicated grieving process* because the suddenness often leaves feelings of anger, guilt, and abandonment.

For to me, to live *is* Christ, and to die *is* gain.
Philippians 1:21

- We now know that there are "stages" of grief as described by various theorists. On hearing of a death, two stages are particularly serious: *shock* and *denial*. *Shock* is an emotional and physical response to the news of a sudden death. The bereaved person may experience a racing heartbeat, shortness of breath, and feelings of unreality.
- *Denial* may follow quickly, and the bereaved person may start doing ordinary things like washing the dishes or balancing a checkbook in an attempt to reestablish normalcy. Denial is usually broken when the person must face up to the many decisions that follow a death.

The Grieving Process

Elisabeth Kübler-Ross and David Kessler developed five stages of grief and loss.

1. **Denial**.[4] The "no, this cannot be real" stage is often the first reaction to learning about the loss of a loved one. Denial is often the first defense mechanism to the loss that has occurred.
2. **Anger**.[5] The "why me?" stage is when people dealing with grief and loss are angry at themselves, others, or the person they lost.
3. **Bargaining**.[6] In the "if I do this, you'll do that" stage of grief and loss, people often find themselves bargaining with God. Often, those in this stage will try to bargain with God for a different scenario to try to remove themself from the pain they currently feel.
4. **Depression**.[7] The "it really happened" stage is when the person realizes the full impact of the death of their loved one. Feelings of apathy, lack of appetite, and lack of energy are common examples of depression. Often, those in this stage can feel a sense of despair, isolation, emptiness, and loss of hope.
5. **Acceptance**.[8] The "I am at peace with what has happened" stage is when the person has come to terms with the finality of the loss. They will still feel the pain of the loss; however, their emotions will begin to stabilize, and they begin to move forward.

3 ASSESSMENT INTERVIEW

Don't be surprised by the variety of responses people have to the death of a loved one. People may do bizarre things in the moments after hearing of a death. It is common for a person to say things like, "Why not me instead?" or "I think I caused it." These are not necessarily true confessions; they are the *cries of a breaking heart*.

Don't rush the grieving process. The anguish is a necessary part of recovery.

Don't tell the person how to feel. Your presence as a loving and attentive listener is your greatest gift to the person who is overwhelmed by grief.

Rule Outs

1. Are you having any physical symptoms as a result of this death? (*Be aware of signs of physical distress; the bereaved person may need medical attention.*)
2. Are you feeling increasingly depressed and suicidal? Is the grief beginning to subside? (*After a certain amount of time, the grief should be lessening. There will always be pain, but if the person is not improving over the course of several weeks, other intervention may be needed.*)

Questions Immediately after a Death

1. Tell me about your loss. Were you present? (*Ask the bereaved to share with you what happened. Talking about the experience is cathartic and will help the bereaved person come to terms with the situation.*)
2. Where are other family members located? (*What kind of a support system exists for helping the person through the experience of loss?*)
3. If the deceased had children, where are they? (*Are there any other individuals who will need help dealing with the loss of the deceased?*)
4. Besides the obvious shock and pain, what else are you feeling right now? (*Probe for feelings like guilt, anger, and fear. Try to identify the source of the feelings—and then make a mental note to talk further about it at a later time.*)

Questions to Help the Grieving Person

1. What are your favorite memories about this person?
2. What did you like best about him [her]?
3. What were his [her] best qualities? What were some things that bothered or irritated you? (*This helps the person realize that the deceased person was not perfect.*)
4. When do you miss this person the most—morning or evening?
5. To whom do you talk when you think about this person?
6. What do you need from the person you're talking to that will help with your grief?
7. Do you still cry when you think of this person?
8. In what ways is your life better for having known this person?
9. In what positive ways can you keep alive the good memories and the joy of having known this person?

> The Bible says that as long as we are here on Earth, we are strangers in a foreign land. There are enemies to be conquered before we return home. This world is not our home; our citizenship is in heaven.
>
> Billy Graham

WISE COUNSEL 4

Remember that your compassionate presence means more than anything to those who are suffering the loss of someone they love. Don't give simplistic answers, and, by all means, don't share Romans 8:28 . . . at least for the first month or two after the funeral. Many people instinctively ask "why"—especially in the death of a child, young person, or someone in their prime—but this isn't an invitation for quick answers to life's biggest mysteries. If they ask this question, it's appropriate to say something like, "I can't give you an answer, but it's a good question for later. We'll talk about it sometime."

Some bereaved people may feel very overwhelmed by the decisions required after a death. Others will argue with family members over decisions, such as cremation versus burial or open versus closed casket. Your first job may be to *help the family and friends come to consensus, but remind them to respect the deceased's wishes, even if they don't agree with them.*

Be affirming, compassionate, and patient. When the time is right (often weeks or even months later, and at the request of the person), share passages of hope and comfort that have been meaningful to you. When a loved one dies, the loss is acute, and knowing that the person is in heaven is not always an immediate comfort to those who are left behind—because they are left behind.

When dealing with a sudden death, *identify a family friend or other volunteer who can help with some of the practical tasks* that must be done for the funeral. Help the bereaved person prioritize what needs to be done. Aid in identifying a funeral home, writing an obituary, calling other family members and friends, and other tasks. It should be noted that the process of grief and bereavement will *not be resolved by things returning to "normal,"* as the person understands it. A death always drastically changes the identity, roles, and responsibilities of the person closest to the deceased. Recovery will come as the bereaved person learns to *cope with and take on the new dynamics and tasks of daily life.*

5 | ACTION STEPS

1. Focus on Basic Needs

For as by a man came death, by a man has come also the resurrection of the dead.

1 Corinthians 15:21 ESV

- Be sure to focus on basic needs—food, shelter, safety. If these needs are not met, the critical emotional issues will be even harder to handle.
- *People who are experiencing shock may neglect hygiene, necessary medications, or meals.*

2. Discover the Best Ways of Coping

- *Assess the level of emotions present by using some of the questions suggested above.*
- Some people process crisis emotions better by being busy while others need to be alone. Help the former to find something simple to do and help the latter find a quiet place to be alone.

3. Seek Social Interaction

- Do not withdraw from social interactions. Find support in your friendships.
- Some friendships will be different (for example, if a spouse has died), but your friends will still want your company, even without the other person.

4. Help the Children

- *If children are involved, counsel the family on strategies for helping them.* Children often feel responsible for a sudden death, and teens can react in particularly complicated ways if a relationship with the deceased was tense.
- Children need, first of all, to feel secure. Reassure them that their family will be okay.
- *If a parent is in acute distress, try to ensure that the children are cared for by a familiar person who is calm.*
- Avoid statements that indicate to a child that God caused the death because He "wanted Mom/Dad/Grandma/Johnny in heaven with Him."
- Demystify death for children. Most funeral directors will openly answer a child's curious questions.
- Help children begin to process feelings of anger, guilt, and abandonment. They need to know that such feelings are normal.

5. Allow Time

- It will take time for the pain to subside.
- You need to truly grieve. The grieving process is healthy.
- *Remind the person, when appropriate, of the stages the grieving person goes through.*

BIBLICAL INSIGHTS 6

But now he is dead; why should I fast? Can I bring him back again? I shall go to him, but he shall not return to me.

2 Samuel 12:23

Precious in the sight of the Lord
Is the death of His saints.

Psalm 116:15

But now Christ is risen from the dead, *and* has become the firstfruits of those who have fallen asleep. For since by man *came* death, by Man also *came* the resurrection of the dead. For as in Adam all die, even so in Christ all shall be made alive.

1 Corinthians 15:20–22

So *we are* always confident, knowing that while we are at home in the body we are absent from the Lord. For we walk by faith, not by sight. We are confident, yes, well pleased rather to be absent from the body and to be present with the Lord.

2 Corinthians 5:6–8

> More than 2.5 million people die every year in the United States, and 60 million worldwide, each leaving behind a variable number of close attachments, roughly estimated as one to five per person.[9]

I have fought the good fight, I have finished the race, I have kept the faith. Finally, there is laid up for me the crown of righteousness, which the Lord, the righteous Judge, will give to me on that Day, and not to me only but also to all who have loved His appearing.

2 Timothy 4:7–8

"Blessed *are* the dead who die in the Lord from now on." . . .
"That they may rest from their labors, and their works follow them."

Revelation 14:13

7 | PRAYER STARTER

Dear Lord, thank You for the life of _____. Our hearts are very heavy that he [she] is no longer here. Although this death may make no sense now, please bring sense from it, and glorify Yourself through it. Give us Your Holy Spirit as a Comforter in the minutes and hours and days to come and help us to understand each other's needs at this time . . .

8 | RECOMMENDED RESOURCES

Graham, Billy. *Nearing Home: Life, Faith, and Finishing Well*. Thomas Nelson, 2011.
MacArthur, John. *Safe in the Arms of God: Truth from Heaven About the Death of a Child*. Thomas Nelson, 2003.
Pitts, Jonathan. *My Wynter Season: Seeing God's Faithfulness in the Shadow of Grief*. Thomas Nelson, 2021.
Wright, H. Norman. *Experiencing Grief*. Broadman & Holman, 2004.

Websites
American Association of Christian Counselors (AACC.net)
Christian Care Connect (Connect.AACC.net)

Decision-Making and the Will of God

PORTRAITS 1

- Gracie has always been a bright student. Now a number of universities have accepted her application for enrollment. For the first time in her life, she feels as though she doesn't have the answer. Which school does God want her to attend?
- Casey has been dating Madison for more than two years. He is thinking of proposing to her, but with a lifelong decision such as this, he wants to make sure that this is what God would have him do.
- A great new job opportunity has just surfaced, but at forty-five, Paul is not sure if he can handle another career change. He is also wondering if his family is up for the challenge. He wishes he knew if this is God's plan.
- Mary wants to get a divorce. She's met another man and wants a counselor to tell her that it's okay for her to make that decision. She thinks the grass is much greener on the other side of the fence.
- Bill and Margaret don't know what to do with their son Jeremy. They paid a lot of money for him to graduate from college, but he has moved back in with them, and he has taken a job that doesn't provide enough income for a place of his own . . . and he seems just fine with his situation. They've made plenty of suggestions, too many in fact. They're exasperated. They believe he's wasting his education and his life, and they're asking for help.

DEFINITIONS AND KEY THOUGHTS 2

- *Do not tell the person what he or she should do*, even if it seems obvious to you. The person is seeking God's will, not yours.
- Encourage the counselee to *wait on God's answer*. He will reveal His will to those who earnestly seek Him. And remember that God is much more patient than we are.
- Do not allow *superstitions* to enter into the decision-making process (such as blindly pointing to a passage in the Bible or following some dream or coincidence). God uses His Word, not luck or superstition.
- God is most interested in a *relationship* in which we lean on Him daily for our strength and guidance. He will not show a person his or her entire life's journey. He wants us to rely on Him throughout our lives.

> I will instruct you and teach you in the way you should go; I will guide you with My eye.
>
> Psalm 32:8

- Decision-making can be *fearful* for some people. They speak of past decisions that ended disastrously. Of course, this doesn't mean that God wasn't in those earlier decisions.
- Be careful not to put too much credence in a person's feelings. *Emotions can be misleading* and may cause a person to sin. Often people will quote Psalm 37:4 and say that God wants to give them the desires of their heart. This is true only after the first half of that verse is fulfilled, which is that they should be delighting themselves in the Lord.

3 | ASSESSMENT INTERVIEW

God has put it in the heart of all Christians to want to know and follow His will. There are, of course, several dilemmas: From time to time, all of us are confused about what His will is for us at that moment, and many people expect God to make every decision crystal clear.

As we study the Bible, we realize some things are, in fact, clear and unmistakable, but many (perhaps most of those we encounter every day), aren't as clear as we'd like. It helps to understand the different types of the will of God:

Directive Will[1]

God's directive will is His specific, absolute, unchangeable, unconditional will. Examples of God's directive will are:

Assemble with others in worship (Heb. 10:25).

Marry only another Christian (2 Cor. 6:14).

Raise children by God's standards (Eph. 6:4).

Obey and honor parents (Eph. 6:1–2).

Support one's own family (1 Tim. 5:8).

Proclaim Christ (Acts 1:8).

Meditate on the Scriptures (Ps. 1:2).

Show love to others (1 Corinthians 13).

Discerned Will

Many of the choices we make each day don't have clear biblical mandates or guidance. Should we eat pizza or a tuna sandwich for lunch? Should we call a friend or relax because we're tired? Should we put this or that at the top of our priority list? The possibilities are endless. In these, we trust the Spirit and our past experiences to shape our minds and hearts, so we make decisions that honor God and promote human flourishing of every kind.

Though God permits sin and evil, He doesn't leave us as helpless, hopeless victims. He promises to use our sins (Rom. 8:28) and the sins people have committed against us (Gen. 50:20) for good if we trust Him. In other words, God's grace and power are

> The Christian life is not merely a matter of getting from here to there . . . from point A to point B. Instead, God's will for us in this life is more about the journey itself.
> Charles R. Swindoll

so great that He wants to redeem every painful event, whatever the cause, to use it for our growth.

Permissive Will

God's permissive will is what He allows to happen. Most of what we see every day is under God's permissive will. The building of a new grocery store, falling interest rates, rising gas prices, the choices we make that glorify God, and the ones we make that do not honor God are all within God's permissive will simply because He permits them to occur.

Questions for Understanding God's Plan

Ask questions that will help the person understand that *God does have a plan and will reveal it*. It's a process that occurs slowly. Often God is fine with any number of possibilities, providing they glorify Him equally. Remember, it's much easier to see God in the rearview mirror than through the windshield. This means that as we look back on our lives, we can usually see how God was working and how He was actively involved. It's much harder to look forward and see the good that He is about to do.

1. Tell me about your relationship with the Lord.
2. Do you think that you initiated this relationship or did God reach out to you?
3. What major decisions have you made in the past?
4. How have you changed as a result of these decisions?
5. Do you believe that God was with you when you made these decisions?
6. If so, how could you tell?
7. What might happen in this current situation if you make the "wrong" decision?
8. Do you think that God will disown you if you make the wrong decision?
9. If you make the wrong decision, do you think God could change His plan to accommodate that wrong decision?
10. How might God direct you toward His will or plan in this decision?
11. How will you know if you have made the right decision?
12. Will any or all of the options you are considering bring glory to God?
13. You are searching for the unrevealed will of the Lord. Do you currently follow what you already know is the revealed will of God as described in His Word?

WISE COUNSEL 4

Faith and action go hand in hand. It is not necessary to make a final decision hurriedly, yet we must also not become complacent and do nothing. We must engage in activities, like searching the Scriptures and prayerfully seeking counsel from mature believers.

When we have God's peace concerning a previous action, we can *receive it as God's confirmation*. This peace is a knowing, a revelation, a confirmation that God is with us and we are walking in His will. If the peace isn't present, then we had better go back to the Lord and continue to seek His will.

5 | ACTION STEPS

1. God Will Show His Will

(Remind the person of James 1:5–6. Assure the person that God wants to reveal His will to him or her even more than the person wants to know it.) God will speak through His Word, through His people, and through prayer. Search the Scriptures, be patient, and pray through the decision at hand.

2. Be Patient

At times it may be necessary to make the decision not to make a decision. In other words, allow yourself the luxury of purposely not deciding until a later time. Often God's will becomes evident after a period of time, and we have to backtrack because we rushed into a decision. During the waiting period, keep seeking God's will.

3. Be Proactive

List the major decisions that you have made in the past. List the results of those decisions. Mark the decisions that you believe God directed.

4. List Options

List as many options as you can think of regarding the current issue.

5. What's Obvious?

Are any of these options automatically outside the will of God? For example, are any illegal or immoral?

6. Keep Praying

Commit yourself to praying over your options for a specified length of time.

7. Get Wise Counsel

Ask advice from a trusted Christian friend or family member regarding this decision.

8. Make the Decision

After the specified amount of time has passed, make a decision and accept that decision as God's will.

> If any of you lacks wisdom, let him ask of God, who gives to all liberally and without reproach, and it will be given to him. But let him ask in faith, with no doubting, for he who doubts is like a wave of the sea driven and tossed by the wind.
>
> James 1:5–6

BIBLICAL INSIGHTS 6

Yet there shall be a space between you and it, about two thousand cubits by measure. Do not come near it, that you may know the way by which you must go, for you have not passed *this* way before.

Joshua 3:4

But [Rehoboam] rejected the advice which the elders had given him, and consulted the young men who had grown up with him, who stood before him.

1 Kings 12:8

I beseech you therefore, brethren, by the mercies of God, that you present your bodies a living sacrifice, holy, acceptable to God, *which is* your reasonable service. And do not be conformed to this world, but be transformed by the renewing of your mind, that you may prove what *is* that good and acceptable and perfect will of God.

Romans 12:1–2

If any of you lacks wisdom, let him ask of God, who gives to all liberally and without reproach, and it will be given to him.

James 1:5

Now this is the confidence that we have in Him, that if we ask anything according to His will, He hears us.

1 John 5:14

> Our failure to hear His voice when we want to is due to the fact that we do not in general want to hear it, that we want it only when we think we need it.
> Dallas Willard

PRAYER STARTER 7

Thank You, Lord, that You promise to give wisdom to those who ask. _____ needs wisdom today to make the right decision. He [she] wants to know Your will and wants to do what You would have him [her] do, but it's just not clear right now . . .

RECOMMENDED RESOURCES 8

Blackaby, Henry, Richard Blackaby, and Claude King. *Experiencing God Workbook: Knowing and Doing the Will of God*. Lifeway, 2007.

Friesen, Garry, and J. Robin Maxson. *Decision-Making and the Will of God: A Biblical Alternative to the Traditional View*. Multnomah, 2004.

Stanley, Charles. *The Will of God: Understanding and Pursuing His Ultimate Plan for Your Life*. Howard Books, 2019.

Willard, Dallas. *Hearing God: Developing a Conversational Relationship with God*. InterVarsity, 2012.

Websites

American Association of Christian Counselors (AACC.net)

Christian Care Connect (Connect.AACC.net)

Depression

1 | PORTRAITS

- Each morning Angela struggles to find the energy to get out of bed. She feels listless and down. Her kids need her, but she can't summon the energy to even interact with them—much less prepare meals or clean the house.
- George is having a hard time thinking clearly. He lost his job and just can't seem to crawl out of the hole he feels he's fallen into. He doesn't interview because he's so down, so he sits around at home and plays on the computer. And he just keeps spiraling downward.
- Sammy has been getting in trouble at school. He has been fighting with his peers and even with his best friends. It seems like little things have begun to set him off and his parents are getting concerned.

2 | DEFINITIONS AND KEY THOUGHTS

- Depression can have a variety of meanings because there are different types of depression. Clinical depression as a disorder is not the same as brief mood fluctuations or the feelings of sadness, disappointment, and frustration that everyone experiences from time to time and that last from minutes to a few days at most. Clinical depression is a more serious condition that lasts weeks to months, and sometimes even years.

> An estimated 21.0 million adults in the United States had at least one major depressive episode. This number represented 8.3% of all US adults.[1]

  - Misdiagnosis of depression is common. It can often be misdiagnosed as anxiety, which is a common affect in many types of depression or other mood disorders. Accurate assessment is the first step to proper treatment.
  - According to the National Institutes of Health, *depression* (major depressive disorder or clinical depression) is a "common but serious mood disorder. It causes severe symptoms that affect how you feel, think, and handle daily activities, such as sleeping, eating, or working. To be diagnosed with depression, the symptoms must be present for at least two weeks."[2]
- Depression differs from sadness, which is a God-given reaction to loss that serves to slow people down so they can process grief. When one is sad, self-respect remains intact, intrinsic hope is maintained, and relief comes after crying and receiving support.

Types of Depression[3]

- Major depression includes symptoms of depressed mood or loss of interest, most of the time for at least two weeks, that interfere with daily activities.

- Persistent depressive disorder (also called dysthymia or dysthymic disorder) consists of less severe symptoms of depression that last much longer, usually for at least two years.

- Perinatal depression occurs during or after pregnancy. Depression that begins during pregnancy is called prenatal depression, and depression that begins after the baby is born is called postpartum depression.

- Seasonal affective disorder comes and goes with the seasons, with symptoms typically starting in the late fall and early winter and going away during the spring and summer. Depression with symptoms of psychosis is a severe form of depression in which a person experiences psychosis symptoms such as delusions (disturbing, false fixed beliefs) or hallucinations (hearing or seeing things others do not hear or see).

- People with bipolar disorder (formerly called manic depression or manic-depressive illness) also experience depressive episodes during which they feel sad, indifferent, or hopeless, combined with a very low activity level. But a person with bipolar disorder also experiences manic (or less severe hypomanic) episodes, or unusually elevated moods in which they might feel very happy, irritable, or "up," with a marked increase in activity level.

Other types of depressive disorders recently added to the diagnostic classification of DSM-5 include disruptive mood dysregulation disorder (diagnosed in children and adolescents) and premenstrual dysphoric disorder (PMDD).

Causes of Depression

- Depression can be caused by *many life issues*, including anger; failure or rejection; family issues, such as divorce or abuse; fear; feelings of futility, lacking control over one's life; grief and loss; guilt or shame; loneliness or isolation; negative thinking; destructive misbeliefs; and stress. This is sometimes referred to as "*reactive depression.*" With this, the depression symptoms may be lowest in the morning and increase throughout the day. *Note*: Persistent reactive depression will change one's chemical balances and may compound depression.

- *Medical and biological factors* can also facilitate depression: inherited predisposition to depression, thyroid abnormalities, female hormone fluctuations, serotonin or norepinephrine irregularities, diabetes, B-12 or iron deficiencies, lack of sunlight or vitamin D, a recent stroke or heart attack, mitral valve prolapse, exposure to black mold, prescription drugs (antihypertensives, oral contraceptives), and recreational drugs (such as alcohol, marijuana, cocaine). When rooted in the biological, it is sometimes referred to as "*endogenous depression.*" With this, sufferers often feel worse in the morning.[4]

Now may the God of hope fill you with all joy and peace in believing, that you may abound in hope by the power of the Holy Spirit.
Romans 15:13

Symptoms of Depression

- Symptoms are many, including decreased energy, fluctuating body weight, depleted concentration, irritability, bouts of crying, hopelessness/despair, a disinterest in pleasurable activities, social withdrawal, and thoughts of suicide.
- The Bible is replete with examples of depression with a variety of reasons and results: David wrote of his depression caused by unconfessed sin (Pss. 38; 51). God used depression to get Nehemiah's attention (Neh. 1–2). Job's devastating losses led him to curse the day he was born (Job 1–3). Elijah was so depressed over the situation with Israel's leaders that he wished to die (1 Kings 19).[5]

3 | ASSESSMENT INTERVIEW

Rule Outs

An estimated 14.5 million US adults aged 18 or older had at least one major depressive episode with severe impairment in the past year. This number represents 5.7% of all US adults.[6]

1. If 10 is extreme sadness, and 1 is feeling well, where are you today on a scale of 1 to 10? (*If the client is on the low side, find out what is causing the sadness. The issue to address may not be depression but other concerns.*)
2. Are you using drugs or alcohol?
3. Are you currently taking any medications?
4. When is the last time you had a thorough physical examination? (*If the counselee hasn't seen his or her doctor recently, give a medical referral.*)
5. Do you have significant mood swings? (*Ask about the existence of mania or hypomania and, if they exist, give a psychiatric referral.*)

General Questions

1. How long have you felt depressed?
2. What was happening in your life when you first became depressed? (*Someone who is depressed needs acceptance and gentleness. The counselee may already be feeling as if he or she has failed in some way. Begin by listening to your counselee's story without judgment.*)
3. Have you been depressed before?
4. Do you have a family history of depression?
5. Do you have difficulty concentrating?
6. Have you lost interest in pleasurable activities?
7. Have you noticed changes in your eating or sleeping patterns?
8. Are you dealing with guilt or fear about anything? (*Fear is prevalent in many kinds of depression—anxiety and depression coexist in 70 percent of those diagnosed with depression.*)
9. What do you see in your future?
10. Have you had any thoughts about injuring yourself or suicide? (*Sometimes the thoughts are vague, such as "It would be better if I were not here." Pay particular attention to anything indicating a means for carrying out these thoughts.*

Someone who is suicidal and imagines having an automobile accident has both a plan and a means to carry it out.)

WISE COUNSEL 4

The most dangerous symptom of depression is *suicidal ideation*. If, as a result of your questions, you discover that the counselee desires to hurt himself [herself], do not hesitate to involve other family members or a mental health professional if necessary. See also the section on Suicide.

If you recommend that your client see a physician, *make sure he or she understands that it is okay to take medications* if needed to get depression under control. Communicate that using medication doesn't mean that the counselee is weak or lacks faith.

ACTION STEPS 5

1. Watch Physical Health

- *(If there would be no health risks, assign your counselee moderate exercise such as a brisk walk.)* Research shows that thirty minutes of moderate daily exercise is very helpful in elevating mood; therefore, I am assigning a daily brisk walk and I'll be checking up. Find a partner to walk with—it makes it harder to avoid the activity if someone is waiting for you.
- Have a medical checkup and work with a doctor on a diet program. Better eating habits (for example, less sugar and more vitamins) can be a big help.

> An estimated 5.0 million adolescents aged 12 to 17 in the United States had at least one major depressive episode. This number represents 20.1% of the U.S. population aged 12 to 17.[7]

2. Get Behind the Scenes

- *Assure the client that you will help them deal with whatever situation might be behind the depression.*
- *(If the counselee has recently suffered a significant loss, acknowledge that loss and begin to help him or her grieve.)* It's okay to feel upset, but you must also look to the light. Your loss is painful but future happiness in Christ is yours.
- Think honestly about what might be other deep sources of the depression.
- Keep a journal in which you write down thoughts that occur over the next couple of weeks regarding what is behind the depression.
- Carry a "daily mood log" and record the times when you feel most depressed. Write down what is happening and what you are thinking at those times.

3. Begin Clear Thinking

- *Challenge the counselee's statements and beliefs. For example, your counselee may say, "I'm totally worthless. I have nothing to give to anyone." Ask pointed questions to draw out the fact that this person does indeed have value.*

- Over the next week prepare a list of ten things you like about yourself—and three of them have to be physical characteristics. I will ask you to tell me those ten things.
- Very few things are really hopeless, and very few situations are "all bad."

4. Get Social Support

- Who are your friends? Are they people who help you counter the depression?
- What social groups are you currently involved in? (*Social isolation will only further his or her depression.*)
- What is your level of church involvement? Who at church could be of help and support?

5. Pay Attention to Spiritual Issues

- Do you have any unconfessed sin that is promoting the depression?
- Do you need to forgive someone as a means of moving toward personal health?
- Are you motivated to connect with Christ? (*When one is motivated by something other than God, frustration and depression can ensue.*)
- Do you believe that God can both remove your depression and provide complete happiness (or joy)?

6 | BIBLICAL INSIGHTS

But [Elijah] went a day's journey into the wilderness, and came and sat down under a broom tree. And he prayed that he might die, and said, "It is enough! Now, LORD, take my life, for I *am* no better than my fathers!"

Then as [Elijah] lay and slept under a broom tree, suddenly an angel touched him, and said to him, "Arise *and* eat." Then he looked, and there by his head *was* a cake baked on coals, and a jar of water. So he ate and drank, and lay down again.

1 Kings 19:4–6

Why are you cast down, O my soul?
And *why* are you disquieted within me?
Hope in God, for I shall yet praise Him
For the help of His countenance.

Psalm 42:5

To console those who mourn in Zion,
To give them beauty for ashes,
The oil of joy for mourning,
The garment of praise for the spirit of heaviness;

> Whether God chooses to heal us or to supply us with sustaining grace, we can rest in knowing He is sovereign over all things (including demons) and He cares for us.
>
> Matthew Stanford

> Approximately 60.1% of adolescents with major depressive episode do not receive treatment.[8]

That they may be called trees of righteousness,
The planting of the LORD, that He may be glorified.

Isaiah 61:3

PRAYER STARTER | 7

Lord, at times we all feel downhearted. Today _____ feels like he [she] is walking in darkness with no way out. I pray, Lord, that You will provide healing and help him [her] discern what is going on deep in his [her] heart. If there is deep pain or loss, guilt or shame, help him [her] to have the discernment to bring it into the light and confess it by Your grace . . .

RECOMMENDED RESOURCES | 8

Hart, Archibald D., and Catherine Hart Weber. *A Woman's Guide to Overcoming Depression*. Revell, 2007.

Jantz, Gregory L. *Healing Depression for Life: The Personalized Approach that Offers New Hope for Lasting Relief*. Tyndale, 2019.

Minirth, Frank, and Paul Meier. *Happiness Is a Choice: The Symptoms, Causes, and Cures of Depression*. Baker Books, 2007.

Tan, Siang-Yang, and John Ortberg. *Coping with Depression*. Baker Books, 2004.

Websites

American Association of Christian Counselors (AACC.net)

Christian Care Connect (Connect.AACC.net)

Discouragement

1 PORTRAITS

- Mark has worked two jobs most of his adult life just to make ends meet. He has three children and a wife who works in the home and has a part-time job outside the home. Recently Mark lost the higher paying of his two jobs. If that weren't enough, their older son was suspended from school the same week for having drugs in his possession. Mark blames himself for not being at home enough.

- Lila is a young woman who has been out of college and in the workforce for almost five years. All her college friends are married, and she longs for a husband and family. This is all she has ever dreamed of. She had a relationship for almost seven years with a Christian high school sweetheart. She blames herself for the breakup, and wonders, *What if?* She sits at home most nights alone in her tiny apartment. A married friend is worried sick about her and doesn't know how to help her.

- Julian's family moved again. Now, as a freshman in high school, he's trying to fit in with a group of kids who have known each other all their lives. His attempts to make friends don't go very well. His parents notice that he's becoming withdrawn.

- Phyllis's husband is having health problems, and the bills are piling up. Both of them are retired, but their pensions aren't covering their expenses. As the months go by and her husband is in and out of the hospital, Phyllis realizes she's losing her husband, her financial stability, and her hope for the future.

2 DEFINITIONS AND KEY THOUGHTS

- Discouragement is a *feeling* of despair, sadness, or lack of confidence. A discouraged person is disheartened. Three underlying causes contribute to discouragement:
    lack of confidence in ourselves
    lack of confidence in God
    lack of hope for the future

- Because discouragement is a feeling or emotion, it can *play games* with our minds. We must learn how to control our minds, and thus our discouragement, and lean on God for strength.

- Joshua was challenged with discouragement as he led the people of Israel into the promised land. God told Joshua, "Be strong and of good courage" (Josh. 1:6).[1]

- God also reminded Joshua that *the key to overcoming discouragement was a personal relationship with Him.* The Lord told Joshua: "This Book of the Law shall not depart from your mouth, but you shall meditate in it day and night, that you may observe to do according to all that is written in it. For then you will make your way prosperous, and then you will have good success" (Josh.1:8).[2]
- Discouraged people often blame themselves or God and ask, *What if . . . ?* This is Satan's trap, his way of trying to have us think, *I blew it* or *God isn't capable.*
- God has a much bigger picture for our lives than we could ever imagine. *Challenges along the way are God's way of refining us*, preparing us for the bigger and better picture—the first prize.
- If not dealt with, discouragement *can lead to depression*, which can stop people in their tracks. People must be taught how to deal with discouragement before it becomes depression.
- Discouragement reveals an *unwillingness to trust God*. It can be dealt a death blow when people consistently cast all their cares on God.
- Discouragement can be *caused by many different circumstances and feelings*:
    - shouldering one's own worries, cares, and fears; then collapsing under the weight
    - out of control events
    - circumstances that were within one's control but were handled poorly
    - failure—occurring either in the present or in the past, or a perceived potential for failure in the future

> The Christian life is not a constant high. I have my moments of deep discouragement. I have to go to God in prayer with tears in my eyes, and say, "O God, forgive me," or "Help me."
>
> Billy Graham

ASSESSMENT INTERVIEW 3

1. What are some things or events that make you discouraged?
2. Do you have control over these things or are they out of your control?
3. Describe yourself using three adjectives.
4. Describe what you think someone else would say about you (a friend, a parent, a coach). (*Note to questions 3 and 4: Sometimes there is an underlying problem of lack of self-confidence that leads to discouragement. If you suspect such a problem, it needs to be addressed.*)
5. When you feel discouraged, what do you do?
6. Do you have a direction or plan for your life?
7. What do you see yourself doing three years from now, five years from now?
8. Is failure an option for you? What does God think about failure?
9. What does God think about you? What do you think about God?
10. Envision yourself failing at something. How does that make you feel?
11. Envision yourself succeeding at something. How does that make you feel?

4 | WISE COUNSEL

Discouragement ought to be the first indication that *it is time to pray*. People may become discouraged as they get overwhelmed and begin to neglect prayer (ironically this is when they need to be relying on God more).

Help the person understand that God uses our trials to shape our personal and spiritual lives for the better, and for His glory. Paul tells us, "We know that all things work together for good to those who love God, to those who are the called according to *His* purpose" (Rom. 8:28).

Many times what leads to discouragement are *events that are out of control*. This is where faith in God comes in. Realizing that God sees the events in our lives before we do should help us not feel so overwhelmed.

There are times when discouragement is a result of *something the client could have controlled* (such as flunking college or being late to work). These events should be seen as wake-up calls and opportunities to improve, not hopeless or disastrous events.

Often the discouraged will need someone to be *accountable* to if this has been a lifelong struggle.

The person needs to be helped to see discouragement as an *opportunity to grow in Christ* and rediscover the person God designed in His image. Help the client to see discouragement as a time to *step back and look at life* and perhaps change some goals or behaviors (consider whether the unachieved goals are in keeping with God's plan for the person's life).

Help the person understand that feelings of discouragement will likely *creep into his or her life from time to time*; this is normal because of our human nature. Share with the person that even when one has confidence in the abilities and greatness of God and has a better grip on handling challenges, it doesn't mean discouragement will never come again.

Look, the LORD your God has set the land before you; go up *and* possess *it*, as the LORD God of your fathers has spoken to you; do not fear or be discouraged.

Deuteronomy 1:21

5 | ACTION STEPS

1. Be Realistic

Understand that discouragement is a part of life and often is a result of things or events that are out of our control. This does not mean that we are failures.

2. Trust God for Wisdom and a Solution

Jesus told His disciples and us, "Peace I leave with you, My peace I give to you; not as the world gives do I give to you. Let not your heart be troubled, neither let it be afraid" (John 14:27). When the future seems dark and bleak, cling to God. Trust Him to bring light into the darkness so you can take the next step forward. He may only give enough light for one step, but that's enough for a good start.

3. Rethink Goals

Pray and ask God for a fresh direction. After prayer and consideration of God's will, make plans for an optimistic future.

4. No "What Ifs"

Stop considering what might have been. This type of thinking will only bring defeat. If you keep looking back at the past, you are going to trip on the future.

5. Don't Focus on Feelings

Stop using feelings to determine how to handle discouragement. Feelings can change drastically with our mood. We must focus on change and doing it with God's help.

6. Keep a Journal

Call your journal "Discouragements That Become Encouragements." Document each discouragement and what was done with God's help to turn it around. You can even write down the ones that have already happened and what you learned in each situation.

7. Be Ready

Be ready for what God may have in mind for you. When you have confidence in God, you will gain confidence in yourself. This will be a huge step toward overcoming discouragement.

> Be strong and of good courage, for to this people you shall divide as an inheritance the land which I swore to their fathers to give them. Only be strong and very courageous. . . . This Book of the Law shall not depart from your mouth, but you shall meditate in it day and night, that you may observe to do according to all that is written in it. For then you will make your way prosperous, and then you will have good success.
>
> Joshua 1:6–8

BIBLICAL INSIGHTS 6

The steps of a *good* man are ordered by the LORD,
And He delights in his way.
Though he fall, he shall not be utterly cast down;
For the LORD upholds *him with* His hand.

Psalm 37:23–24

For a righteous *man* may fall seven times
And rise again,
But the wicked shall fall by calamity.

Proverbs 24:16

And let us not grow weary while doing good, for in due season we shall reap if we do not lose heart.

Galatians 6:9

Being confident of this very thing, that He who has begun a good work in you will complete *it* until the day of Jesus Christ.

Philippians 1:6

Casting all your care upon Him, for He cares for you.

1 Peter 5:7

7 | PRAYER STARTER

Dear Lord, Your child is discouraged today. He [she] feels unable to get past this, unable to do better. He [she] feels that he [she] has disappointed You and doesn't know where to turn. Help _____ see that You are the God of second chances. Show _____ the path You want him [her] to go, the changes You want him [her] to make as a result of this discouraging time . . .

8 | RECOMMENDED RESOURCES

What we call despair is often only the painful eagerness of unfed hope.

George Eliot

Allen, Jennie. *Get Out of Your Head: Stopping the Spiral of Toxic Thoughts*. Penguin Random House, 2020.

Cloud, Henry, and John Townsend. *What to Do When You Don't Know What to Do: Discouragement and Depression*. Integrity Publishers, 2009.

Lucado, Max. *Unshakable Hope: Building Our Lives on the Promise of God*. Thomas Nelson, 2018.

Wright, H. Norman. *Real Solutions for Overcoming Discouragement, Rejection, and the Blues*. Vine Books, 2001.

Websites
American Association of Christian Counselors (AACC.net)

Christian Care Connect (Connect.AACC.net)

Divorce

PORTRAITS | 1

- Jennifer is served with divorce papers after her husband has an affair with a coworker. She is devastated and begs him to attend counseling, but he has no interest in saving the marriage.
- Doug's wife walked out two years ago, leaving him alone to care for their three-year-old son. "She didn't want to be a mother anymore," he says. He wonders if he should file for divorce and move on with his life.
- Emily's husband has beaten her since they were married five years ago. He always apologizes, and she always takes him back, but then it happens again and the cycle is repeated. "As a Christian, I feel I have to stay with him," she explains, "but I'm tired of being a punching bag."
- Luke and Cathryn fight constantly over everything. "I'm worried our fighting is hurting the children," Cathryn says. "I think they'd be better off if we'd divorce. At least they would have a peaceful home."

DEFINITIONS AND KEY THOUGHTS | 2

- Divorce and recovery will be something *today's pastors will deal with much more* than their predecessors.
- About 40 to 50 percent of married couples in the United States divorce. The divorce rate for subsequent marriages is even higher.[1]
- Today, about one in four Americans (27 percent) is a practicing Christian. Divorce rates are lower among this group when compared to the general population and other faith segments, including non-practicing Christians.[2]
- Thirty-one percent of American young adults say they have already gotten married, while 43 percent of those who have not reached this relationship milestone say they want to get married in the next ten years.[3]
- Many children continue to battle with consequential unhappiness even ten to fifteen years after the divorce of their parents.[4]
- In many ways (emotionally, relationally, and often financially), divorce feels like a death—the death of a marriage, a family, and a dream. No one, especially a Christian, enters marriage expecting the marriage to end in divorce.

> So they are no longer two, but one flesh. Therefore what God has joined together, let no one separate.
>
> Matthew 19:6 NIV

Scriptural View of Divorce

- Marriage is one of the few institutions given by God for human flourishing. From the beginning, it has promised intimacy, security, joy, and strength. Paul says that this union is a picture of Christ's love for us and His commitment to us (Eph. 5:25–33).
- Malachi 2:16 says that the *Lord hates divorce*. The rest of the verse reveals that Malachi was speaking to men who were disloyal to their wives. God's compassion toward the injured party is clear.
- Romans 12:15 says that we should "weep with those who weep." People recovering from the trauma of a broken marriage *need the church* to:
    share in their sorrow
    offer compassion
    give reassurance that their church family will not reject them
    impart hope that God will somehow bring good out of this
    offer opportunities to serve in the church

Biblical Reasons for Divorce

- *Sexual activity outside the marital covenant* breaks the marriage vow. In Matthew 19:9, Jesus said that if a spouse has committed this type of sin, the other spouse is free to divorce and remarry. This does not mean divorce is required in instances where sexual sin has been committed, but it is permitted.
- Some maintain that *the abandonment* of a believer by a nonbelieving spouse leaves the believing spouse free to divorce the deserter (see 1 Cor. 7:15).

Reasons for Separation

- *Physical abuse* is not addressed in the Bible as a reason for divorce, but nowhere does Scripture specifically command a woman to stay in a home where she or her children are being physically abused. Separation (not divorce) is necessary for physical safety. Restoration should be predicated on *true repentance and by a significant change* in the abuser's behavior that lasts for an extended period of time. The church can serve as a protector of the abused by helping them find a safe place to stay, counseling, providing economic assistance, and using church discipline to hold the abusive spouse accountable.
- *Mental or verbal abuse* is not a biblical reason for divorce, although in some cases, such as severe belittling and demeaning behavior, it can be a cause for separation. Restoration should follow the pattern established for physical abuse (above).
- *Chemical addictions* to drugs or alcohol that result in harmful behavior to the spouse or children can be a reason for separation. Restoration should follow the pattern established for physical abuse (above).
- *Physical neglect*, such as not providing appropriate food, clothing, shelter, or supervision for the children, or physical abuse can result in life-threatening situations. The spouse should remove the children or the addict from the home to

provide a safe environment for the children. Restoration should again follow the pattern outlined above with the church functioning in the role of a safe haven.

Consequences of Divorce

- Divorce creates *new problems* in exchange for the old ones (see under Wise Counsel below).
- Divorce *devastates children*. Research shows that, for most children, the pain they feel from the breakup of their home is just as painful ten years after the divorce as it was at the time of the divorce. The pain follows them into adulthood and affects their personalities and life choices.

ASSESSMENT INTERVIEW | 3

For Couples Contemplating Divorce

When a couple comes to counseling with divorce as an option, *you are usually the last stop before a lawyer.*

Rule Outs

1. Do either of you have reason to believe that you are in physical danger from the other?
2. Has there been any type of abuse (physical, verbal, or sexual) to either of you or your children? (*If there has been physical or sexual abuse, the first step is to get the abused spouse and children away from the abuser and to a safe place. Counseling cannot begin until this takes place. After the abused person is safe, the couple can meet for counseling with the counselor and a representative of the church, such as an elder or pastor, present. It is a good idea if both genders are represented in the core counseling times.*)

General Questions

1. What has prompted you to come to counseling at this time?
2. What do you hope the outcome of counseling will be?
3. Tell me about your marriage. How long have you been married?
4. Do you have any children?
5. How did you meet?
6. What first attracted you to each other?
7. How did you know this was the person you wanted to marry?
8. What was your first fight about?
9. When did the problems that bring you here today first arise?
10. What have you tried already to solve these problems?
11. Do you feel there is any hope for reconciliation?
12. Do you both want a divorce? Why or why not?
13. What would it take for you to want to reconcile?
14. Do either of you think you have biblical grounds for divorce?

> Marriage should be honored by all, and the marriage bed kept pure, for God will judge the adulterer and all the sexually immoral.
>
> Hebrews 13:4 NIV

15. What are they?
16. Are you both believers?
17. How is your walk with the Lord?
18. Tell me about your background, your parents, and your siblings. What was growing up like for you?
19. Are there any divorces in your family or among your friends?
20. What do you think divorce will accomplish for you?
21. How do think the divorce will affect your children?
22. Would you like to see what the Bible says about divorce?

For a Victim of Divorce—A Person Divorced against His or Her Will

When a victim of divorce comes for counseling, it is a positive sign that he or she feels worthy of help, even though the person's *self-worth may have been demolished* by the divorce.

Reinforce his or her decision by reminding the person that the Bible says only *the wise seek counsel* (Prov. 12:15).

Rule Outs

1. On a scale of 1 to 10, with 10 being joy and 1 being hopelessness, where would you put yourself? (*You will want to rule out the presence of clinical depression.*)
2. Do you feel down much of the day on most days?
3. Have you had any thoughts of hurting yourself or others? (*If you feel the client is a danger to self or others, refer him or her to a professional counselor immediately.*)
4. Have you been worried about things lately? How much of your day are you worried about something? (*You want to rule out the presence of anxiety.*)

General Questions

1. What brought you here today?
2. What do you hope the outcome of counseling will be?
3. Tell me about your marriage. How did you meet your spouse?
4. What attracted you to him or her?
5. Did you notice any character qualities that gave you concern?
6. Did your feelings change during the marriage? How?
7. How did your parents feel about your spouse?
8. When did you first realize there were problems?
9. How did your spouse tell you he or she wanted to end the marriage?
10. What were your feelings?
11. What did you say and do?
12. Who did you go to for help?
13. Were they helpful?
14. What was the reaction of your family? Your spouse's family?
15. Do you have any children? How old are they?
16. How did they react when they heard?

Draw close to Him and let your marriage be the overflow of that. When things are right with God, your marriage can actually become what it was designed to be. Peace comes when both parties come to an agreement. Agree on God—agree on His holiness and the supremacy He deserves in your lives.

Francis Chan

17. How are they doing now?
18. What feelings have you gone through? Be honest.
19. Have you been able to talk about your feelings to anyone?
20. How do you express your anger?
21. Do you go to a support group?
22. What support do you have around you?
23. How are you and your children doing financially?
24. How does that make you feel?
25. What is your relationship with the Lord like?
26. Do you feel the Lord has rejected you or forgotten about you?
27. Let's see what the Bible says about that.

WISE COUNSEL | 4

For Couples Contemplating Divorce

Share what God says about divorce. Explain that *God hates divorce* because of the hurt and devastation it brings to people. He still loves the people involved.

Make clear that the only biblical reasons for divorce are constant sexual sin (by one or both of the partners in violation of the marital covenant) and abandonment.

Make it clear that people are not commanded to divorce in these situations but are allowed to. *Forgiveness and restoration* are also an option when true repentance is embraced by the partner who has violated the marital covenant.

Empathize with the pain and hurt both spouses are going through, but share with them the new problems divorce will bring:

- financial difficulty of providing for two households
- probability of custody battles
- stress of single parenthood, with no one to help
- guilt from seeing the children's world torn apart
- dealing with sending children back and forth between the parents
- anger
- grief
- depression
- hopelessness

> The mere mention of the word carries a huge weight of sorrow and loss and tragedy and disappointment and anger and regret and guilt. Few things are more painful than divorce. It cuts to the depths of personhood unlike any other relational gash.
>
> John Piper

For Victims of Divorce

Assure the counselee that *God sees his or her troubles. It grieves Him* to see the person hurt like this (Isa. 40:27–28).

Using the Scripture passages under Biblical Insights, let victims of divorce know that God loves them and totally accepts them. He *understands their feelings of betrayal and rejection* because He was also betrayed and rejected.

Explain *the importance of grieving* and the time it takes.

Grieving usually takes *two to five years and consists of five stages*: denial, anger, bargaining, depression, and acceptance. A person usually goes through these stages many times in different order until healing occurs.

Validate the evil done against the victim. Emphasize that, though the person is a victim, he or she can *become a survivor*.

Give hope that *God can bring good* out of this (Rom. 8:28).

Share with the person that other people may judge him or her unjustly; the victim will be tempted to feel shame because of the divorce. It is important that he or she *not accept that shame*. The person must put it back on the spouse who wronged him or her. Express that the person will never be truly healed and released until he or she *forgives himself [herself] and the spouse*. As long as he or she lives with anger and resentment, the victim is not free from these feelings. (For more, see the section on Forgiveness.)

> Marriage and family are important to God, but just as important to him are the individuals within those marriages and families.
>
> Leslie Vernick

5 | ACTION STEPS

For Couples Contemplating Divorce

1. Put the Divorce on Hold

- Wait for a time and attend marriage counseling if you have not yet done so.
- Begin to meet with a trained marriage mentoring couple who can encourage and instruct you.
- Considering the devastation a divorce causes for all involved, isn't it worth your best efforts to save this marriage if you can? At the end of the marriage mentoring and counseling, you can revisit your decision and see if there is any reason to be hopeful.

2. Go to Marriage Mentoring and Counseling

- (*Have on file the names of several good Christian marriage counselors who have a record of success in helping couples restore their marriages.*) Call one of these recommended counselors.
- Work with pastoral staff to determine how and when to utilize marriage mentoring and professional counseling.

3. Read Books

- *Suggest to the couple the list of books at the end of this section.*
- Many people were once where you are today and they now have healthy and fulfilling marriages. It is helpful to read what has helped others.

For Victims of Divorce

1. Go to a Recovery Group

- Start attending a divorce recovery group. Many larger churches have these groups. (*Research and recommend.*)
- Some groups last a specific number of weeks and some are 12-step programs that meet every week indefinitely.

2. Go to Counseling

- Start individual counseling on a weekly basis. You need someone to whom you can be accountable.
- Make a commitment to meet with a counselor once a week.

3. Make No Major Decisions

- Do not make any major life decisions for at least a year without running it by your counselor or pastor.
- This helps guard against making poor decisions while you are still emotionally vulnerable.

4. Develop No New Relationships

- Do not rush into any new dating relationships.
- Focus on letting God fill the emptiness inside you. You need to heal before entering another relationship.

5. Pursue Church Involvement

- Get involved in church and join a Sunday school class.
- Seek out friends of the same sex to whom you can talk and with whom you can do activities.
- When you feel up to it, serve and help others.

BIBLICAL INSIGHTS 6

They said to Him, "Why then did Moses command to give a certificate of divorce, and to put her away?"

He said to them, "Moses, because of the hardness of your hearts, permitted you to divorce your wives, but from the beginning it was not so."

Matthew 19:7–8

Nevertheless let each one of you in particular so love his own wife as himself, and let the wife *see* that she respects *her* husband.

Ephesians 5:33

If any brother has a wife who does not believe, and she is willing to live with him, let him not divorce her. And a woman who has a husband who does not believe, if he is willing to live with her, let her not divorce him. For the unbelieving husband is sanctified by the wife, and the unbelieving wife is sanctified by the husband; otherwise your children would be unclean, but now they are holy. But if the unbeliever departs, let him depart; a brother or a sister is not under bondage in such *cases*. But God has called us to peace. For how do you know, O wife, whether you will save *your* husband? Or how do you know, O husband, whether you will save *your* wife?

1 Corinthians 7:12–16

Marriage *is* honorable among all, and the bed undefiled; but fornicators and adulterers God will judge.

Hebrews 13:4

7 PRAYER STARTER

Lord, we know that You hate divorce. You hate what it does to people. You hate the death it causes of a marriage, a family, a dream. And yet, it is a sad reality. We want Your will, Lord. We want what is best for all concerned. I pray today for . . .

8 RECOMMENDED RESOURCES

Chapman, Gary. *Loving Your Spouse When You Feel Like Walking Away: Real Help for Desperate Hearts in Difficult Marriages.* Northfield Publishing, 2018.

Clinton, Tim. *Before a Bad Goodbye.* Thomas Nelson, 1999.

Cloud, Henry, and John Townsend. *Boundaries in Marriage.* Zondervan, 2002.

Feldhahn, Shaunti. *The Good News About Marriage: Debunking Discouraging Myths About Marriage and Divorce.* Multnomah, 2014.

Hart, Archibald D. *Helping Children Survive Divorce.* Thomas Nelson, 1997.

Thomas, Gary. *Sacred Marriage: What If God Designed Marriage to Make Us Holy More Than to Make Us Happy?* Zondervan, 2015.

Websites
American Association of Christian Counselors (AACC.net)
Christian Care Connect (Connect.AACC.net)

Domestic Violence

PORTRAITS | 1

- Marge stares in the mirror at the new bruise on her face. She had never imagined that this would be happening to her. She knows her husband, Paul, is sorry; he told her so again and again last night after he saw the marks on her face where he had hit her. This morning before he left for work, he promised that it wouldn't happen again if she would just give him another chance.

- Janet doesn't know what to do. The wedding is only weeks away, and she had always thought that she and Randy had made such a good couple. But lately he is becoming more controlling of her time and demands to know where she is going when he isn't with her. He is also getting jealous when some of her friends spend time with her. But last night was the worst. When she disagreed with him, he actually grabbed her arms and shook her. She was afraid. But surely he will calm down once they are married, won't he?

- Tom is afraid. Marsha has always had a temper and occasionally slaps him when she gets angry. But last night she had been drinking, and when she attacked him, she really tried to hurt him. Tom knows he couldn't fight back, but he doesn't know how much more of it he can take.

> About 1 in 4 women and nearly 1 in 10 men have experienced contact sexual violence, physical violence, and/or stalking by an intimate partner during their lifetime and reported some form of IPV-related impact.[1]

DEFINITIONS AND KEY THOUGHTS | 2

The US Office on Violence Against Women (OVW) defines *domestic violence* as a "pattern of abusive behavior in any relationship that is used by one partner to gain or maintain power and control over another intimate partner." Domestic violence can happen to anyone regardless of race, age, sexual orientation, religion, or gender. It can take many forms such as physical abuse, sexual abuse, emotional abuse, economic abuse, and psychological abuse.[2]

Domestic violence or intimate partner violence (IPV) may follow a three-step circular pattern.

1. *Tension builds* until the abuser loses control.
2. *Battering occurs.* The batterer sometimes feels that the victim deserves it or that he or she needs to teach the victim a lesson. Rationalization about the battering and minimization of the consequences of the abuse are common.

3. *There is remorse.* The batterer is sorry and asks for forgiveness. The tension is gone and he or she asks for reconciliation. The batterer may make promises that "it will never happen again" and behave in very loving and contrite ways.

> » The third stage of the cycle looks a great deal like true repentance. However, it is due only to an absence of tension and the feeling on the part of the abuser that the victim has "learned her [or his] lesson." When this situation changes and the tension again increases, the battering can recur.

> » Domestic violence is fueled by the *batterer's need to control.* When the victim tries to break the cycle, she or he can be in danger of more battering.

> » *Biblical headship* in a marriage is based on love and servant leadership, not on the man's control over his wife and certainly not on physical coercion.

> » Abusers and victims of domestic abuse often *grew up in abusive homes.*

> » Many of the predictors of domestic violence are *present in the dating relationship.* Some of these predictors are:
> use of force or violence to solve problems
> a male abuser's need to prove himself by acting tough
> rigid ideas of what men and women should be like
> the victim's fears of the abuser's anger

> » In public, abusers can often be charming and personable but *behave entirely different in private.* In counseling sessions, abusers can seem quite reasonable and can try to influence you, portraying their wives as irrational or rebellious and wanting you to see their side.

Consequences

Physical

There are many negative health outcomes associated with domestic violence and IPV. "These include a range of conditions affecting the heart, muscles and bones, and digestive, reproductive, and nervous systems, many of which are chronic. Survivors can experience mental health problems such as depression and PTSD symptoms. They are at higher risk for engaging in behaviors such as smoking, binge drinking, and sexual risk activity."[4]

Psychological

Abused girls and women often experience adverse mental health conditions, such as depression, anxiety, and low self-esteem. Women with a history of IPV experience increased levels of substance use, and antisocial and suicidal behavior.

Social

Children who witness IPV are at greater risk of developing psychiatric disorders, developmental problems, school failure, violence against others, and low self-esteem. Women in violent relationships have been found to be restricted in the way they gain access to services, take part in public life, and receive emotional support from friends and relatives.

Over 43 million women and 38 million men have experienced psychological aggression by an intimate partner in their lifetime.[3]

When IPV occurs in adolescence, it is called teen dating violence (TDV). TDV affects millions of US teens each year. About 11 million women and 5 million men who reported experiencing contact sexual violence, physical violence, or stalking by an intimate partner in their lifetime said that they first experienced these forms of violence before the age of 18.[5]

Vulnerability of Victimization

Several factors are related to IPV: history of physical abuse, prior injury from the same partner, having a verbally abusive partner, economic stress, partner history of alcohol or drug abuse, childhood abuse, being under the age of twenty-four, marital conflict, male dominance in the family, and poor family functioning.

ASSESSMENT INTERVIEW | 3

If a couple comes into counseling together and you *suspect abuse, speak to each separately* to get an accurate understanding of the situation. To avoid putting the victim in danger, simply say that it is *your practice* to speak to each member of the couple individually.

Rule Outs

1. Do your fights ever get physical? (*This is an easier question to answer than one about violence or abuse.*)
2. Do either of you use alcohol or drugs?
3. Do you feel safe with your spouse? (*If you have any questions about the presence of abuse, do not try to address marital issues with the couple together until the issue of safety is thoroughly addressed.*)

General Questions

1. Has your spouse ever hurt you physically or tried to physically intimidate you?
2. If yes, when was the last time it happened?
3. How often does the abuse happen?
4. Have you ever tried to get help?
5. What have you done to get help?
6. Has it worked?
7. Does your spouse go through the cycle of tension, battering, and then remorse? (*See Definitions and Key Thoughts above.*)
8. Describe what usually happens.
9. Are you afraid for your children's safety?
10. Do you have a plan for safety if the abuse happens again?
11. Have you confided in anyone else about this abuse? What was their response? (*This can show you if there are any barriers you may have to overcome to help the individual get help.*)

> IPV is a significant public health issue that has many individual and societal costs. About 35% of female IPV survivors and more than 11% of male IPV survivors experience some form of physical injury related to IPV.[6]

4 | WISE COUNSEL

The first issue is safety. Working out a plan of safety with the victim is essential. Sometimes what keeps a victim in the abusive situation is the lack of *resources to escape.* Be sure you investigate this need.

5 | ACTION STEPS

The following steps are specific actions for the counselor to take.

1. Provide for Safety

- *Reassurance of the person's safety (and that of any children involved) is the first priority.*
- *Empower the victim to separate from their abuser if necessary.*

2. Have a Plan

- *Help the person develop a plan for the next time abuse occurs.*
- *Be sure the victim has numbers to call—police, a family shelter or hotline, and a trusted friend or counselor. These numbers should be in an easily accessible place.*
- *If the victim decides to leave, where will they go? Who will they call?*
- *Advise the victim to have bags with essentials packed and in an easily accessible location so he or she and the children can leave quickly if needed.*
- *The victim should photocopy important documents and have them packed as well.*
- *Think through how the victim can access money, car keys, and important documents if she does need to leave suddenly.*
- *If he or she needs to leave at some point after an abusive incident, tell them that no argument or discussion should happen at this point, but she should calmly exit and go to a location they have predetermined with the people at that location (if the place is with a friend or family member).*

> Ten percent of women and 2% of men report having been stalked by an intimate partner.[7]

3. Follow Up

- *After the first session, put a follow-up plan in place for the victim to get continued help.*

4. Provide Reassurance

- *Reassure the person that abuse is never "deserved" and is always wrong.*
- *A husband's role of headship in a marriage never includes the right to control or abuse. A wife's role never includes the right to control or abuse, nor does it include submitting to abuse.*

5. Assess Relationships

- *Assess how much support the person has and encourage him or her to reach out to others for help.*
- *A victim of abuse is often isolated, both out of shame over the situation and due to the abuser's need to control.*

BIBLICAL INSIGHTS 6

Husbands, likewise, dwell with *them* with understanding, giving honor to the wife, as to the weaker vessel, and as *being* heirs together of the grace of life, that your prayers may not be hindered.

1 Peter 3:7

Then [Abimelech] went to his father's house at Ophrah and killed his brothers, the seventy sons of Jerubbaal, on one stone. But Jotham the youngest son of Jerubbaal was left, because he hid himself.

Judges 9:5

And you, fathers, do not provoke your children to wrath, but bring them up in the training and admonition of the Lord.

Ephesians 6:4

Fathers, do not provoke your children, lest they become discouraged.

Colossians 3:21

> Data from US crime reports suggest that about one in five homicide victims are killed by an intimate partner. The reports also found that over half of female homicide victims in the US are killed by a current or former male intimate partner.[8]

PRAYER STARTER 7

Today we're worried and frightened, Lord. Your children are in need of great help. One needs help handling anger so that he [she] no longer is abusive; the other needs help to know how best to deal with this situation and get his [her] spouse the help he [she] needs . . .

RECOMMENDED RESOURCES 8

Hawkins, David. *In Sickness and in Health: The Physical Consequences of Emotional Stress in Marriage*. Harvest House, 2019.

Hawkins, David. *When Loving Him Is Hurting You: Hope and Help for Women Dealing with Narcissism and Emotional Abuse*. Harvest House, 2017.

Kroeger, Catherine Clark, and Nancy Nason-Clark. *No Place for Abuse: Biblical and Practical Resources to Counteract Domestic Violence*. InterVarsity, 2001.

Langberg, Diane. *On the Threshold of Hope: Opening the Door to Healing for Survivors of Sexual Abuse*. Tyndale, 1999.

Vernick, Leslie. *The Emotionally Destructive Marriage: How to Find Your Voice and Reclaim Your Hope.* WaterBrook, 2013.

Websites

American Association of Christian Counselors (AACC.net)

Christian Care Connect (Connect.AACC.net)

National Domestic Violence Hotline (TheHotline.org) or 1-800-799-7233

Eating Disorders

PORTRAITS 1

- Lindsay binged a few times during middle school and early high school. She doesn't like vomiting, so she uses laxatives afterward and exercises a lot.
- Madeline and Maggie are twelve-year-old twins whose anorexia started in part because of their intense competition with each other. They obsess over who eats the least and exercises the most.
- Don is a seminary student who finds that he is very good at keeping track of his food intake. After he graduates, his food obsession goes with him to his job as a youth pastor.
- Jennifer would binge and purge for weeks every time she started dating someone new or broke up with a boyfriend. After getting married in her early twenties, her bingeing stops for a while. When it returns, she starts getting cavities from the vomiting and finally decides she has to tell her husband.
- Suzanne is the daughter of a soldier, and her family moves every few years. At each new school, she has trouble fitting in. When she is in junior high, she begins eating to have a feeling of pleasure. As she gains weight, others distance themselves from her, which is okay with her since it gives her an excuse to remain lonely and disconnected. By the time she graduates from high school, she weighs over three hundred pounds.

DEFINITIONS AND KEY THOUGHTS 2

- Persons with eating disorders are characterized by a primary *obsession with food* (either eating a lot or not eating enough) and compulsive behaviors related to eating. Often these behaviors are illegitimate attempts to gain control and deal with *anxiety and stress*.
- Compulsive overeating and milder forms of obsession with food or weight can also be considered eating disorders if the practices produce *unhealthy and obsessive behaviors* and/or altered thought processes or body image.

> Nine percent of the US population or 28.8 million Americans will have an eating disorder in their lifetime.[1]

Anorexia Nervosa[2]

- People with anorexia nervosa *avoid* food, *severely restrict* food, or eat *very small quantities* of only certain foods. Even when they are dangerously underweight, they may see themselves as overweight. They may also weigh themselves repeatedly.

- There are *two* subtypes of anorexia nervosa: a *restrictive* subtype and *binge-purge* subtype.
    - » *Restrictive:* People with the restrictive subtype of anorexia nervosa place severe restrictions on the amount and type of food they consume.
    - » *Binge-Purge:* People with the binge-purge subtype of anorexia nervosa also place severe restrictions on the amount and type of food they consume. In addition, they may have binge eating and purging behaviors (such as vomiting, use of laxatives and diuretics, etc.).

- *Symptoms* include:
    - » Extremely restricted eating and/or intensive and excessive exercise
    - » Extreme thinness (emaciation)
    - » A relentless pursuit of thinness and unwillingness to maintain a normal or healthy weight
    - » Intense fear of gaining weight
    - » Distorted body image, a self-esteem that is heavily influenced by perceptions of body weight and shape, or a denial of the seriousness of low body weight

- Over time, these symptoms *may also develop*:
    - » Thinning of the bones (osteopenia or osteoporosis)
    - » Mild anemia and muscle wasting and weakness
    - » Brittle hair and nails
    - » Dry and yellowish skin
    - » Growth of fine hair all over the body (lanugo)
    - » Severe constipation
    - » Low blood pressure, slowed breathing and pulse
    - » Damage to the structure and function of the heart
    - » Drop in internal body temperature, causing a person to feel cold all the time
    - » Lethargy, sluggishness, or feeling tired all the time
    - » Infertility
    - » Brain damage
    - » Multiorgan failure

- Anorexia can be *fatal*.
- Anorexia nervosa has *the highest mortality (death) rate* of any mental disorder.
- People with anorexia may die from medical conditions and complications associated with starvation; by comparison, people with other eating disorders die of suicide.

There are 10,200 deaths per year as a direct result of an eating disorder, equating to 1 death every 52 minutes.[3]

Bulimia Nervosa[4]

- People with bulimia nervosa have *recurrent episodes* of eating unusually large amounts of food and feeling a lack of control over these episodes.

- This binge-eating is *followed* by behaviors that compensate for the overeating, such as forced vomiting, excessive use of laxatives or diuretics, fasting, excessive exercise, or a combination of these behaviors.
- Unlike those with anorexia nervosa, people with bulimia nervosa *may maintain* a normal weight or be overweight.
- Symptoms include:
  - » Chronically inflamed and sore throat
  - » Swollen salivary glands in the neck and jaw area
  - » Worn tooth enamel and increasingly sensitive and decaying teeth (a result of exposure to stomach acid)
  - » Acid reflux disorder and other gastrointestinal problems
  - » Intestinal distress and irritation from laxative abuse
  - » Severe dehydration from purging
  - » Electrolyte imbalance (too low or too high levels of sodium, calcium, potassium, and other minerals), which can lead to stroke or heart attack

Binge-Eating Disorder[5]

- People with binge-eating disorder *lose control* over their eating.
- Unlike bulimia nervosa, periods of binge-eating are not followed by purging, excessive exercise, or fasting. As a result, people with binge-eating disorder are often overweight or obese.
- Symptoms include:
  - » Eating unusually large amounts of food in a specific amount of time, such as a two-hour period
  - » Eating fast during binge episodes
  - » Eating even when full or not hungry
  - » Eating until uncomfortably full
  - » Eating alone or in secret to avoid embarrassment
  - » Feeling distressed, ashamed, or guilty about eating
  - » Frequently dieting, possibly without weight loss

Common Barriers to Treatment

There are often multiple barriers that keep a person from receiving proper treatment for an eating disorder.

Access: Sometimes finding treatment from someone who specializes in eating disorders is difficult.

Considering it an act of will: There are emotional, spiritual, and interpersonal complexities involved in the healing of eating disorders. Persons with an eating disorder cannot simply "will themselves" out of it.

Denial: Persons with eating disorders can have distorted body images and may deny the level of harm they inflict on themselves.

Females are two times more likely to have an eating disorder.[6]

Fear of treatment: Treatment involves discomfort and facing pain and hurt, and it can be a difficult and frightening process. This prevents some persons with eating disorders from seeking treatment.

Financial barriers: Unfortunately, many treatments for eating disorders are expensive.

Idols: With eating disorders, food is not about sustenance; it is a preoccupation and obsession similar to idolization. The person's world and priorities revolve around food.

Lack of faith: Persons with eating disorders may not believe any person or treatment can help with their affliction.

Minimizing the problem: Many delay treatments because they minimize the grasp the problem has on their lives, and they believe it might go away on its own.

Pride: It's not easy to admit to one's self, others, and God that something is out of control.

Shame and guilt: Secrecy and shame and guilt may shroud eating disorders for long periods of time. It is very hard for persons to admit there is a problem. It is embarrassing to admit to not eating or to bingeing and vomiting.

3 ASSESSMENT INTERVIEW

You will probably be *approached by a family member* who is concerned about someone's eating. Your questions need to be probing but nonjudgmental. The family members might be inclined to *blame themselves* for the eating problem or to deny the problem.

First, *rule out immediate medical problems.* Then ask the remaining questions. Some are directed at family members, while others are for the person who is having eating problems. We have used female pronouns because most often those with eating disorders are girls or women.[7]

Rule Outs

Each year, there are 53,918 ER visits due to eating disorders.[8]

1. If you [your loved one] have been starving yourself [herself], how long have you [has she] been doing it?
2. What do you [does she] weigh? (*If her weight is 10 percent or more below the lowest recommended weight for her age and height, she should be taken to a doctor for a thorough medical exam. Medical conditions are always a significant concern for those with eating disorders.*)
3. If you [your loved one] purge by vomiting, share how long has this been going on? (*If the answer is that this has been going on for some time, encourage the individual to have medical and dental exams to rule out medical conditions caused by vomiting.*)

Questions for the Caring Adult

1. What statements does this person make related to body image and fat?
2. Does this person view herself as fat, even if she is very thin?
3. Has this girl been asked to gain weight? If so, how did she respond?

4. How long has she been starving herself/bingeing and purging/overeating?
5. What was childhood like for her? Are there issues of control or perfectionism in the home?
6. Is this girl facing a transition (*such as from middle school to high school, from high school to college, from a familiar neighborhood and school to a new one*)?
7. Are you aware of any bullying?
8. How has this girl been influenced by social norms related to beauty?
9. Have you noticed her being particularly sensitive to such expectations?

Questions for the Counselee

1. Do you ever feel helpless? If so, when?
2. How do you handle such feelings?
3. Describe a time when you felt angry, frustrated, or afraid. How did you express those feelings?
4. What were meals like in your family of origin?
5. In your home, was there much focus on food while you were growing up?
6. Has anyone ever told you that you're beautiful? Who and when?
7. How did that make you feel?
8. Why do you think the person said that?
9. Describe your relationship with your parents and siblings. What kind of a child were you?
10. Have you been experiencing any type of bullying or shaming in person or online?
11. Do you sometimes feel as though you aren't good enough?
12. What advantage does weight loss (purging) afford you? How does it make you feel about yourself?
13. What disadvantages have you seen from those actions?

WISE COUNSEL 4

Do not attempt to treat an individual whose symptoms are affecting their health. A person whose eating disorder is endangering their life or well-being should be in the hospital or an inpatient treatment program.

Even if the person with the eating disorder must be hospitalized, there is also a *family that is hurting*. Focus on them and their needs. Help them avoid blaming themselves or their child. Instead, help them have hope for recovery.

Keep reminding everyone involved that *God is always working* and there is always hope for recovery. Eating disorders are very difficult but not impossible to overcome.

Watch for *evidence of suicidal feelings* (see the section on Suicide) and get help immediately if you see signs.

If the behavior has gone on for some time, it would be best to *seek the assistance of a professional* who is a specialist in eating disorders. The person's *health will continue to be compromised* until they get help.

5 | ACTION STEPS

1. Identify a Target Weight

- It is important to identify an ideal weight and target weight. Ideal weight refers to the best weight for a person when the person's height and body type are taken into account. The body mass index (often abbreviated as BMI) is the most accurate measure of ideal weight, but few persons can easily work with this index.
  - A target weight is the lowest safe weight; it is the bare minimum you want someone with an eating disorder to be at. Target weight is calculated as 90 percent of midpoint of the ideal weight. It is best to have agreement on a target weight with a doctor or dietician because persons with eating disorders often try to negotiate this number.

2. Focus on Relationships

- *You will want to build a positive relationship with the person with the eating disorder. These individuals tend to have a very hard time being open and accepting help. You will need much patience and you will need to be willing to speak the truth. Let the young woman know that she must be willing to hear the truth.*
- *Encourage family members to show unconditional love to the person with the eating disorder. Do not criticize or compare or ask questions in a manner that causes the person to feel condemned.*
- Healing relationships with people and with God are essential to the recovery process.

3. Take the Focus off Food

- *Unless the girl is in immediate danger from starvation or electrolyte problems, examine what weight loss means to this person, what eating stands for, and what she most fears about eating.*
- *Help the family to take the focus off food at home. They need to see that focusing on food is part of the disease, not the solution.*

4. Watch for Triggers

- *Help the young woman to see what triggers her bingeing behaviors and try to identify situations that aggravate it.*
- *Help her see what is behind her actions. Chances are, some kind of anxiety and stress are driving these actions.*

5. Change Thinking Patterns

- *Gently question the girl's thinking. Help her begin to see the lies behind the behaviors that are trapping her.*

6. Examine Perfectionism

- *Examine her perfectionism. Chances are she holds herself to standards to which she does not hold her loved ones.*
- *Help her examine these standards and how they square with God's truth revealed in Scripture.*

7. Keep a Journal

- *Encourage the person to write in a journal about her feelings and the events of each day. She may have difficulty identifying feelings. Help her view her feelings as normal and acceptable.*

BIBLICAL INSIGHTS | 6

Now the mixed multitude who were among them yielded to intense craving; so the children of Israel also wept again and said: "Who will give us meat to eat? We remember the fish which we ate freely in Egypt, the cucumbers, the melons, the leeks, the onions, and the garlic; but now our whole being is dried up; *there is* nothing at all except this manna *before* our eyes!"

Numbers 11:4–6

> $64.7 billion is the yearly economic cost of eating disorders.[10]

No temptation has overtaken you except such as is common to man; but God is faithful, who will not allow you to be tempted beyond what you are able, but with the temptation will also make the way of escape, that you may be able to bear it.

1 Corinthians 10:13

All things are lawful for me, but all things are not helpful. All things are lawful for me, but I will not be brought under the power of any. Foods for the stomach and the stomach for foods, but God will destroy both it and them. Now the body *is* not for sexual immorality but for the Lord, and the Lord for the body.

1 Corinthians 6:12–13

PRAYER STARTER | 7

Dear Lord, thank You that _____ is seeking help. Please help him [her] to accept himself [herself] and know that he [she] is loved. Help his [her] family to get beyond their concern or guilt so they can work on showing love to their child. Please comfort this family, Lord, and be very close to them. Heal their hearts and minds, and protect _____ from medical problems. Please be with them every step of the way to healing . . .

8 RECOMMENDED RESOURCES

Alcorn, Nancy. *Starved: Mercy for Eating Disorders*. WinePress, 2007.

Arterburn, Stephen, and David Stoop. *The Life Recovery Workbook for Eating Disorders: A Bible-Centered Approach for Taking Your Life Back*. Tyndale, 2020.

Barbosa, Jenna. *Tenacious Grace: Redefine Your Relationship with Food and End Emotional Eating*. Author Academy Elite, 2020.

Epstein, Rhona. *Food Triggers: End Your Cravings, Eat Well and Live Better*. Worthy Books, 2013.

Jantz, Gregory L., and Ann McMurray. *Hope, Help, and Healing for Eating Disorders: A New Approach to Treating Anorexia, Bulimia, and Overeating*. WaterBrook, 2010.

Schaffer, Jenni. *Life Without Ed: How One Woman Declared Independence from Her Eating Disorder and How You Can Too*. McGraw-Hill, 2003.

Organizations

Gurze Books specializes in eating disorder publications (1-800-756-7533 or Gurze .com).

Remuda Ranch provides inpatient and residential programs for women, girls, and boys suffering from anorexia, bulimia, other eating disorders, and related issues. Their Christian programs offer hope and healing to patients of all beliefs (1-800-445-1900 or RemudaRanch.com).

Websites

American Association of Christian Counselors (AACC.net)

Christian Care Connect (Connect.AACC.net)

National Eating Disorders Association (NationalEatingDisorders.org)

The Center: A Place of Hope (APlaceOfHope.com)

Envy and Jealousy

PORTRAITS | 1

- Marilyn spends most of her days looking at the latest fashion trends. Her husband, Tom, complains that they are never able to get ahead because of Marilyn's constant spending.
- Although Jake has advanced education and a successful career, he finds himself resenting Peter's ability to be the life of the party and make everyone laugh. He thinks, *If I had Peter's personality, I would be able to be everyone's best friend too!*
- Maria can't seem to control her tongue. She feels it is almost impossible to resist the temptation to pass along to her friends the latest "scoop" on someone in the church.
- Steve was thankful that his friendship with Dan was one in which they could commiserate over the hardships and trials they were both experiencing. Now that Dan seems to be receiving one blessing after another, Steve finds that he is resentful that Dan's life has taken a turn for the good.
- Jealous of her sister, her friends, and her neighbors, Angela is now jealous of her husband's new coworker. Wallowing in anger and self-pity, she allows her jealousy to consume her emotions and taint her marriage. Feeling smothered and wrongly accused, her husband begins pulling away in frustration. She is becoming panicky, predicting that her husband will leave her or have an affair, and she is behaving in a way that increases the odds of her dark predictions coming true.

DEFINITIONS AND KEY THOUGHTS | 2

- Jealousy and envy are siblings, the perverse children of a *toxic mix* of anger, anxiety-based insecurity, and an obsessive habit of comparing oneself (usually poorly) with others.[1]
- There is also a *root of fear* in most jealousy—the fear of losing the love or praise of one's object of love or affection.[2]
- *Envy* wants what someone else has.
- *Jealousy* is being fearful that something one has attained will be taken. Jealousy also involves a triangle—three people, one of which is the jealous person becoming fixated on a (usually misperceived) rival, who is viewed as competing for the attention of the third person.[3]

- Scripture says that love as "strong as death" will produce powerful jealousy that is "*as* cruel as the grave" (Song of Sol. 8:6).[4]
- *Envy* may be defined as *wanting what someone else has,* whether it is status, possessions, lifestyle, relationships, or characteristics.
- Left unchecked, envy can develop into *malice, contempt, and destruction* of others (see 1 Sam. 18:9 to see envy in the life of Saul).
- Envy manifests itself in the *resentment* of others' prosperity.
- Envy will be *evident in one's dislike of another.* The envious person will not necessarily be aware that the dislike is prompted by envy.
- Envy is fueled by the *expectation of deserving* more success and recognition than another person. Envy, therefore, is *closely linked to pride and greed.*
- *Envy is the opposite of love.* Love rejoices over the good of another. Envy seeks the destruction of another for the benefit of oneself.
- Envy is ultimately a *rebellion* against one's own finiteness and God's provision. When people struggle with envy, they reject God's provision as well as how God uniquely created them to be.
- Scripture tells us that the Lord is "a jealous God" (Exod. 34:14), but the Lord's jealousy is righteous. God is jealous for the church (2 Cor. 11:2). Paul warns us, however, not to provoke the Lord to jealousy (1 Cor. 10:20–22).[5]

Causes of Envy and Jealousy

Dissatisfaction with God's provision: The person may see only what God *hasn't* provided rather than what God has provided.

Comparison with others: From early on, many have been conditioned to see themselves only in comparison to others—being smarter than, not as attractive as, more popular than, and so on.

Pride: Envy is driven by the false notion that a person "deserves" to have a life focused on his or her own personal gain and satisfaction.

Low self-esteem or seeking significance: When people don't feel good about themselves, they will constantly try to soothe their pain by seeking significance in their circumstances rather than finding their deepest needs met by Jesus Christ.

Value of worldly gain: People may seek money, status, appearance, talents, or achievements as evidence of their value and "place" in the world.

Expressions of Envy and Jealousy

Envy can be disguised in a multitude of ways. Here are the most common manifestations:

Resentment toward others: The person may be highly critical and judgmental of another person or persons.

Competition in relationships: The desire to be the "top dog" in relationships may be indicative of a struggle with envy. The person may exhibit a drive toward overachievement and a superior attitude toward others.

Depression: The person may become highly self-critical because he or she has not achieved what is desired and what the other person has.

Lack of contentment: We live in a culture in which the media bombards us with the false notion that achieving more material gain will lead to greater happiness. A person struggling with envy is rarely content with what God has provided.

Gossip about others: Envious people constantly criticize the object of their envy.

Idolizing or putting others on a pedestal.

Dissatisfaction with life: People who are jealous often have thoughts of *If only . . .*

Stages of Envy and Jealousy

Initial Stage: The first stage of envy is desiring what someone else is or has.

Scorn or Disdain: When a person does not face his or her own envy, it can *lead to scorn or disdain* for another person, simply because this person is a reminder of what is lacking. This is expressed in contempt.

Malice: Envy can also *develop into malice.* People desire to destroy the good they see in another's life, believing that if they cannot have what another person has, they will destroy any pleasure the other person has from it.

Domination of Relationships: Jealousy, when carried to extremes, can dominate a relationship. Some spouses, having faced abuse or abandonment in their childhood, bring this pathology into a marriage. *Unresolved issues* from one's past can be the impetus for developing a vicious cycle of dysfunctional jealousy.

A Consuming Cycle: A chronically jealous partner will use self-pity, lies, threats, and other manipulations to control a relationship. When the other resists, the jealous person reacts by becoming more controlling. As time goes by, this cycle gains speed and heads toward disaster.

> But if you have bitter envy and self-seeking in your hearts, do not boast and lie against the truth. This wisdom does not descend from above, but *is* earthly, sensual, demonic.
>
> James 3:14–15

ASSESSMENT INTERVIEW 3

Often other issues mask envy. A person may speak of *the unfairness of life* or *express resentment* toward someone else. The person may have a *need to always be the best* at every task undertaken.

Be aware that the issue of resentment may also be a *lack of forgiveness* in which the person experienced hurt from someone else and desires revenge.

Listen to the core issue. Is it that the person is resentful toward what someone has done to him or her? Is it because someone else has achieved something that he or she has not?

Do not label the person as being "envious" or "jealous." Listen and acknowledge the person's struggle and experience.

In a study on comparison, researchers found more than 10% of daily thoughts involved making a comparison of some kind.[6]

1. What is the situation that has prompted such difficult feelings for you?
2. Do you get upset when others advance in their career or social standing?
3. Do you find that it is difficult for you to celebrate the blessings of some of those around you?
4. Do you sometimes feel that God has disappointed you in His provision?
5. Do you find yourself often thinking, *If only I* _____ (fill in the blank with what you wish were different in your life)?
6. Where do you find that most of your money goes?
7. Do you feel secretly pleased when someone you admire experiences a setback?
8. Do you sometimes want to sabotage another's blessings?
9. Do you struggle with feeling critical and/or judgmental of others?
10. Do you find that you are not content unless you are the "best" at something?
11. Do you struggle with depression?
12. Would you identify more with the best and brightest rather than with those on the fringe of a group?
13. Do you find that you tend to put others on a pedestal?
14. Tell me about your marriage.
15. How do you feel about your spouse's friendships or activities?
16. Has your spouse ever given you reason to doubt his [her] faithfulness or love for you?

4 WISE COUNSEL

The core to overcoming envy or jealousy is *threefold*:

- understanding God's love
- being content with His provision
- loving others as God loves you

Envy and jealousy are *futile attempts* to fill one's deepest longings for significance and security by seeking what someone else has or by controlling what someone else does.

The person who is struggling should be gently and consistently pointed to the *love and sufficiency of Jesus Christ*.

In addition, *offer encouragement* until the person is willing to address this issue and look honestly at his or her own sin.

ACTION STEPS | 5

1. Be Honest

- We all deceive ourselves in a multitude of ways. While we may not feel we are experiencing envy or jealousy, these feelings may be disguised in many different forms, such as criticism, contempt, gossip, self-pity, and manipulation.
- Ask God to reveal your motivations and feelings. Write down in a journal or private notebook what God has shown you in your heart.
- Confess your heart attitudes to Christ.

2. Focus on Jesus Christ

- God sees you as His own beloved child.
- Commit yourself and the day to God, asking for His guidance and presence throughout the day.

3. Develop a Lifestyle of Gratitude and Worship

- Count your blessings.
- Read the Psalms as personal prayers, praising God for all He is and what He has done.
- At the end of each day, reflect on the unexpected blessings you received throughout the day. Thank God for His constant love and care.

4. Avoid Activities That Encourage Comparison

- Spend time in malls only when there is a specific item you need to purchase.
- Read books that encourage reflection on the beauty of life and external blessings we have as believers.
- Minimize exposure to social media, magazines, TV, and other platforms that focus on material gain.

5. Interrupt Feelings of Envy

- Pray for God's blessing to be poured out on the person whom you envy and give thanks for God's provision for that person.
- Remind yourself of Jesus's counsel that "one's life does not consist in the abundance of the things he possesses" (Luke 12:15). Ultimately, "things" are shallow substitutes for the presence of God in your life.
- Remind yourself of who you are as one of God's chosen children. "From the beginning [God] chose you for salvation through sanctification by the Spirit and belief in the truth" (2 Thess. 2:13).

- Ask yourself what it is about the person that causes you to envy him or her. Does this person have strong social skills? Is he or she deeply compassionate? Thank God for the redeeming qualities you see in this person and ask God to form those qualities in your own heart. Then you will move from envy to admiration. Affirm and give thanks for the qualities that God has established in your own heart.

6. Interrupt Feelings of Jealousy[7]

- Be honest with yourself—back off from controlling or manipulative statements.
- Spend time with God. Immerse yourself in prayer and God's Word. Ask Him to transform your need for security into dependence on and confidence in Him.
- Transform your mind. Instead of allowing your anxious thoughts to lead to dark suspicions, ask God to cleanse your heart and mind. Ask Him to help you truly love—"love does not envy . . . thinks no evil" (1 Cor. 13:4–5). Remember all the positives in your relationship with the person of whom you are jealous. Do something—right then—to show your love. Make a call; send an email.

7. Grow

- Create a plan to develop the gifts and abilities God has uniquely given you.
- Evaluate your spiritual gifts and talents.
- Practice spiritual disciplines. Examples are prayer, fasting, solitude, study, sacrifices, worship, fellowship, meditation, and memorization.
- Spend time memorizing Scripture. Make a commitment to fast and pray for a particular situation in your life.
- Ask God to bring believers into your life who can encourage you in your relationship with Christ.

8. Consider Follow-Up

- *For some people, a chronic struggle with envy may be indicative of deeper unresolved pain from their past in which working with a professional therapist might be the best course of action.*

6 BIBLICAL INSIGHTS

You shall not covet your neighbor's house; you shall not covet your neighbor's wife, nor his male servant, nor his female servant, nor his ox, nor his donkey, nor anything that *is* your neighbor's.

Exodus 20:17

Then Saul was very angry, and the saying displeased him; and he said, "They have ascribed to David ten thousands, and to me they have ascribed *only* thousands. Now *what* more can he have but the kingdom?"

1 Samuel 18:8

For I am jealous for you with godly jealousy. For I have betrothed you to one husband, that I may present *you* as a chaste virgin to Christ.

2 Corinthians 11:2

Therefore, laying aside all malice, all deceit, hypocrisy, envy, and all evil speaking.

1 Peter 2:1

> A sound heart *is* life to the body, But envy *is* rottenness to the bones.
> Proverbs 14:30

PRAYER STARTER 7

Lord, we want to thank You, first of all, for Your great blessings in Your child's life. He [she] knows that You have done great things, but today he [she] struggles with the pain of desiring more. Help him [her] today, Lord, to understand the great gifts he [she] has from Your hand and the great contributions he [she] can make to Your kingdom. Help him [her] learn contentment . . .

RECOMMENDED RESOURCES 8

Idleman, Kyle. *Gods at War: Defeating the Idols That Battle for Your Heart.* Zondervan, 2018.

Laurie, Greg. *The Best Is Yet to Come: Faith for Today, Hope for the Future.* Multnomah, 2005.

TerKeurst, Lysa. *Finding I AM—Bible Study Book: How Jesus Fully Satisfies the Cry of Your Heart.* Lifeway Press, 2017.

Websites

American Association of Christian Counselors (AACC.net)

Christian Care Connect (Connect.AACC.net)

Fear and Anxiety

1 PORTRAITS

- Janice is always on the alert. Her timid voice and shy manner indicate she is on constant watch for potential hazards. As an only child born to a single mother, Janice feels she was born to be her mother's scapegoat. When she was young, Janice can remember waiting for her mother to come home and feeling her whole body become tense. She never knew what would happen when her mother returned. As an adult, Janice is always wary of potential harm. She even finds that she becomes tense when there is nothing to be anxious about.

- Nadine is considered a loner. Little does anyone know that she has a deep fear of being in groups. Nadine becomes overwhelmed with panic when she is in a restaurant eating with her coworkers. Even though it seems irrational, she fears saying something foolish, spilling food on her shirt, or beginning to stutter. When she is alone with one person, she is fine, but in a group, even making eye contact with someone seems painful.

- Steve hurt his neck in an accident, and he has lived with pain and numbness in his arm for several years. Finally, he goes to the doctor, who has him get an MRI. When Steve is ready to go into the machine, the technician asks, "Do you have any problem with closed spaces?" Steve answers, "No, I don't." But after only fifteen seconds in the MRI machine, he has a full-blown panic attack. He has had many others on airplanes, so now he takes medication whenever he flies.

> For God has not given us a spirit of fear, but of power and of love and of a sound mind.
>
> 2 Timothy 1:7

2 DEFINITIONS AND KEY THOUGHTS

Fear

- While most people experience fear as a negative emotion, *fear also has a positive component.* If you find that you have turned down a one-way street and see a car heading directly at you, fear triggers an autonomic response that sends a signal to your brain to "flee" the potentially dangerous situation.

- Fear becomes a problem when a person is *afraid of things that are not real* or when the feeling of fear is *out of proportion* to the real danger present.

- Fear is an emotion that draws a person into a *self-protective mode.*

- More often than not, fears are related to *what a person perceives* as a threat to his or her safety and security. The person may fear losing his or her job, having his or her home burglarized, or having conflict in a relationship.

Anxiety

- *Anxiety is a constant fearful state*, accompanied by a feeling of unrest, dread, or worry. The person may not be aware of what is creating the fear.
- Anxiety is aroused by *a number of factors*:
  » external situations (viewing the nightly news, a fast-paced lifestyle)
  » physical well-being (lack of sleep, blood sugar imbalance)
  » modeling (parents who were highly anxious)
  » trauma (in situations that may be similar to experiences of the past that caused great pain)
- Anxiety's *symptoms* can include inability to relax, tense feelings, rapid heartbeat, dry mouth, increased blood pressure, jumpiness or feeling faint, excessive perspiring, feeling clammy, constant anticipation of trouble, and constant feeling of uneasiness.[2]

> An estimated 19.1% of US adults had any anxiety disorder in the past year.[1]

Phobias

- A *phobia* is "a persistent, excessive, unrealistic fear of an object, person, animal, activity or situation. It is a type of anxiety disorder."[3]
- A person with a phobia "either tries to avoid the thing that triggers the fear or endures it with great anxiety and distress."[4]
- Phobias are fears that are out of proportion to the object, situation, or activity feared. For example, one may have a fear of spiders. A person exhibits a phobia when he or she sees a small spider on the ceiling of a room and refuses to enter the room ever again.

Panic Attacks and Disorder[5]

- People with panic disorder have "sudden and repeated attacks of fear that last for several minutes or longer. These are called panic attacks."
- Panic attacks are characterized by "a fear of disaster or of losing control even when there is no real danger."
- A person may also have a strong physical reaction during a panic attack. It may feel like having a heart attack. Panic attacks can occur at any time, and many people with panic disorder worry about and dread the possibility of having another attack.
- A person with panic disorder may become "discouraged and feel ashamed because he or she cannot carry out normal routines like going to school or work, going to the grocery store, or driving."

- Panic disorder often begins "in the late teens or early adulthood. More women than men have panic disorder. But not everyone who experiences panic attacks will develop panic disorder."

Relational Fears

- There are four major relational fears that people experience that can significantly alter their quality of life: fear of *failure*, fear of *rejection*, fear of *abandonment*, and fear of *death or dying*.

3 | ASSESSMENT INTERVIEW

1. When do you find yourself feeling afraid or anxious?
2. How long and to what extent has this fear or anxiety been occurring for you?
3. What situation/object/person causes you the most distress?
4. Do you find there are times when you are more anxious than others? If so, when?
5. Of the things that cause you fear, which seem reasonable and which seem more unreasonable?
6. When do the feelings of anxiety go away?
7. How have you tried to cope with the anxiety?
8. Do you have any health problems and/or medications that may contribute to the anxiety?
9. What would your life be like if you were free of this anxiety?

4 | WISE COUNSEL

Fear and anxiety are *defused by knowledge*. The more a person can defuse the perceived threat, the less anxiety he or she will experience.

Generally, the fearful person has established an *irrational belief system* that is creating anxiety for him or her. *Try to gain an understanding* of what lies or deceptions are contributing to the anxiety.

Most anxiety reactions are *learned behavior*. Be intentional in your efforts to encourage the person to develop hope that he or she will be able to overcome the anxiety or fears by learning new behaviors rooted in truth.

Anxiety can be *contagious*. Those who experience strong anxiety tend to elicit anxiety reactions in those who are around them. You need to be aware of your own anxiety level and how you cope personally with anxiety when it occurs. Remember that this could be a familial pattern. It is good to see how fear was exhibited and handled in the family of origin. Also, these patterns could be passed down to children and it is important for the parent to understand that they could be affecting their children with their fear.

Be patient with the person as he or she sorts through the feelings of fear. Changing patterns takes time.

ACTION STEPS | 5

1. Change Thought Patterns

- It is important to dispute negative thoughts and lies with the truth of Scripture (Phil. 4:8). There are many Scriptures about fear. *It may be good to explain positive fear (fear of the Lord) and negative fear (fear of things in this world).*

2. Focus on God

- *Help the person move his or her focus from fear to the character of God (1 Peter 5:7).*
- God wants you to trust and relinquish all fears to Him, especially through prayer (Phil. 4:4–6).
- To have peace, keep your thoughts on God (Isa. 26:3).

3. Watch for Triggers

- *Assist the person in trying to minimize activities and input that induce anxiety.* Encourage the employment of coping skills when these activities or situations cannot be avoided.

> Worry is a cycle of inefficient thoughts whirling around a center of fear.
>
> Corrie ten Boom

4. Move Forward

- *Help the person learn from setbacks and resolve to continue to face down the fears.*
- *Gently encourage the person to take careful steps to face their fears.* Have safe people be with them as they do these actions. *Make sure these safe people are aware of the fear and have some skills in reminding the person to slow down their breathing and to help the fearful individual think rationally.*
- When you are becoming afraid, move your focus to the external world and others rather than the internal feelings of anxiety.

5. Develop Relationships

- *Assist the person in finding supportive, positive relationships.*

6. Be Patient

- Growth takes time.
- God will work in your life to overcome the anxiety that is keeping you from living life to the fullest.
- Try to keep an eternal perspective.

7. If Prescribed, Use Medications

- A doctor may prescribe medications to help alleviate inordinate fears or phobias. These enable people to think more clearly so they can make decisions without being dominated by their fears. As an individual employs coping skills and works on increasing his or her knowledge in order to combat the fear, medication could be lowered in order to wean the person off. This is only to be done with a doctor's permission.

6 | BIBLICAL INSIGHTS

If you should say in your heart, "These nations are greater than I; how can I dispossess them?"—you shall not be afraid of them, *but* you shall remember well what the LORD your God did to Pharaoh and to all Egypt: the great trials which your eyes saw, the signs and the wonders, the mighty hand and the outstretched arm, by which the LORD your God brought you out. . . . You shall not be terrified of them; for the LORD your God, the great and awesome God, *is* among you.

Deuteronomy 7:17–19, 21

> An estimated 31.1% of US adults experience an anxiety disorder at some time in their lives.[6]

Trust in the LORD. . . .

Delight yourself also in the LORD. . . .

Commit your way to the LORD. . . .

Rest in the LORD, and wait patiently for Him;
Do not fret because of him who prospers in his way,
Because of the man who brings wicked schemes to pass.

Psalm 37:3, 5, 7

Surely He shall deliver you from the snare of the fowler
And from the perilous pestilence.
He shall cover you with His feathers,
And under His wings you shall take refuge;
His truth *shall be your* shield and buckler.
You shall not be afraid of the terror by night,
Nor of the arrow *that* flies by day,
Nor of the pestilence *that* walks in darkness,
Nor of the destruction *that* lays waste at noonday.

Psalm 91:3–6

Trust in the LORD with all your heart,
And lean not on your own understanding;
In all your ways acknowledge Him,
And He shall direct your paths.

Proverbs 3:5–6

PRAYER STARTER | 7

Today a precious child of Yours is frightened, Lord. He [she] is frightened about the fear that has taken hold of his [her] life and left him [her] feeling helpless and hopeless. He [she] wants to serve You, Lord, but this anxiety is debilitating him [her] to the point that he [she] can barely function. He [she] needs the healing touch of Your hand, Lord, and wisdom to handle this anxiety . . .

RECOMMENDED RESOURCES | 8

Hart, Archibald D. *The Anxiety Cure*. Thomas Nelson, 2001.

Jantz, Gregory L. *The Anxiety Reset: A Life-Changing Approach to Overcoming Fear, Stress, Worry, Panic Attacks, OCD and More*. Tyndale, 2021.

Lucado, Max. *Anxious for Nothing: Finding Calm in a Chaotic World*. Thomas Nelson, 2019.

Simpson, Amy. *Anxious: Choosing Faith in a World of Worry*. IVP Books, 2014.

Young, Ed. *Know Fear: Facing Life's Six Most Common Phobias*. Lifeway Christian Resources, 2003.

Websites

American Association of Christian Counselors (AACC.net)

Christian Care Connect (Connect.AACC.net)

Forgiveness

1 PORTRAITS

It takes two to reconcile but only one to forgive.

- Gabriel cannot bring himself to attend his parents' fiftieth wedding anniversary celebration. Their lack of interest in his life and his family has hurt him so much that he wants nothing to do with them—let alone to honor them for fifty years of marriage.
- Becky cannot sleep at night. She keeps having nightmares about her mother, who abused her as a child. Even though her mother has been dead for ten years, Becky still cannot forgive her for the pain she caused.
- Joanne's "best friend" lied about her to her boyfriend, causing him to break up with her. Now Joanne's friend and her former boyfriend are dating. Every time Joanne sees them at school, she feels betrayed all over again and can't stop thinking about it.
- Tom finds out his coworker has been criticizing him to the boss and making negative comments about his work. The boss promotes his coworker and demotes Tom. Tom can't stop thinking of ways to get even with his coworker.

2 DEFINITIONS AND KEY THOUGHTS

What Forgiveness Is and Is Not

Unforgiveness is a state of resentment, bitterness, hatred, hostility, anger, fear, and stress toward an individual who has transgressed against another in some way. *Unforgiveness is a cancer that eats away at the very soul of a person.*

Forgiveness occurs when the cold feelings of unforgiveness are changed to warm, loving, compassionate, caring, and altruistic emotions because of a heartfelt transformation.[1]

In Luke 7:40–47 Jesus tells us the truth that those who have been forgiven much love much.

Explain to the person you're counseling the following definitions and parameters of forgiveness. Forgiveness

- does not mean that any wrongs done to you were acceptable.
- does not diminish the evil done against you, nor is it a denial of what happened.
- is a key part of not letting those wrongs hurt you any longer.

- does not take away the consequences the other person will face because of his or her sin.
- is letting go of your desire to hurt the other person. Simply put, forgiveness means you "cancel a debt."
- is a difficult and uncomfortable process. When you make a decision to forgive, God provides the grace and strength to forgive and to maintain a heart of forgiveness.
- is not weakness. It is the most powerful thing you can do. Refusing to forgive allows Satan to continue to hurt you; forgiveness stops the destructive power of Satan in one's life.
- is not reconciliation.
- does not depend on the other person's actions, and it is not probationary (for example, saying, "I will forgive you as long as you aren't drinking").
- does not require you to become a "doormat" nor does it require you to allow the offender to hurt you again.
- is a gift you *give* to the offender. Trust, on the other hand, *must be earned*. You must set boundaries.
- does not wait for the offender to repent. Unlike God, who provides forgiveness when we repent, humans cannot demand repentance before granting forgiveness.
- is about how much you trust God to take care of you.
- is experiencing empathy for the offender, humility about your own sinfulness, and gratitude for being forgiven by God and others.

> Human power alone is not sufficient to reach full forgiveness. There is an element of forgiveness that is divine. It cannot be reached without God.
>
> Frank Minirth

Reasons to Forgive

- Forgiveness sets you free to move on with your life.
- It refuses to let the person who hurt you have any power over your life.
- It opens up your relationship with God (see Matt. 5:43–48).
- It keeps you from becoming bitter and thus protects those around you.
- It keeps you from becoming like the person who hurt you.
- Unforgiveness doesn't hurt the perpetrator at all; it hurts only *you*.
- Scripture commands us to be forgiving (Matt. 18:21–35).

ASSESSMENT INTERVIEW 3

When a person seeks help to forgive, it is because the inability to forgive has started to *disrupt his or her personal, emotional, or spiritual life.*

The inability to forgive (due to the stress it creates) may be the source of physical problems, such as lack of energy, sleeplessness, headaches, joint pain, or back pain. It also may be the root cause of *depression or anxiety*.

Sometimes the person *does not realize* that the origin of his or her problem is a lack of forgiveness. Therefore, a counselor may need to gently lead him or her to this knowledge.

Consider the following assessment questions:

1. Can you tell me about your background?
2. What do you think is the source of your concern?
3. What led you to come to counseling?
4. What do you hope to accomplish?
5. What incident or incidents are you having trouble forgiving?
6. How did the incident(s) make you feel?
7. What can you tell me about the person who hurt you?
8. What have you already tried to do to help you forgive?
9. How have you protected yourself from being hurt again by this person?
10. How can you tell that you haven't forgiven this person?
11. Did you ever see any examples of forgiveness in your home while you were growing up?
12. When is the first time you can remember someone offending you? How did you handle it?
13. Can you see a pattern in how you respond when people offend you?
14. Do those responses help or hurt you?
15. What does God say about forgiveness?
16. What do you think forgiveness is?
17. Has anyone forgiven you for something? What did that look like? How did you feel?

4 WISE COUNSEL

Share with the person some *information about real forgiveness* as described above. Often a person has not forgiven because he or she doesn't understand what forgiveness is.

Forgiveness is best understood as an act and a process. When a person forgives, his or her heart will begin to heal. We can forgive when we realize that we have been forgiven by God (Eph. 4:31–32).

If the person doesn't want to let the offender "off the hook," explain that forgiveness *lets* the counselee *off the hook* and protects him or her from the destructive power of unforgiveness, setting the person free to move on with life.

Identify Emotions

One of the most important roles you can play in the life of someone who has been deeply offended is to validate the person's perception of the wrong. Many people go to great lengths to avoid the pain of the offense: they minimize ("It wasn't that bad"), excuse the offender ("He couldn't help it"), or deny the impact of it ("I'm used to it by now").

Empathize with the person and acknowledge the evil that has occurred. Encourage the person to grieve the offense and the losses that have resulted from any wrong committed against him or her. Explain that hurt and anger are not sinful; they are normal responses to an offense.

It is important to identify and express one's feelings toward the offense committed; how the person felt during the offense and how he or she feels now.

Draw from a Deep Well

Author Philip Yancey once wrote that forgiveness is "the unnatural act" because everything in us cries out for revenge. People live with bitterness—which is anger that has festered—because they depend on their own wisdom and strength to find a way to feel better about what happened. To them, the only remedy is revenge, either overt revenge by actively hurting the offender or covert revenge by using gossip, passive-aggressive behavior, or avoiding the person altogether.

Jesus has given us a better way. Paul wrote, "Let all bitterness, wrath, anger, clamor, and evil speaking be put away from you, with all malice. And be kind to one another, tenderhearted, forgiving one another, even as God in Christ forgave you" (Eph. 4:31–32). When we draw from the deep well of God's forgiveness for our own sins, we'll have the motivation and the capacity to forgive those who have hurt us. Wounded people wound people, but forgiven people forgive people.

Set Boundaries

Work with the person to decipher what must be done to keep the offender from hurting the counselee again. This involves the way in which the person maintains an ongoing relationship with the offender. For instance, he or she can be polite (safe boundaries) without being a best friend (unsafe boundaries). Likewise, he or she can listen without taking advice.

Minimize time with unsafe people. Unsafe people are those who hurt without regard for the damage it creates in another's life.

Do not look for approval from a person who will likely cause pain.

Help the person recognize that he or she does not need another's approval to live a free and fulfilling life. The only approval he or she needs is God's.

> Sixty-two percent of American adults say they need more forgiveness in their personal lives, according to a survey by the nonprofit Fetzer Institute.[2]

Recognize God's Hand

Know that God can use the offense to promote personal and spiritual growth and dependence on Him for His plan and glory.

Ask for the intervention of the Holy Spirit to heal the emotional wounds of the client.

Ask God to help the client love the offender. It is said that any action that is not motivated by compassion is sinful. Since those who transgress are often lost, broken, or hurting, even the one who was wronged can feel pity and compassion for the offender.

Praying for the offender will help the client's feelings move from wanting revenge to not wanting harm and finally to wanting the best for the transgressor. When the client reaches the latter stage, he or she will know real freedom. When the client asks God not to hold the sin against the offender, they will truly know peace, but do not push the client here. It is a difficult thing for anyone to do.

5 | ACTION STEPS

Everett Worthington Jr., author of *The Handbook of Forgiveness*, has developed a useful acrostic for navigating the process of forgiveness. It is known as R-E-A-C-H:

Recall the Hurt[3]

- It is difficult but necessary to recall the hurt.
- *Don't minimize or deny the person's pain.*
- *Don't make excuses for the offender.*
- Recalling your hurt is not for the purpose of finger-pointing but a means to objectively review what has occurred.
- Journaling is a great way to work through anger and hurt. It organizes your thoughts and helps you acknowledge the truth in black and white.
- Sometimes writing a letter to the offender is helpful, but *don't mail the letter.*

Empathize with the Person

> But if you do not forgive men their trespasses, neither will your Father forgive your trespasses.
>
> Matthew 6:15

- Write a letter as if you were the offender. *This should not be done if the offender has physically or sexually abused the individual.* You should write about thoughts, feelings, insights, and pressures. Make this a letter of apology. Consider how difficult it is to do this.
- By placing yourself in the shoes of the person who transgressed, you can begin to understand why the person did what he or she did.
- This does not remove blame from the individual but does serve to show that people who hurt are often hurting deeply themselves.

Altruistic Gift of Forgiveness[4]

- Think about the "giving" of forgiveness. Think of a time when you did something wrong and were forgiven. Reflect on the wrongdoing and guilt you felt. How did it feel to be forgiven? Would you like to give that gift of forgiveness to the person who hurt you?
- Write a blank check of forgiveness. Write in your journal that this day you have released the offender from the debt he or she owes you.
- You may want to write down the offenses the person has done and then write "Canceled" or "Paid in Full" over them.
- Through this step, also recall the great mercy and grace of God toward you.

Commit Publicly to Forgive

- Write a certificate or letter of forgiveness stating that you will not ruminate on the wrongs done to you anymore, but don't send it.
- By participating in some outward expression of forgiveness, such as writing a letter, you will be more prone to remember that you have forgiven and are thus freed from the plague of "unforgiveness."
- Tell your family and/or friends about your decision to forgive. By disclosing your forgiveness to others, you will be held accountable to your decision to forgive the transgressor.

Hold On to Forgiveness

- Hold on to forgiveness when doubts arise.[5]
- There is a difference between remembering a transgression and lacking forgiveness.[6]
- Make "Stones of Remembrance." After God parted the Jordan River so the Israelites could go through on dry land, God told Joshua to have each tribe choose a stone to be piled up as a memorial to what great things God had done that day. Those stones served as a remembrance for the people and their children in times to come (Josh. 4). It is good to have something "concrete" to help you remember the day you set your offender free.
- Remember to forget! When Corrie ten Boom was reminded of an offense someone had done to her, she responded, "I distinctly remember forgetting that." Though you may never really forget, you can remember that you forgave.

BIBLICAL INSIGHTS 6

He shall restore its full value, add one-fifth more to it, *and* give it to whomever it belongs, on the day of his trespass offering. And he shall bring his trespass offering to the Lord, a ram without blemish from the flock, with your valuation, as a trespass offering, to the priest.

Leviticus 6:5–6

And when [David] had called for Absalom, he came to the king and bowed himself on his face to the ground before the king. Then the king kissed Absalom.

2 Samuel 14:33

I, *even* I, *am* He who blots out your transgressions for My own sake;
And I will not remember your sins.

Isaiah 43:25

And you know, when you've experienced grace and you feel like you've been forgiven, you're a lot more forgiving of other people. You're a lot more gracious to others.

Rick Warren

Then Peter came to Him and said, "Lord, how often shall my brother sin against me, and I forgive him? Up to seven times?"

Jesus said to him, "I do not say to you, up to seven times, but up to seventy times seven."

Matthew 18:21–22

But if you do not forgive, neither will your Father in heaven forgive your trespasses.

Mark 11:26

7 | PRAYER STARTER

Lord, Your servant has been deeply hurt. He [she] wants to let go, to be free of the pain, but he [she] is finding it very difficult. The emotions go all over the place and he [she] doesn't want this pain affecting one more waking moment. Please help him [her] let this go. Please help him [her] forgive the offender as he [she] has been forgiven by You. Please give him [her] life once again . . .

8 | RECOMMENDED RESOURCES

Kendall, R. T. *Total Forgiveness*. Charisma House, 2007.

TerKeurst, Lysa. *Forgiving What You Can't Forget: Discover How to Move On, Make Peace with Painful Memories, and Create a Life That's Beautiful Again*. Thomas Nelson, 2020.

West, Matthew. *Forgiveness: Overcoming the Impossible*. Thomas Nelson, 2013.

Worthington Jr., Everett L. *Handbook of Forgiveness*. Brunner-Routledge, 2005.

Websites

American Association of Christian Counselors (AACC.net)

Christian Care Connect (Connect.AACC.net)

Grief and Loss

- Mark doesn't know what the matter is—it has been almost two years since his wife, Sue, died and he feels as if nothing has changed. He still can't believe that she is really gone. After Sue's accident, Mark's friends were supportive and his church brought meals and prayed for him, but nothing seemed to help. There are days, more of them than he cares to admit, when he thinks it would have been better if he had been in the car with Sue and had died too.
- Tina can't seem to stop crying. She is angry with herself for agreeing to move and with her husband, Bill, for forcing them to move a thousand miles from family and friends. She misses everyone, her church, the friends she grew up with, and most of all her family. She doesn't want to be here and certainly doesn't want to make friends. The phone bill is huge but she doesn't care. She just wants to go back home.
- Rob can't drive past the hospital without feeling that sick clenching feeling in his gut. He spent hours watching his dad struggle with cancer. Rob just can't seem to care about anything else—his days, and sometimes nights for that matter, had revolved around doing whatever he could to make sure his dad made it, and now his dad is gone.

DEFINITIONS AND KEY THOUGHTS 2

- Grief is intense emotional suffering caused by a loss.[1]
- Grieving is like entering the valley of shadows. Grief is not fun. It is *painful*. It is *work*. It is *a lingering process*. It is a healing journey that can last anywhere from one to three years, and for some a lifetime. Some people never get through the process of grieving.
- A *sudden death* can be more difficult to grieve because there is no warning and no chance to say goodbye and begin to prepare for the loss.
- Grief is not always just about death. It can also be faced in a *divorce, life transition, disaster, or misfortune*.
- Grief is actually a *complex set of emotions*, all of which are "normal." People who are grieving may experience their loss psychologically through feelings, thoughts, and attitudes; socially as they interact with others; and physically as it affects their health.

- Often friends don't know how to help someone who is grieving and may try to "cheer him up" or "get her mind off her loss." This can actually add to the burden as the person who is grieving has to either avoid friends or "fake it" rather than have the chance to share his or her true feelings.
- Sometimes loss is cumulative and *awakens memories of early losses* that were never fully grieved.
- Someone who is grieving may experience *intense feelings of guilt* for aspects of the relationship with the person who has died or the grieving person may feel as if he or she is being punished.
- Sometimes the feelings of anger and sadness are *projected onto God* and the grieving person experiences God as distant and uncaring.
- Often sadness and loss can *intensify during certain times of the year*, such as the month that the person died, family holidays, and the person's birthday or anniversary.

Stages of Grief

Grief can be felt in many different ways. Grief has several stages that were originally identified by Elisabeth Kübler-Ross (*On Death and Dying*):[2]

1. *Denial or isolation:* Intellectually, bereaved people may comprehend what has happened, but their emotions may not experience the pain yet; they may feel numb.[3]
2. *Anger:* Often this anger is released toward others. The bereaved may even get angry with God. Grieving people become preoccupied with memories of what has been lost and may withdraw for a time.
3. *Bargaining:* In the case of impending death, the grieving individual may bargain with God for more time—a time of negotiations.
4. *Depression:* A time of sadness, disconnection. Bereaved people beat themselves up emotionally as they blame themselves for not somehow preventing the loss. They feel disorganized and don't know how to move on with life. Depression may set in.
5. *Acceptance:* Reorganizing their life, filling new roles, and reconnecting with those around them are all healthy and important facets of the healing process. A key part of this process is the ability to learn how to feel and express the pain more truly without denial and avoidance.

As helpful as it may be to learn about these stages, they are not neatly packaged states that a person experiences sequentially; rather, they are a cycle, and the bereaved may experience more than one at a time and go back and forth through the stages. Some have even likened it to a vortex where a person continues to "spin around" in these emotions for a time.

The goal of grieving is *not to get things back to normal*. After a loss, one's entire life may change. The goal is to find and accept a new "normal."

As a culture, we seem to have an intolerance for suffering; we tend to want those who have experienced a loss of any kind to get on with their lives as quickly as possible. Often, by minimizing the impact of significant losses, pathologizing those whose reactions are intense, and applauding those who seem relatively unaffected by tragic events, we encourage the inhibition of our own grief.

H. Norman Wright

ASSESSMENT INTERVIEW | 3

Rule Outs

1. To determine if the grieving process has cycled downward into a debilitating depression ask: "On a scale of 1 to 10, with 1 being great and 10 being extremely depressed, where would you put yourself today?" (*If depression is evident, see also the section on Depression.*)
2. Do you have any thoughts of hurting yourself? (*If suicidal tendencies are evident, see the section on Suicide and get other help immediately.*)

General Questions

Note: These are directed toward someone who is grieving over a death but could be recast for the person who is grieving loss for other reasons.

1. How are you feeling?
2. What happened? Can you tell me the story?
3. What did you like most about the person?
4. Was the death sudden? (For example, was it a sudden accident or death at home?)
5. Where were you when the death occurred? (*Listen for ways that the person may be blaming himself [herself] or feeling guilty for what has happened. For example, was he or she driving the car that had the accident? Was he or she the passenger who survived a car accident while the other person did not? Process those feelings with the grieving person.*)
6. How did you feel after the death?
7. What emotions have you had since the death?
8. What emotions do you currently feel most often?
9. Does this loss remind you of any other loss that you have experienced?
10. Who else knows what you have been going through? Who is supporting you emotionally and spiritually?
11. What does the loss mean for you personally? What are you having to do now that is hard for you? Can we figure out some ways to make it easier?
12. At what level are you functioning right now? Tell me about a typical day.
13. When are your best times?
14. When are your worst times?

> But I do not want you to be ignorant, brethren, concerning those who have fallen asleep, lest you sorrow as others who have no hope. For if we believe that Jesus died and rose again, even so God will bring with Him those who sleep in Jesus.
>
> 1 Thessalonians 4:13–14

WISE COUNSEL | 4

Address any issues the person may have of *wanting to die* or not having a reason to live and give a referral for immediate professional care and/or medication, if necessary.

Assess how the person is *functioning in daily life* and what help he or she might need. Reassure the person that the process will *take time* and that the range and intensity of emotions he or she is experiencing are normal.

Remind the grieving person that everyone's grieving experience is unique, while at the same time *normalizing the process* by identifying it as one you have seen with all persons suffering some important loss.

5 | ACTION STEPS

1. Be Patient

- Give yourself the time it takes to heal emotionally.
- Keep a routine, get lots of rest, and try not to attempt too much but direct your energies toward healing.
- It is okay to break down emotionally from time to time. This is all a part of the process.

2. Maintain Friendships

The reality is that you will grieve forever. You will not "get over" the loss of a loved one; you will learn to live with it. You will heal and you will rebuild yourself around the loss you have suffered. You will be whole again but you will never be the same. Nor should you be the same nor would you want to.

Dr. Elisabeth Kübler-Ross

- Let others comfort you and share in your journey toward healing.
- Do not become isolated from people but rather seek meaningful connection with others.
- Make a list of friends to call.
- Locate a grief support group.
- Keep going to church and Bible studies.

3. Feel the Pain

- The intensity of your pain is normal and eventually it will begin to subside. The pain will probably never disappear completely, but it will become bearable.
- Trying to avoid the "terrible pain" only prolongs the grief.
- Trying to avoid a loss by hiding the feelings will only cause problems in other areas—emotionally, spiritually, or physically.[4]
- Dealing with loss in a healthy manner can be a major avenue to growth and life-transforming change.
- You must move forward by experiencing the grief, while at the same time rejoining the living through acts of giving and receiving.
- Keep a journal, and sometimes write to your loved one or about what you have lost. It helps you work through those difficult emotions.

4. Realize Grief Is Normal

- Grief encompasses a number of changes. It appears differently at various times, and it comes and goes in people's lives.[5]
- It is a normal, predictable, expected, and healthy reaction to a loss.

- *Grief is each individual's personal journey, and his or her manner of dealing with any kind of loss—no matter how minor or severe it may appear to others—must be respected. It should be gently challenged only when prolonged in a manner that is detrimental to the person and his or her relationships.*

5. Heal

- *Help the grieving person process any guilt and anger he or she is feeling.*
- *Help him or her redirect energy from excessive "if onlys" and wishing that things could be different to a focus on healing.*
- *There are still positives happening in life; it is a good reminder that not all is bad.*

My flesh and my heart fail; *But* God *is* the strength of my heart and my portion forever.
Psalm 73:26

BIBLICAL INSIGHTS 6

Then David lamented with this lamentation over Saul and over Jonathan his son.

2 Samuel 1:17

He is despised and rejected by men,
A Man of sorrows and acquainted with grief.
And we hid, as it were, *our* faces from Him;
He was despised, and we did not esteem Him.

Surely He has borne our griefs
And carried our sorrows;
Yet we esteemed Him stricken,
Smitten by God, and afflicted.

Isaiah 53:3–4

Jesus said to her, "I am the resurrection and the life. He who believes in Me, though he may die, he shall live. And whoever lives and believes in Me shall never die. Do you believe this?"

John 11:25–26

But I do not want you to be ignorant, brethren, concerning those who have fallen asleep, lest you sorrow as others who have no hope. For if we believe that Jesus died and rose again, even so God will bring with Him those who sleep in Jesus.

1 Thessalonians 4:13–14

And God will wipe away every tear from their eyes; there shall be no more death, nor sorrow, nor crying. There shall be no more pain, for the former things have passed away.

Revelation 21:4

The five stages—denial, anger, bargaining, depression, and acceptance—are a part of the framework that makes up our learning to live with the one(s) we lost. They are tools to help us frame and identify what we may be feeling. But they are not stops on some linear timeline in grief.
Dr. Elisabeth Kübler-Ross

7 PRAYER STARTER

Lord, we wish we understood Your thoughts and Your plans, but sometimes we admit that we just don't get it. We don't understand why You would take a loved one from us. We don't understand why You would allow this to happen when You knew what it would do. Yet, Lord, we want to trust You . . .

8 RECOMMENDED RESOURCES

Hodges IV, Samuel, and Kathy Leonard. *Grieving with Hope: Finding Comfort as You Journey Through Loss*. Baker Books, 2011.

Wright, H. Norman. *Experiencing Grief*. Broadman & Holman, 2004.

Wright, H. Norman. *Recovering from Losses in Life*. Revell, 2006.

Zonnebelt-Smeenge, Susan, and Robert DeVries. *The Empty Chair: Handling Grief on Holidays and Special Occasions*. Baker Books, 2001.

Zonnebelt-Smeenge, Susan, and Robert DeVries. *Getting to the Other Side of Grief*. Baker Books, 2019.

Websites

American Association of Christian Counselors (AACC.net)

Christian Care Connect (Connect.AACC.net)

Guilt

- For the first ten years of her marriage, Lydia lived in a house on the street behind her parents. She visited them every day, and her mother helped babysit her children. She was always very close to her parents. Then her husband got a job in a new location. Lydia feels tremendous guilt over moving away from her parents, who had become quite dependent on her.
- When Glen was nine years old, he was told to go home right after school to check on his great-aunt, who lived with them. He was asked by a friend to play football in the park and decided his great-aunt would be fine for a bit longer. When he arrived home an hour late, there was an ambulance at his house. Aunt Muriel had suffered a heart attack. She passed away that day, and Glen carried the guilt with him into his adult life.
- Marjorie stole some money years ago from a previous employer. It wasn't a lot of money, and she had gotten away with it undetected. However, recently she became a Christian and feels a lot of guilt over what she did.

> As far as the east is from the west, *So* far has He removed our transgressions from us.
> Psalm 103:12

DEFINITIONS AND KEY THOUGHTS **2**

- Guilt is a *feeling of deep regret or remorse* caused by feeling responsible for something.
- Guilt can *lead to shame* if the feelings of guilt are based on an act or acts that were thought to be wrong.
- There is a difference between *feeling guilty* and *actually being guilty*. If a moral law has been violated, a person is guilty, regardless of whether or not he or she feels guilty. On the other hand, just feeling guilty doesn't mean that a moral law has been violated.[1]
- It is important to clarify whether the guilt is caused by a *sinful act* or *from regret*.
- *True guilt* is caused by sin and is God's way of calling us to repentance and restitution.
- *False guilt* is guilt we place on ourselves because of regret for past acts, failure to live up to our own or someone else's expectations, or even causes that are unknown to us.

- Just to add a twist of complexity, sometimes the guilt can *appear to be false or invalidated* but underneath there is some sin that has been committed.

Dealing with False Guilt

- Often obsessive feelings of guilt over a situation in which the person committed no identifiable sin come from a sense of unworthiness rooted in *the person's childhood.* He or she may have been blamed or punished for things that he or she didn't do, or may have been called worthless.
- It helps for the individual to *tell his or her story*, not to ask forgiveness but to verbalize his or her feelings and get them out in the open.
- It may help for the person to *verbalize those feelings to the one* who makes him or her feel guilty. Often the person on the receiving end will affirm that he or she had no reason to feel guilty and this can provide some relief. This *can backfire*, so prepare the person for that possibility.
- If not comfortable sharing with the other person, the client needs to deal with the guilt by *giving it to God* (this is necessary anyway). This is the first step to healing.
- A person with extreme guilt over something that was not a sinful act needs to work on squaring his or her views of self and behavior with the truth as revealed in Scripture so that he or she can be *released to a life of peace and freedom in Christ.* This process will help the person experience a closeness to God that will enable him or her to realize the depths of God's love and mercy.

Dealing with True Guilt

- Guilt caused by sin requires an understanding of *confession and forgiveness.*
- This kind of guilt is healthy when *triggered by the Holy Spirit working in the conscience.* The individual should desire to do something about the sinful behavior.
- Confession, request for forgiveness, and/or restitution must happen if possible (that is, if the person hurt is still alive, or if restitution is able to be made in any form). Please be sure that if you are working with someone who has physically or sexually abused someone, that they do not re-traumatize the victim. Confession can happen to God, but there is a possibility that this "confession" could be used as a way to get back to the victim.

3 ASSESSMENT INTERVIEW

Rule Outs

1. Tell me about your energy level and your physical condition. (*You're looking for signs of depression and the psychosomatic symptoms guilt can cause.*)
2. Are you having any thoughts of hurting yourself? (*You are looking for suicidal ideation.*)

General Questions

First, seek to identify if the guilt is true or false, then proceed with the correct set of questions below.

1. Tell me what brings you to see me today.
2. Can you connect your feelings with particularly painful past events you've experienced? Tell me about it.
3. What have you done about the feelings of guilt related to this event?
4. What do you think you did wrong?

Questions If It Is True Guilt

1. Is this guilt affecting your life today? If so, how?
2. What have you done to deal with your sin?
3. What can you do to rectify the situation—confess, apologize, make restitution?
4. Have you shared this guilt with anyone?
5. If you have confessed your sin, do you feel forgiven by God?
6. How do you understand God's grace?

Questions If It Is False Guilt

1. Since no sin was committed, why do you think that you still carry feelings of guilt?
2. *If this is an abuse situation, the person will often feel that they have done something to make the abuse happen. It is important to remind them that they had no control over what the abuser did. It was the abuser's choice.*
3. Have you shared this guilt with anyone?
4. Tell me about your childhood. How were you disciplined as a child?
5. How was/is your self-image? How might it affect the way you experience guilt?
6. How might the way you were raised affect the way you feel guilt?
7. Have others made you feel guilty? If so, how?
8. Do you think it would help to talk to these people? Why or why not?

> When addressing guilt, the first step may be to identify the source of our burdens. While genuine, biblical guilt stems from poor moral judgment, false guilt can originate from a variety of circumstances—such as faulty teaching, unpleasant childhood memories, perfectionist tendencies, and low self-esteem.
> Charles Stanley

WISE COUNSEL 4

A person who seeks help for false guilt probably has *issues of unworthiness and self-worth*. These often are rooted in childhood. If people were always made to feel that they could not do anything right or were always being blamed for things that were out of their control, then they have more than likely carried these feelings into adult life. They need to be reminded of *God's unconditional love*. Letting people talk about their past provides an opportunity to begin the healing process.

The person dealing with true guilt needs to be given action steps that will pave the way for *confession, forgiveness, and restitution*.

Guilt can trap a person into a life of *unfulfillment and heartache*. The person will never be free to experience God's best until the guilt is released.

5 ACTION STEPS

1. Pay Attention to the Feelings

- Guilt, like physical pain, is a signal that something is wrong.[2]
- *Guilt and shame aren't the same thing.* Objective guilt is the realization of a wrong committed; shame is the conclusion that either true or false guilt has made us worthless and helpless to change.

2. Determine the Source

- Are the guilt feelings because of sin or because of some issues that were out of your control?
- Seek God patiently. Just because you feel guilty doesn't mean you have sinned; yet, you may need to let God peel back some layers to reveal a sin long forgotten that needs to be repented.
- If the guilt feelings are out of your control, you still need to find a way to resolve them.

3. Identify True Guilt

- If you are feeling guilty because you have committed a sin, what steps will you take to receive forgiveness from God?[3]
- What steps will you take to receive forgiveness from and/or make restitution to the person?
- If an apology or restitution cannot happen (for example, the person has passed away), then plan a way to deal with the guilt. Write a letter to the person and do a "ceremony" of sorts when your guilt can be given to God.
- Realize that "telling all" can be a way of inflicting more pain on others. Permanent relief from moral guilt comes from God's forgiveness, not necessarily public confession. The scope of the confession should not exceed the scope of the sin.[4]

4. Identify False Guilt

- If the guilt is self-worth related, make a list of all the things God has done for you, including paying the price to save you. (*Note: provide suggestions and Scripture to back it up.*)
- Continuing to punish yourself for being human is useless. Do what you can and move on.[5]

Guilt is an excellent warning light that says something is wrong. Yet when it persists too long, it provides fuel for Satan's lies and strangulates spiritual growth.

Ed Welch

5. Move On

- Once you've confessed, apologized, and/or made restitution, don't beat yourself up anymore. Leave it with God.
- Turn off the mental tape player. Satan, not the Holy Spirit, is the accuser (Rev. 12:10). Satan wants to create feelings of condemnation resulting in unnecessary guilt. Turn him off![6]
- Keep a "guilt pot." Anytime you feel guilt creeping in, write that guilt feeling on a piece of paper and throw it in the pot. (The pot will remind you that God is the Potter, always at work on you, and you are merely the clay—Isa. 64:8.)

6. Keep Active

- Do things for other people.
- Practice being forgiving in your relationships.
- By providing encouragement to someone else, you will receive encouragement back and this will increase your feelings of self-worth.

BIBLICAL INSIGHTS 6

So he said, "I heard Your voice in the garden, and I was afraid because I was naked; and I hid myself."

Genesis 3:10

At the evening sacrifice I arose from my fasting; and having torn my garment and my robe, I fell on my knees and spread out my hands to the LORD my God. And I said: "O my God, I am too ashamed and humiliated to lift up my face to You, my God; for our iniquities have risen higher than *our* heads, and our guilt has grown up to the heavens."

Ezra 9:5–6

Then Jesus said to those Jews who believed Him, "If you abide in My word, you are My disciples indeed. And you shall know the truth, and the truth shall make you free. . . . Most assuredly, I say to you, whoever commits sin is a slave of sin. And a slave does not abide in the house forever, *but* a son abides forever. Therefore if the Son makes you free, you shall be free indeed."

John 8:32, 34–36

There is therefore now no condemnation to those who are in Christ Jesus, who do not walk according to the flesh, but according to the Spirit.

Romans 8:1

When God is involved, anything can happen. Be open. Stay that way. God has a beautiful way of bringing good vibrations out of broken chords.

Charles Swindoll

129

7 PRAYER STARTER

Lord, guilt can be so powerful. On the one hand, we know You use it to show us where we have gone wrong, where we need to confess, ask for forgiveness, or make restitution. On the other hand, it can also become like a prison that keeps us from living for You . . .

8 RECOMMENDED RESOURCES

Allen, Jennie. *Get Out of Your Head: Stopping the Spiral of Toxic Thoughts*. Water-Brook, 2020.

Batterson, Mark. *If: Trading Your If Only Regrets for God's What If Possibilities*. Baker Books, 2016.

Burton, Valorie. *Let Go of the Guilt*. W Publishing, 2020.

Cook, Alison, and Kimberly Miller. *Boundaries for Your Soul: How to Turn Your Overwhelming Thoughts and Feelings into Your Greatest Allies*. Thomas Nelson, 2018.

Thompson, Curt. *The Soul of Shame: Retelling the Stories We Believe About Ourselves*. IVP Books, 2015.

Websites

American Association of Christian Counselors (AACC.net)

Christian Care Connect (Connect.AACC.net)

Homosexuality

- Shane painfully recalls feeling different from his brothers. "I remember feeling so alone. While my brothers were out competing in sports, I was quite content in my room drawing." He continues, "My dad and I never got along. He was a high pressure 'corporate type' and was always putting me down for my 'sissy' interests. As I got older, I became increasingly aware of a longing for other men. I fought fantasies of being hugged and touched by another man. Finally, in college, I decided that I couldn't battle these feelings anymore and gave in to having sex with men. Yet even then, I realized it wasn't the sex I was wanting, but love."
- Leah is the youngest daughter with five older brothers. She recalls seeing pictures of herself in preschool dressed by her mom in overalls and T-shirts. With the exception of her ponytail, it was difficult to determine if she was a boy or a girl. In grade school Leah often received the brunt of her brothers' wrestling competitions. She despised being born a girl. In high school Leah developed a close friendship with a girl named Emily, who was two years older and took a special interest in Leah. Leah experienced tenderness from Emily that she had never experienced from her mom or anyone growing up. Emily's care for her awakened within Leah a deep need to be loved. With time, they developed a sexual relationship. As the relationship progresses, Leah starts to see not only how controlling Emily is but how dependent on her she has become. Somehow Emily's love is not enough to take Leah's deep soul pain away.
- Henry speaks in a quiet and controlled manner as he shares the recent news of his son "coming out." "Sure, Jay and I have had a difficult relationship, but I just saw it as his own willfulness. He always seemed to want to push me away. I see this as just another attempt to rebel against everything my wife and I believe in."

DEFINITIONS AND KEY THOUGHTS **2**

- Homosexuality refers to an orientation and a behavior. The homosexual orientation is when a person is *sexually attracted* to members of the same sex. Homosexual behavior refers to any sexual activity between members of the same gender.[1]
- Sexual orientation is a common term used to describe a person's sexual identity in relation to the gender or genders that they are sexually attracted to.

- Sexual orientation is divided into several categories including: heterosexual (emotional, romantic, or sexual attractions to members of the other sex), gay/lesbian (emotional, romantic, or sexual attractions to members of one's own sex), and bisexual (emotional, romantic, or sexual attractions to both men and women).[2]

- Gender identity has been divided into many categories. Each category reflects a person's specific sense of how they define their own gender. Gender identity, according to some, has been explained as "fluid" or "on a spectrum." Some people may identify as one gender one day and a different one another day. Some identify as multiple genders. God's Word is clear, however, that He made them male and female (Gen. 1:27).

- Currently research does not support the existence of a "gay" gene, and no conclusive evidence for the biological basis of homosexuality has been found. According to current scientific and professional understanding, the core attractions that form the basis for adult sexual orientation typically emerge between middle childhood and early adolescence. These patterns of emotional, romantic, and sexual attraction may arise without any prior sexual experience.[3]

- Even in the unlikely case of such evidence being discovered, such would only prove what is already known—that people are fallen beings, physically, emotionally, and spiritually imperfect. An inborn tendency toward a particular sin does not justify that sin; it reinforces the need for a Savior.[4]

- Homosexuality can be rooted in a variety of psychological, biological, social, and spiritual factors.

- Some other factors that are believed to play a part in the development of same-sex preferences are:
  » personality
  » sexual abuse
  » exposure to pornography
  » experimentation
  » social factors
  » cultural influences
  » developmental issues
  » early childhood experiences/family dynamics

- Heterosexual and homosexual behaviors, like all human behaviors, are a matter of choice. People choose what to do with their desires. Just like someone may want to lie about something, they have the choice to do it or not. Even though there may be urges or desires, it does not mean that a person must act on them or that they are beneficial.[5]

- Those struggling with unwanted same-sex attractions can experience freedom from these attractions. These persons can find healing from past wounds and experience redemption from sinful behavior patterns as they seek to live in obedience to God.

- God's intent for sexual expression is within a covenant marriage between a man and a woman (see Gen. 2:24; Heb. 13:4). Hence, any sexual behaviors outside of a husband/wife relationship in marriage, such as adultery and fornication, are denounced in Scripture, along with homosexual behavior.

- In Romans 1:24–27, the practice of homosexuality is referred to as sin due to fallen human nature. In 1 Corinthians 6:9–10 and 1 Timothy 1:9–11, Paul lists homosexual practices alongside drunkenness, fornication, murder, and other vices.[6]

- In 1 Corinthians 6:11, Paul preaches to those who have been sanctified from sinful lifestyles, such as homosexuality, and celebrates their deliverance with the words: "Such were some of you. But you were washed, but you were sanctified, but you were justified in the name of the Lord Jesus and by the Spirit of our God."[7]

> Then Jesus said to his disciples, "Whoever wants to be my disciple must deny themselves and take up their cross and follow me."
>
> Matthew 16:24 NIV

ASSESSMENT INTERVIEW | 3

If the Person Is Struggling with Unwanted Same-Sex Attraction or Behaviors

1. Tell me why you came to see me today. (*The person may have come only because someone made him or her. If that's true, you need to know it from the beginning.*)
2. Are you a Christian? If so, how did you come to know the Lord and what is your relationship with God like now? (*You're trying to determine if the person wants to follow God and is struggling with temptation/behaviors.*)
3. What are your thoughts when you have feelings or desires that are bothering you?
4. Are these just "feelings" or have you acted on them in some way? (*Let the person describe his or her emotional tension and choices. Don't judge or condemn. Listen carefully and make open-ended follow-up statements like, "Tell me more about that."*)
5. If you have been acting out your sexual desires, how long has this pattern been occurring? (*Evaluate the extent of the behavior—was it an experimentation, or have they decided that they want to pursue this lifestyle?*)
6. Tell me about your family life. What is [was] your relationship with your mom like? What is [was] your relationship with your dad like?
7. Have you ever experienced any of the following?
   » sexual abuse
   » exposure to pornography
   » experimentation with the same sex
8. Are you part of a local church or Christian fellowship? (*If so, does the church provide support or resources for those who are seeking healing from unwanted same-sex attraction?*)
9. Have you told anyone that you are close to about what you have been going through? What was their response?

If the Person Is the Parent of an Individual with Unwanted Same-Sex Attraction or Behaviors

1. What has been your reaction to finding out about your child's sexual feelings or orientation? (*The person may have a variety of reactions, such as feeling shock, betrayal, sadness, and/or fear.*)
2. Describe what your relationship has been with your child in the past.
3. Can you ever remember a time when your child could have experienced some type of sexual abuse, seen pornography, or was exposed to any sexual acts as a child? (*If there was a time, it would be important for the parent to check with the child to see if something did happen. It is not to say that this incident "made the child have same-sex attraction," but it could have contributed to it. This is where healing may need to start for the parent and child; for the parent to acknowledge that something happened, and the child experienced something that harmed them. It may be important for the parent to apologize for not recognizing the incident sooner or for ignoring something that the child was trying to communicate.*)
4. Describe your relationship right now.
5. What has your child communicated to you about their expectations of you now that they have shared this information?
6. How do you feel about your own role in this situation? (*It is important to evaluate how the person is seeing his or her own effectiveness as a parent. There may be guilt or regret as to how he or she parented this child.*)
7. How do you feel your child is handling this?
8. Does your child feel free to express their feelings to you?

4 | WISE COUNSEL

Those struggling with unwanted same-sex attraction or homosexuality who are seeking counseling may have *repressed many fears, anxieties, hostilities, and painful memories for a long time.* They may have believed it was unsafe to share with anyone their true feelings but found it too unbearable to face them alone. Therefore, it is crucial that you *communicate a deep respect for the person and acknowledge their fear.*

The pathway to healing from unwanted same-sex attraction can be long and not easy but is extremely rewarding. Ultimately, the course of healing and redemption for the client is found in a *deep love from and radical obedience to Jesus Christ*, while at the same time facing honestly the wounds and sins of the past. God is not intimidated by any sin; He loves unconditionally.

What does unconditionally really mean? Paul says it the best in Ephesians 3:17–19: "And I pray that you, being rooted and established in love, may have power, together with all the Lord's holy people, to grasp how wide and long and high and deep is the love of Christ, and to know this love that surpasses knowledge—that you may be filled to the measure of all the fullness of God." This love "surpasses knowledge," which means we as humans can't understand it because it is so enormous!

> Many Christians want to follow Jesus, but they're unwilling to deny themselves and take up their cross daily.
>
> Christopher Yuan

The outcome of the healing journey is to be a person who walks with integrity, willing to sacrifice all fleshly desires to be identified deeply with Christ. As with any born-again Christian, this is difficult and has many mountain and valley experiences.

ACTION STEPS | 5

If the Client Has Unwanted Same-Sex Attraction

1. Seek Help from a Professional Counselor or Pastor

- *Ultimately the person will need to work with a counselor or pastor who has training in this arena.*

2. Address the Issues

Explain that in counseling with the professional, the client will need to address particular issues in the process of healing:

- Submit your sexuality to God, seeking forgiveness for behavior and choices.
- Choose to change behavior—terminate homosexual relationships and choose not to frequent places where homosexual relationships or activity are encouraged.
- Find healing of your full identity in Christ and accept yourself as a child of God.
- Deal with the shame and guilt of your past.
- Face the pain of the deficit in relationship with the same-sex parent or of opposite-sex abuse.
- Establish healthy same-sex friendships.

If the Person Is the Parent of Someone with Unwanted Same-Sex Attraction or Behavior

1. Examine Your Heart

- God does not view one sin as more heinous than others. We have all sinned and fall short of God's glory.
- Examine your own heart before God and be aware of your own personal struggles and temptations so that you are prepared to show your child the same love and forgiveness God has shown you.

2. Avoid Condemnation

- "Coming out" is often not an intentional act to hurt the parent. *More often than not, the child has kept secret the feelings he or she has struggled with so as not to hurt the parent.*
- Think before you speak. Let your child know that you will need time to process the information.

3. Avoid Lecturing

- Avoid lecturing on all the risks and problems with homosexuality.
- Rarely does someone respond positively when being told what he or she shouldn't do.
- Put yourself in the situation. Respond how you would want to be treated.
  - The ultimate goal is to speak "truth in love."

> Flee from sexual immorality. All other sins a person commits are outside the body, but whoever sins sexually, sins against their own body.
>
> 1 Corinthians 6:18 NIV

4. Maintain the Relationship

- Let your child know that you want to maintain a relationship.
- Acceptance of your son or daughter does not mean agreement or affirmation with his or her choices.
- Withdrawing your love and affection will only make the relationship more difficult.

5. Pursue Dialogue

- Talk with your child and *listen*. It may be tough but try to get your child to share the reasons behind his or her choices. Take this slow; it may take multiple conversations.
- As you dialogue, you will become more comfortable sharing your concerns. At this point, your child may be more open to listening once you have listened.

6. Pray Constantly

- Pray diligently for God's truth and compassion to speak into your son or daughter's heart.

7. Find a Support Group

- You may want to join an organization that seeks to minister to homosexuals and where parents can learn more about God's redemptive plan for healing.

8. Maintain Boundaries

- You can still have boundaries in your home. Just as you would not allow your child's opposite-sex boyfriend [girlfriend] to sleep with your child on visits, this must not happen with a homosexual partner either.
- Even if they consider themselves "married," you must stand by your values, especially if younger siblings are still in the home.

6 | BIBLICAL INSIGHTS

Now before they lay down, the men of the city, the men of Sodom, both old and young, all the people from every quarter, surrounded the house. And they called to Lot and said to him, "Where are the men who came to you tonight? Bring them out to us that we may know them *carnally*."

Genesis 19:4–5

You shall not lie with a male as with a woman. It *is* an abomination.

Leviticus 18:22

For this reason God gave them up to vile passions. For even their women exchanged the natural use for what is against nature. Likewise also the men, leaving the natural use of the woman, burned in their lust for one another, men with men committing what is shameful, and receiving in themselves the penalty of their error which was due.

Romans 1:26–27

And even as they did not like to retain God in *their* knowledge, God gave them over to a debased mind, to do those things which are not fitting; being filled with all unrighteousness, sexual immorality . . . who, knowing the righteous judgment of God, that those who practice such things are deserving of death, not only do the same but also approve of those who practice them.

Romans 1:28–29, 32

> One very difficult aspect of sin is that my sin never feels like sin to me. My sin feels like life to me, plain and simple. My heart is an idol factory, and my mind is an excuse-making factory.
>
> Rosaria Champagne Butterfield

PRAYER STARTER 7

Lord, You love Your precious child. You created him [her] and You have a plan for his [her] life. He [she] is struggling today with their desires and feels helpless to overcome the challenges they bring . . .

RECOMMENDED RESOURCES 8

Butterfield, Rosaria. *Openness Unhindered: Further Thoughts of an Unlikely Convert on Sexual Identity and Union with Christ*. Crown and Covenant Publications, 2015.

Carson, D. A, and Mark Yarhouse. *How Should We Think about Homosexuality?* Lexham Press, 2022.

Dallas, Joe. *When Homosexuality Hits Home: What to Do When a Loved One Says, "I'm Gay"*. Harvest House, 2015.

Perry, Jackie Hill. *Gay Girl, Good God: The Story of Who I Was, and Who God Has Always Been*. B&H, 2018.

Yarhouse, Mark. *Sexual Identity and Faith: Helping Clients Find Congruence*. Templeton Press, 2019.

Websites

American Association of Christian Counselors (AACC.net)

Christian Care Connect (Connect.AACC.net)

Loneliness

1 PORTRAITS

- David's wife of forty-five years recently became ill and requires around-the-clock medical attention in a nursing home. David spends every moment he can beside his wife at the facility but does not know how to be alone at night. None of his children live in the area, and he has become increasingly lonely.
- All of Dawn's friends are married and are starting to have children of their own. She loves celebrating with her friends and is happy for them, but she has been single since college and is losing hope. All she dreams about is to be married and have a family of her own.
- Josh has dedicated his life to his job. He is young, talented, and is quickly rising in the ranks of his company. All he can do is think about the next project or check his email once he leaves the office, leaving no time for friends or social connections. His coworkers consider him a workaholic, but he works to mask the feelings of loneliness he experiences when he gets back to his luxurious but empty apartment.
- Mark is from a broken home. His mom is an alcoholic, and his dad drifts from job to job. Both of them have broken too many promises to count. As a young adult trying to find his way, Mark has a hard time trusting anyone. It's safer to just isolate and remain alone. He wants to find meaningful relationships, but he's afraid people will withdraw when they find out about his parents. He lives with the conclusion that no one cares, no one understands, and no one could possibly want a relationship with him.
- Lucia's husband died ten years ago, just after he retired from his job as an engineer. They had a lot of fun together. Her son and daughter live in two different cities, both about a thousand miles away. They call sometimes, but they're busy with growing families of their own. Lucia's health is fading, and she doesn't feel like getting out very often. There aren't many people left to visit with—she's the last person still alive in her circle of good friends.

2 DEFINITIONS AND KEY THOUGHTS

- Loneliness is a human response to being alone because God created humans with *a need for relationships*.[1]
- Loneliness:

- » is an uncomfortable feeling of *isolation*
- » is a negative feeling of being *disconnected* from others and causes a person to feel *alienated*
- » happens when a person feels there is *no one* with whom to share joys and disappointments
- » can result in an overwhelming feeling of *sadness*
- » can cause a person to become *despondent* if nothing is done about it
- From the moment of birth, humans seek attachment and connection.
- Since humans are made in the image of a triune God (who exists in relationship), humans too are *made for relationship*. This is evidenced in Genesis 2:18, where God sees Adam alone in the garden of Eden and says it is "not good."
- Humans need both *intimacy with God* (vertical relationship) and *intimacy with other people* (horizontal relationship).
- Due to our sinful nature, *intimacy is difficult to achieve* and people often experience loneliness.

Types of Loneliness

Situational Loneliness[2]

- A response to physical or emotional separation.
- Death, divorce, life transitions, and personal mobility are the *most common causes* of situational loneliness.
- In situational loneliness, intimate relationships are severed, changed, or forever disrupted in some way.
- The loneliness may be brief and contained or deep and overwhelming.
- The person knows there are those who care, whose support is, perhaps, only a phone call away, but the *situation (a job or school) demands separation*.
- The *intense longing* that accompanies the separation is compelling and sometimes overwhelming.
- When the separation is *extensive* (such as through death), the loneliness is *more difficult to handle*.

Emotional Loneliness[3]

- *Emotional separation* can also lead to loneliness.
- People can feel lonely when they are surrounded by those with whom they perceive *little or no intimate connection*. The loneliest people are often *in crowds*.
- This sense of *disconnectedness* accentuates the loneliness and often leads to greater despair.
- This kind of loneliness is often felt as a *form of anxiety*, driving some to frantic efforts at *superficial connection*.
- When physical separation is coupled with emotional separation, the loneliness can seem unbearable.

America's loneliness epidemic is getting worse, with three in five adults (61%) reporting they are lonely, a seven percentage-point increase from 2018, according to Cigna's 2020 Loneliness Index.[5]

Chronic Loneliness[4]

- *Chronic loneliness* can result from persistent feelings of not belonging or being understood.
- Chronic loneliness is often rooted in deeply held personal beliefs of social deficits.
- The person feeling chronically *alone and isolated* has *no hope of "connecting"* again in the future.
- Chronic feelings of loneliness can lead to *deep personal isolation and despair*, often ending in angry, violent alienation or suicide.
- A lack of social insight or understanding may also be a factor in chronic loneliness. It would be important for the counselor to determine if the client has lacked social training from parents or may have a disability, such as autism, that makes it hard to understand social cues.

3 | ASSESSMENT INTERVIEW

1. Do you ever feel that it is hard for you to connect with others?
2. What do your relationships look like?
3. If I were to see you with your group of friends, what would I see?
4. How would you describe yourself? (*You are looking for words like "invisible," "loner," "keep to myself," "don't fit in."*)
5. How would you describe your closest relationship?
6. Does the feeling of loneliness ever go away? If so, what are you doing when it does?
7. If something bad were to happen, who would you call? Why?
8. Do you ever feel left out? Do you feel like anyone really knows you well?
9. What have your previous friendships or relationships looked like?
10. What does a typical day look like for you?
11. What are some of your interests and hobbies?
12. Are you involved in a church small group or other activity involving others?
13. What does connection with others look like to you?

4 | WISE COUNSEL

Help the client to be able to identify the root or source of their loneliness. Are the feelings based on a certain circumstance or a situation that can be changed? Or is it something that is out of their control? Being able to identify the root of the feelings of loneliness will be a big first step before the counselee can begin to feel connected with others. Let them know that they are not alone in this.

A person's loneliness can be a healthy part of their grieving process as they deal with a loss. This is a natural response and can pass if the person does not let the loneliness cause isolation from others.[6] Even though it may sound counterproductive, there may be a time when God requires a person to be alone to heal from the loss.

God will bring people into and out of our lives at various times, but He does not leave us. A person might not always have the same trusted friend to confide in, or they may have to find new friends to connect with. People will come and go, but God is constant.

ACTION STEPS 5

1. Recognize the Feeling

- *Have the person experiencing loneliness express the feeling during counseling.*
- Have them put their thoughts and feelings in writing, whether in a journal or letter, as a way to determine the source of the loneliness.
- Provide some social or spiritual changes to help them move out of loneliness (*for example, join a small group at church, volunteer in the community, ask an acquaintance to go to dinner or coffee, and spend daily time with the Lord through reading Scripture and prayer*). Your client may try to avoid this, but it is important to help them realize that they need to do something if they want to move out of loneliness.

2. Seek God

- Loneliness can draw one closer to God or further away from Him. Remind the client that God wants relationship and wants His children to be dependent on Him—for everything. The way to connect with God is through prayer and Bible reading.
- If social relationships are lacking, remind them to enjoy time in their relationship with God. He is the closest friend they will ever have. He will never leave or disappoint them (Heb. 13:5).
- Help them learn to focus on the fact that God has a will and a plan for each day and each season of life.

3. Get Involved

- Encourage the client to join a church small group, community organization, support group, sports team, or hobby club.
- Volunteering can be a great way to help others and at the same time engage in meaningful relationships.
- Encourage them to do more than just attend church, and to get involved in an area that they have a passion for (worship team, volunteering, youth group, etc.).
- Help them search for those who may be in a similar situation. Many churches and community organizations have groups for those seeking community with others.

A new report from the National Academies of Sciences, Engineering, and Medicine (NASEM) points out that more than one-third of adults aged 45 and older feel lonely, and nearly one-fourth of adults aged 65 and older are considered to be socially isolated.[7]

- Guide the client to attend social gatherings (work, church, or social events) and introduce themselves to those they don't know. Have them practice with you and remind them to be confident.
- Tell someone about Jesus. Nothing will change your perspective in life more than telling someone about a God who loves them unconditionally.

4. Be Confident

- Loneliness can be overcome in time.
- Remember that no one is truly alone when they are in relationship with God.

6 | BIBLICAL INSIGHTS

And the LORD God said, "*It is not good that man should be alone; I will make him a helper comparable to him.*"

Genesis 2:18

> I have become a stranger to my brothers,
> And an alien to my mother's children.
>
> Psalm 69:8

> Fear not, for I *am* with you;
> Be not dismayed, for I *am* your God.
> I will strengthen you,
> Yes, I will help you,
> I will uphold you with My righteous right hand.
>
> Isaiah 41:10

Live from the abundant place that you are loved, and you won't find yourself begging others for scraps of love.

Lysa TerKeurst

> Yea, though I walk through the valley of the shadow of death,
> I will fear no evil;
> For You *are* with me;
> Your rod and Your staff, they comfort me.
>
> Psalm 23:4

Let your conduct *be* without covetousness; *be* content with such things as you have. For He Himself has said, "I will never leave you nor forsake you."

Hebrews 13:5

7 | PRAYER STARTER

Your child has come today with a burden, Lord. He [She] is facing what You called "not good" from the very moment of creation—people should not be alone. He [She] knows he [she] has You, dear Lord, and I pray that during this lonely time, Your presence and friendship will be all the more real to him [her]. Then I pray that You will show him [her] places he [she] can serve, people he [she] can help, things he [she] can do to break out of this pattern . . .

RECOMMENDED RESOURCES 8

Clinton, Tim, and Gary Sibcy. *Why You Do the Things You Do: The Secret to Healthy Relationships.* Thomas Nelson, 2006.

Early, Justin Whitmel. *Made for People: Why We Drift into Loneliness and How to Fight for a Life of Friendship.* Zondervan, 2023.

Jeremiah, David. *Overcoming Loneliness.* Turning Point, 2017.

Mayfield, Mark. *The Path Out of Loneliness: Finding and Fostering Connection to God, Ourselves, and One Another.* NavPress, 2021.

TerKeurst, Lysa. *Uninvited: Living Loved When You Feel Less Than, Left Out, and Lonely.* Thomas Nelson, 2016.

Websites

American Association of Christian Counselors (AACC.net)

Christian Care Connect (Connect.AACC.net)

Love and Belonging

1 PORTRAITS

- Years after her divorce, Kathy realizes she married someone just like her dad: controlling, condemning, and distant. She concludes sadly, "I guess I didn't think I deserved anyone better than that, anyone who would love me and treat me with respect."

- Robert's son is an addict. Robert can't bring himself to let his son experience the consequences of his choices. He tells his friends, "I love him. If I don't help him, who will?" Robert's life revolves around his son's addiction and the "moveable disasters" of his broken relationships, debts, and terminated employment.

- Susan was sexually abused every time her uncle came to visit, which was several times a year. This lasted from the time she was ten until she left for college. She always wondered if her parents knew what she and her uncle were doing on their "special times together." Now, as a young adult, Susan detests the thought of having a relationship with a man, even when some very nice young men show interest in dating her. She's afraid she'll be hurt again, and she's terrified someone will ask why she's so emotionally withdrawn.

- Richard grew up in a home with very little affection. He tried to win his parents' approval in every possible way: making good grades, being funny, and jumping to help with household chores before they could even ask. He was compulsively driven to help people—that was the only way he knew to be noticed and earn acceptance. He drifted from one circle of friends to another. These connections always started out well, but the people soon realized Richard was too needy . . . too clingy. Richard was trying so hard, but he didn't fit in anywhere.

2 DEFINITIONS AND KEY THOUGHTS

Love is being so completely oriented to another—in thought, feeling, and behavior—that their best interests and desires become as important, if not more so, than your own.

- First Corinthians 13:4–8 describes several characteristics of love:
    Love suffers long and is kind.
    Love does not envy.
    Love does not parade itself.
    Love is not puffed up.
    Love does not behave rudely.

Love does not seek its own.

Love is not provoked.

Love thinks no evil.

Love does not rejoice in iniquity.

Love does rejoice in the truth.

Love bears all things.

Love believes all things.

Love hopes all things.

Love endures all things.

Love never fails.

- In Romans 12:9–10, Paul writes "*Let* love *be* without hypocrisy. . . . *Be* kindly affectionate to one another with brotherly love." Paul continues on, speaking about love's other remarkable qualities (vv. 11–21):

  Love is fervent in spirit and service, strong and intense.

  Love is joyful, patient, prayerful, generous, and hospitable.

  Love blesses persecutors, refusing revenge.

  Love is compassionate and humble.

  Love is peaceable.

  Love overcomes and destroys evil.

  Love hates or abhors what is evil.

- All people need to feel like they *belong*. Ephesians 1:4–6 states explicitly that we are chosen for belonging with God, "just as He chose us in Him before the foundation of the world, that we should be holy and without blame before Him in love, having predestined us to adoption as sons by Jesus Christ to Himself, according to the good pleasure of His will, to the praise of the glory of His grace, by which He made us accepted in the Beloved."

- Truly happy and contented people will attribute their well-being first to God, and then to their *friends and family*. What they're saying is, "I have been blessed by the love I have been able to receive from others."

- While everyone has an emotional need for love and belonging, the *level of that need may vary* from person to person. Some are perfectly content with feeling loved by and belonging to a few close people, while others thrive on being loved and accepted by a wide variety of people.

- We all need to be loved and accepted, but *no one will be loved by everyone*. A person may receive love from a number of individuals yet *be focused on the one person* who will not accept him or her.

- When we love others, regardless of whether it's warranted or not, we are *freeing ourselves to be loved* as well.

Love Languages

- In his book *The 5 Love Languages*, Gary Chapman describes five different "love languages" or ways that people say, "I love you" (see Recommended Resources at the end of this section). Based on these adapted questions from that book, we need to help the client determine his or her love language:

Words of Affirmation. Do you need verbal praise and encouragement? Do you thrive on verbal praise, tone of voice, kindness, and thank you? Do you love it when people compliment you to your face and to others (directly and indirectly)? Do you love getting notes and emails? Do you need verbal affirmation? Do you do this for others you care about?

Quality Time. Do you love having people's undivided attention? Do you like it when people come over and just hang out? Do you like to plan activities to do with others? Do you like quality conversations? Do you enjoy the give-and-take of asking questions and listening? Do you really like to get inside people's heads and find out what they're thinking?

Gifts. Do you like visual symbols of love? Gifts can come in any shape or size—maybe someone just brings you a cup of coffee at work or tosses a candy bar your way. The cost doesn't matter; it's truly the thought that counts. Do you find yourself doing this for others?

Acts of Service. Do you like to *do* things for others, and have them help you out as well? Someone steps in to help on a project; someone washes your car; someone makes you dinner—and you eagerly do the same types of things for your friends.

Physical Touch. Are you a "toucher"? Do you give pats on the back and hugs—all of which mean nothing but friendship? Do you appreciate that kind of physical touch from others?

Determining your own love language, and *understanding the love language of those around you,* will go a long way to communicating the love that is truly there.

3 ASSESSMENT INTERVIEW

Nobody comes into counseling saying they need to feel loved and that they need to belong. Instead, *not receiving love and belonging will exhibit itself* with the following symptoms: feeling depressed, lacking energy, having no zest for life, having no desire to be social, not feeling fulfilled.

The following questions should be addressed only after some of the aforementioned symptoms have been ascertained:

1. What are your hobbies?
2. Do you share these hobbies with other people?
3. What organizations do you belong to?
4. What is a typical Saturday or day off like for you?
5. Whom do you love?
6. How do you show that love?
7. Of the five love languages (noted above), which is yours?
8. What do you think are the love languages of those closest to you?
9. Who loves you? How do these people show it?
10. Do you think that some people may be showing you love in a different "language," and you're just not understanding it?

11. Do you think that you are showing love to some people but that your "language" is different from theirs, and they aren't understanding it?
12. Do you deserve to be loved by others?
13. Who doesn't love you?
14. Do you think that everyone should love you?
15. How do people get to know you?
16. Do you think that they are getting to know the real you, not the you that you want others to see but the deeper you?

WISE COUNSEL 4

We love because God first loved us. If you are going to be a change agent in someone's life, love needs to be so given over to them that they feel that you prize and value them like no one else on this earth.

ACTION STEPS 5

1. Be Realistic

- Everyone needs to feel loved and accepted, but no one will be loved and accepted by everyone.
- It is unreasonable to expect that your friends or family will never be upset or disappointed.

2. Refuse to Be Offended

- It doesn't matter who your friends are or what family you belong to or where you work, the opportunity to be offended will come. Wherever people are together, sparks will fly. Do not take the opportunity to be offended.
- Too many people leave friends, jobs, organizations, or even marriages because they have been offended. This is not the answer to problems in relationships. You must work through these situations if you expect to grow and mature into the person God wants you to be.

3. Get Involved

- Find an activity that will force you to associate with other people. It doesn't matter what activity or hobby you choose. The goal is to get into a situation where other people will get to know you better.
- Join a club or organization or ministry that you haven't been a part of before—and be committed for no less than three months of involvement.
- Write in a journal about the social interaction you experience.
- Call someone at least once a week from the ministry or club you join.

4. Pay Attention to the Primary Love Language

- Love in the way others want to be loved.
- Be aware of your own love language.

6 | BIBLICAL INSIGHTS

Two *are* better than one,
Because they have a good reward for their labor.
For if they fall, one will lift up his companion.
But woe to him *who is* alone when he falls,
For *he has* no one to help him up.

Ecclesiastes 4:9–10

This is My commandment, that you love one another as I have loved you. Greater love has no one than this, than to lay down one's life for his friends.

John 15:12–13

[Love] bears all things, believes all things, hopes all things, endures all things.

1 Corinthians 13:7

Beloved, let us love one another, for love is of God; and everyone who loves is born of God and knows God.

1 John 4:7

7 | PRAYER STARTER

Thank You for the love You have shown us through Your Son, dear Lord. Thank You for the others You have placed in our lives. Your child has come today with a feeling of not belonging, of not being loved. I pray that You will reveal to him [her] the special person You created him [her] to be, and show him [her] that love from others is often the result of showing love . . .

8 | RECOMMENDED RESOURCES

Chapman, Gary. *The 5 Love Languages: The Secret to Love That Lasts.* Northfield Publishing, 2015.

Eggerichs, Emerson. *Love and Respect: The Love She Desires Most; The Respect He Desperately Needs.* Thomas Nelson, 2004.

Goff, Bob. *Love Does: Discover a Secretly Incredible Life in an Ordinary World.* Thomas Nelson, 2012.

Gottman, John, and Nan Silver. *What Makes Love Last? How to Build Trust and Avoid Betrayal.* Simon & Schuster, 2013.

Johnson, Sue, and Kenny Sanderfer. *Created for Connection: The "Hold Me Tight" Guide for Christian Couples.* Little Brown Spark, 2016.

Parrott, Les. *Love Like That: 5 Relationship Secrets from Jesus.* Thomas Nelson, 2020.

Stuart, Ben. *Single, Dating, Engaged, Married: Navigating Life and Love in the Modern Age.* Thomas Nelson, 2017.

Websites

American Association of Christian Counselors (AACC.net)

Christian Care Connect (Connect.AACC.net)

Mental Illness

1   PORTRAITS

- Angie has been anxious about her job ever since her boss hired three new employees. Two of her coworkers were fired the same week as the new hires started. Angie has trouble concentrating on her current projects and is on edge every time her boss comes to her office.
- Jaylen's wife has noticed that her husband has seemed down for weeks and doesn't seem to enjoy social activities like he once did. Jaylen has become more quiet and at night is constantly restless. She is scared to ask him how he feels but is concerned about him.
- Sarah's parents are very worried about her sudden changes in behavior and how impulsive she has become. She dresses in all black and wears dark makeup and tells her parents to call her "Lucy."
- Matthew recently returned from military service overseas. His wife, Carmen, wants to celebrate having Matthew home by taking him and the kids to the local parade in town. They are having a great time until the fireworks start going off and Matthew becomes alarmed and begins looking for cover. For the next few nights, Carmen can hear Matthew breathing heavily. He sweats and often wakes up screaming.

2   DEFINITIONS AND KEY THOUGHTS

- A mental illness is "a condition that affects a person's thinking, feeling, behavior or mood. These conditions deeply impact day-to-day living and may also affect the ability to relate to others."[2]
- Mental illness is often referred to as a mental health disorder or a mental health condition.
- Mental illness is common. The latest statistics reveal that:
  - » 1 in 5 US adults experience mental illness each year.
  - » 1 in 20 US adults experience serious mental illness each year.
  - » 1 in 6 US youth aged 6–17 experience a mental health disorder each year.
  - » 50% of all lifetime mental illness begins by age 14, and 75% by age 24.[3]

Types of Mental Illness

- There are two broad types of mental illness:
  - » Any Mental Illness (AMI) is defined as "a mental, behavioral, or emotional disorder. AMI can vary in impact, ranging from no impairment to mild, moderate, and even severe impairment (e.g., individuals with serious mental illness as defined below)."
  - » Serious Mental Illness (SMI) is defined as "a mental, behavioral, or emotional disorder resulting in serious functional impairment, which substantially interferes with or limits one or more major life activities. The burden of mental illnesses is particularly concentrated among those who experience disability due to SMI."[5]
- Mental health and mental illness are not the same thing. They are often mistakenly used as interchangeable terms.
- Mental health refers to daily function and psychological and emotional well-being.
- A person can experience poor mental health and not be diagnosed with a mental illness.[6]

> 65.5% of US adults with serious mental illness received treatment in 2019.[4]

Causes and Risk Factors of Mental Illness[7]

- A number of factors can contribute to the cause of mental illness, including but not limited to the following:
  - » Early adverse life experiences, such as trauma or a history of abuse (for example, child abuse, sexual assault, witnessing violence, etc.)
  - » Experiences related to another ongoing (chronic) medical condition, such as cancer or diabetes
  - » Biological factors, such as genes or chemical imbalances in the brain
  - » Use of alcohol or recreational drugs
  - » Few friends or few healthy relationships
  - » Having feelings of loneliness or isolation

Symptoms of Mental Illness[8]

- Each mental illness will have its own presenting problems, but common symptoms of mental illness are:
  - » Excessive worrying or fear
  - » Feeling excessively sad or low
  - » Confused thinking or problems concentrating and learning
  - » Extreme mood changes, including uncontrollable "highs" or feelings of euphoria
  - » Prolonged or strong feelings of irritability or anger
  - » Avoiding friends and social activities
  - » Difficulties understanding or relating to other people

» Changes in sleeping habits or feeling tired and low energy

» Changes in eating habits such as increased hunger or lack of appetite

» Changes in sex drive

» Difficulty perceiving reality (delusions or hallucinations, in which a person experiences and senses things that don't exist in objective reality)

» Inability to perceive changes in one's own feelings, behavior, or personality ("lack of insight" or anosognosia)

» Overuse of substances like alcohol or drugs

» Multiple physical ailments without obvious causes (such as headaches, stomach aches, vague and ongoing "aches and pains")

» Thinking about suicide

» Inability to carry out daily activities or handle daily problems and stress

» An intense fear of weight gain or concern with appearance

Common Types of Mental Illness

- These are some common types of mental disorders:
  » Psychotic disorders are those that result in bizarre, paranoid, or delusional thinking. The most common is schizophrenia. Individuals with psychotic illnesses manifest the symptoms most often thought of as "crazy"—seeing or hearing things that aren't there, making bizarre connections between unrelated events, or showing grossly inappropriate responses to ordinary occurrences.
  » Mood disorders are those that primarily affect a person's emotional stability. The most common are depression and bipolar disorder (formerly called manic depression). Individuals afflicted with depression feel discouraged and hopeless almost every day, have lost interest in activities in which they used to take pleasure, and sometimes consider or attempt suicide. Those with bipolar disorder exhibit cycles of wildly changing emotions and behaviors.
  » Anxiety disorders are characterized by extreme nervousness, panic, or phobias. Persons suffering from anxiety disorders cannot calm down, feel panicky much of the time, and have physical symptoms of constant nervousness. Those with post-traumatic stress may experience flashbacks of trauma and may react to loud noises or other reminders of the precipitating event.
  » Personality disorders are disturbances in thinking and behavior that are a part of a person's basic character. They result in lifelong patterns of counterproductive behavior. Unlike the above mental disorders, personality disorders do not often respond to medications or short-term therapy.
- There are many other types of disorders, some associated only with children, but there is not enough space here to deal with them all. These disorders can be found in the *Diagnostic and Statistical Manual of Mental Disorders*. There have been many versions of this manual, so please make sure that you are looking at the most recent edition as some disorders and/or symptoms have changed.

Treatment of Mental Illness

- Mental illness is not short-term, but it is also not necessarily permanent. By definition, a mental illness must endure for a certain minimum period of time before a mental disorder can be diagnosed. For example, to be diagnosed with major depressive disorder, the client must have symptoms persisting for at least two weeks.

- Mental disorders can resolve after treatment with counseling and/or medication, or simply the passing of time. Some mental disorders can be intermittent, meaning that they can come and go in a person's life depending on stresses or circumstances that increase or decrease symptoms.

- Mental illnesses can be lifelong and cause ongoing problems for those with them and for their families. A person with this type of mental illness can find ways of reducing their symptoms through therapy and/or medication.

- If someone is mentally ill, he or she is not simply "odd" or "crazy." Diagnosis of mental illness should never be applied without professional assessment. Mental illnesses are—by definition—a serious health condition.

- Misdiagnosis and improper treatments are common. Far too many suffer needlessly when given a diagnosis that does not fit the person's symptoms. Ongoing assessment is needed to make sure that another diagnosis or an added diagnosis should be considered for the individual. The failure to understand the multiple reasons people suffer—including the distinction between sin, mental illness, and demonic influence—has significant consequences.[9]

- Some treatments for mental illness require collaborative care of doctors, psychologists, counselors, social workers, health educators, nutritionists, physical therapists, family members, etc.[10] If an individual would like to include others in his or her treatment, such as a pastor or spiritual mentor, this can also be beneficial for healing or maintenance.

Mental illness is a significant issue that the church must address. The church and mental health professions must value the contribution each can make and work together to relieve human suffering.[11] The church must learn and be aware of mental illness and how these illnesses or impairments can affect people in their congregation, but also understand that their scope of aiding such an individual may be limited due to the physical and psychological nature of the issue. This is not to say that the pastor or spiritual mentor should not be involved; on the contrary, they should be an integral part. What is important is that this pastor or spiritual mentor be aware of the fact that they might not know everything there is to know about the mental illness and be willing to learn from the psychological personnel involved in the person's life.

3 | ASSESSMENT INTERVIEW

Keep in mind that much that passes for "insanity" in the general population is simply a brief crisis due to extreme circumstances. *Don't jump to conclusions* or place labels on people.

Some people with mental disorder struggle for *just a short time*. Others are able to live nearly normal lives with regular medication and supportive counseling. Some will *suffer from constant emotional and behavioral chaos*, inability to maintain relationships or jobs, and difficulties with the law and with substance abuse. People's responses to medications vary widely, and some disorders (such as bipolar disorder) cause symptoms that make afflicted individuals unlikely to stay on the medication.

With some forms of mental illness, *there is the risk of violence* due to severe depression, feelings of hopelessness, or aggression. Ask the rule-out questions below to assess for the potential for violence. All the questions are directed toward the family member or concerned friend of an individual with mental illness, but they could also be asked directly to the individual.

> 50.6% of US youth aged 6–17 with a mental health disorder received treatment in 2016.[12]

Rule Outs

1. Has your family member ever been violent?
2. Does he [she] have access to weapons?
3. Has he [she] ever expressed feeling threatened? (*If so, turn to Action Steps 1 and 2.*)
4. Does your family member seem despondent or hopeless?
5. Has he [she] ever attempted suicide? (*See the section on Suicide for more information on how to handle this situation.*)
6. [If a woman] Has she recently had a baby?
7. Who could be endangered if this person becomes violent?

General Questions

1. Has anyone in this person's family ever been under the care of a psychiatrist or admitted to a psychiatric hospital?
2. If so, what reason was given?
3. Are you aware of a diagnosis?
4. What makes you think that this person has a mental disorder?
5. Describe the history of this person's most significant relationships. (*Unstable relationships—or lack of any personal relationships—may be an indicator of underlying mental problems.*)
6. Has this individual ever been convicted of a crime? If so, what crime and when?
7. Does this person ever speak in bizarre ways?
8. Does this person express fear that people are "after" him [her]?
9. Does this person describe hearing or seeing things that are not there? (*Questions 7–9 are all symptoms of psychosis.*)
10. Does this person show cycles of emotions or behaviors?
11. Does he [she] ever go for long periods with little sleep?

12. Does he [she] ever spend a lot of money recklessly or act grandiosely and above the law? (*Questions 10–12 are symptoms of bipolar disorder.*)

WISE COUNSEL | 4

Though only a small percentage of persons with mental disorder become violent, you should still *be vigilant for the risk of violence.*

People who are *paranoid*—who believe that others are working against them, perhaps in an elaborate plot—can feel threatened enough to strike out at others. *Mania*—feeling grandiose and on top of the world—can also breed violence when the manic individual is crossed.

Never risk the safety of yourself, your family, or your congregation members by naively thinking that violence will not occur. If a situation is escalating, it is better to *call 911* unnecessarily than to overlook the potential of violence.

Police and paramedics are *trained to assess the situation* and bring to local emergency rooms people who are exhibiting signs of mental problems. At the emergency room, medical professionals should be available to assess the individual and decide on a course of action. You can help by reporting your concerns to the police or paramedics. You may feel that you are betraying that person's trust, but please remember that it is better for them to not like you or even hate you than it is for them to be injured, to injure someone else, or to be dead themselves. Oftentimes a person whom you call emergency personnel to help with or that person's family will thank you later.

> The average delay between onset of mental illness symptoms and treatment is 11 years.[13]

ACTION STEPS | 5

Encourage the family member or concerned friend of a mentally ill person to take the following action steps.

1. Lessen the Risks

- If there is any risk of violence, get professionals involved immediately.
- If needed, remove any weapons (guns, knives, anything else sharp) and ropes, scarves, sheets, or belts, as well as drugs, from the home. Try to observe the person until help arrives.

2. Protect Yourself

- If you are with the person who is expressing extreme anger or paranoia, you should get out of the way.
- Do not block the individual's exit. Instead, let him or her leave and then call 911.

3. Get Professional Help

You should talk with a professional if your loved one is

- threatening violence
- causing financial hardship
- abusing substances (see also the section on Addictions)
- participating in dangerous or destructive behavior
- disappearing without explanation

4. Get Medical Help

- Often, medications can play a role in treating severe mental disorders and conditions.
- Medical personnel can also assist someone who is trying to hurt themselves or others in a way that other people who are not trained in such matters can't.

5. Join a Support Group

- There are many support groups for those who love persons with mental disorders. The best-known is NAMI, the National Alliance for the Mentally Ill, which sponsors both support and advocacy across the country.
- Other groups can be found by contacting your church or local mental health agencies.

6. Get Practical Help

- Local mental health agencies should have information about financial help, health insurance, supportive counseling, and other interventions that can aid persons with mental disorders and their families.
- Persons with *severe mental illnesses* who need ongoing help may benefit from programs such as day treatment or supportive living facilities.

7. Get Spiritual Help

- God is for those with mental disorders. Be sure to be spiritually sensitive and unbiased in your love for them.
- Help the person with mental disorder understand his or her need for Christ. Is he or she a Christian? Does he or she know the plan of salvation? Does he or she understand what Jesus can do in his or her life? (See John 1:12; Rom. 3:23; 6:23.) Ask a pastor or spiritual mentor to get involved and be an active helper in this time of need.
- Pray for wisdom regarding your approach to helping the person with mental disorder. Does he or she need advice, encouragement, education, correction,

Anxiety disorders are the most common mental health concern in the United States. Over 40 million adults in the US (19.1%) have an anxiety disorder. Meanwhile, approximately 7% of children aged 3–17 experience issues with anxiety each year. Most people develop symptoms before age 21.[14]

Suicide was the tenth leading cause of death overall in the United States, claiming the lives of over 48,000 people. In 2021, suicide was among the top 9 leading causes of death for people ages 10–64. Suicide was the second leading cause of death for people ages 10–14 and 20–34.[15]

a support system, insight, confession, verbal reinforcement, modeling, or confrontation?

8. Live in Peace

- Do not blame the person with a mental illness. Blaming the person is like blaming a patient for his or her heart attack. There are some things in the person's control, but oftentimes with mental illness, the person acts outside of his or her normal self.

BIBLICAL INSIGHTS | 6

But the Spirit of the LORD departed from Saul, and a distressing spirit from the LORD troubled him.

1 Samuel 16:14

That very hour the word was fulfilled concerning Nebuchadnezzar; he was driven from men and ate grass like oxen; his body was wet with the dew of heaven till his hair had grown like eagles' *feathers* and his nails like birds' *claws*.

Daniel 4:33

The thief does not come except to steal, and to kill, and to destroy. I have come that they may have life, and that they may have *it* more abundantly.

John 10:10

PRAYER STARTER | 7

Dear Lord, we know that You care deeply about each of Your children. We come to You now asking for Your help, guidance, and support in a time that feels very strange and scary. We do not know why this has happened, but we know that You have some type of purpose for all that happens. Please help us to look to You for rest, guidance, and most of all unconditional love . . .

RECOMMENDED RESOURCES | 8

Clinton, Tim. *The Care and Counsel Bible.* Thomas Nelson, 2019.

Clinton, Tim, and Jaren Pingleton. *The Struggle Is Real: How to Care for Mental and Relational Health Needs in the Church.* Westbow Press, 2017.

Grcevich, Stephen. *Mental Health and the Church: A Ministry Handbook for Including Children and Adults with ADHD, Anxiety, Mood Disorders, and Other Common Mental Health Conditions.* Zondervan, 2018.

Langberg, Diane. *Suffering and the Heart of God: How Trauma Destroys and Christ Restores.* New Growth Press, 2015.

Simpson, Amy. *Troubled Minds: Mental Illness and the Church's Mission*. IVP Books, 2013.

Stanford, Matthew. *Grace for the Afflicted: A Clinical and Biblical Perspective on Mental Illness*. InterVarsity, 2017.

Websites

American Association of Christian Counselors (AACC.net)

Christian Care Connect (Connect.AACC.net)

Money and Financial Hardship

PORTRAITS | 1

- Carl and Laura's credit card debts are out of control. Carl can't get Laura to stop spending, so they are constantly overwhelmed with bills they cannot pay. Carl wants a counselor to talk some sense into Laura.
- Bill just lost his job due to the downsizing of the company. He is trying to find work, but the job market is tough. He's struggling with believing God's care for him is sufficient in the midst of this crisis.
- Sherry's husband of twenty years ran off with another woman. After all the negotiating between the lawyers, Sherry is left with virtually nothing. She hasn't worked for years—how will she make ends meet?

DEFINITIONS AND KEY THOUGHTS | 2

- For most people, the topic of money can be one of the most stressful things to talk about.
- Money has to be *mastered* or it will master us.[1]
- *Jesus talked more about money* than about any other single topic. Why? "Where your treasure is, there your heart will be also" (Matt. 6:21).[2]
- A person who comes for counsel about money will need advice about handling the difficult financial situation, but he or she also needs something deeper—an understanding that, amid the difficulty, *God still cares and will meet his or her needs.*
- It may be important to help the counselee make some *lifestyle changes* that can help with the crisis. If the crisis is the result of personal irresponsibility, the counselee needs to make changes that will keep this crisis from happening again.

ASSESSMENT INTERVIEW | 3

Practical Questions

1. What do you consider to be the cause of the financial crisis you're in today? (*If spouses, do they agree on the source of the problem?*)
2. What do you think needs to happen for you to get out of this crisis?

The average American debt totals $103,358. That includes mortgage loans, home equity lines of credit, auto loans, credit card debt, student loan debt, and other debt like personal loans.[3]

3. How has this crisis affected you and your family?
4. How are you currently coping with the situation?
5. Who usually handles the bills in your home?
6. Describe the process for handling your monthly financial commitments.
7. In one column, let's put your needs, and in another column, let's put your wants. Do you see anything that jumps out at you?
8. What is the shortfall between what you have and what you need to meet your commitments?
9. In what areas can you pare back and save some money?
10. Do you think you can commit to "tightening your belt" for a while?
11. What lifestyle changes do you need to make to keep this money crisis or problem from happening again?
12. Will you commit to these changes?

Spiritual Questions

1. What does your relationship with God look like?
2. Do you practice tithing?
3. How do you feel about prayer? Do you think you can pray about this situation?
4. In what ways have you seen God answer your prayers?
5. In what ways do you still want Him to answer?
6. What answers may not be helpful for you right now?
7. Is there any sin that may have led you into this situation? Do you wish to repent of that sin?
8. What do you think God wants to teach you through this situation?

4 | WISE COUNSEL

Some issues your counselee may be facing:

Perspective: The person may be so completely overwhelmed that he or she cannot function in life and loses perspective on what really matters. You need to help the counselee see that there *is* a way out if he or she takes a breath and begins to think creatively and implement some action steps.

Prayer: The person may feel he or she cannot pray because the situation is his or her fault. You need to help the counselee understand that, no matter what the cause of the crisis, God wants him or her to pray about it.

Blame: The person blames the entire problem on someone else and focuses too much on that person. You need to help him or her see that spending all of his or her time thinking about the anger is not helping the financial situation.

Quick Fix: The person is focused on some speedy way to get out of the problem (like winning the lottery or filing for bankruptcy). Help him or her see that financial management is going to be hard work. It will take some belt-tightening and lifestyle changes to solve the problem and ensure it doesn't happen again.

ACTION STEPS | 5

1. Get Perspective

- *The client needs to get his or her perspective back. Ask him or her to say aloud:* "Money will not solve all my problems." Sure, money is important, but the more important issue is what God wants to do in your life.
- Credit card companies are not staying awake at night worrying about *you*.
- Go do something free and enjoyable. You have today—enjoy it. Keep on living. Walk the dog, hug your kids, or borrow a movie from the library or a friend.
- Set new priorities. Give back to God and God promises to provide (see Mal. 3:10; Acts 20:35).

> Collectively, US student loan borrowers owe a total of $1.7 trillion in student debt, according to Federal Reserve data.[4]

2. Pray

- Is it okay to pray about money? Yes, of course. In the middle of a financial crisis, as in any crisis or suffering, God wants you to run to Him.
- In addition to praying about your financial crisis, pray for guidance and wisdom.
- If you caused the financial problem, ask God to forgive you and to help you learn so it will not happen again.
- God is concerned about *all* of life. His goal is to make you more like Him. Your financial crisis can be part of that growth.

3. Deal with the Immediate Problems

- Face the problems and decide what sacrifices or changes may be necessary in the short term, such as:
    Is there sin? Look it in the face and deal with it.
    Do you need professional help (such as for a gambling addiction)?
    Communicate with creditors; set up payment plans.
    Put the credit cards on ice (literally), so you can't get to them. Cut up as many as possible.
    What other fires need to be put out?
    Is there anything that you can sell that you do not need? Can you stop any monthly subscriptions you are not using?

4. Develop a Plan

- Prepare a budget. Start with your income; figure fixed payments (rent or mortgage, tithe, utilities, car payments, insurances), then regular expenses per month (such as food and gas), then other monthly payments (creditors—start with minimum payment amounts).

- List all the creditors you owe, from lowest total to highest total.
- After working your budget, how much money can you put toward the creditors' bills? If only the minimum (such as with credit cards), start there. (If you can't even make minimums, you will consider other options in number 5 below.) List each bill and the monthly amount you will pay beside it.
- Decide how much additional money you can pay toward each creditor's bill. Try to pay off first the bill with the highest interest rate, while paying the minimum on the others. When the first one is paid off, go to the one with the next highest interest rate, and so on.
- Prepare a worksheet that lists all bills. Organize them according to due dates and which will be paid with which paycheck during the month. Make this reproducible so you can use it each month, checking off payments as you go.

The borrower is servant to the lender.

Proverbs 22:7

5. Get Help

- Brainstorm ways to get additional money to help retire debts. (*Be sure the counselee understands that any additional money must go toward the debt, not to raise his or her standard of living.*)

  Sell something of value.

  Consider consolidating your debt. Take out a home equity loan or refinance an existing mortgage.

  Take on a new job (spouse goes to work outside the home, or money is earned at home by babysitting, tutoring, and so on).

  Get a loan from family or friends (be careful with this one).

  Obtain advice from an accountant or financial advisor who can help keep you on track (see also Recommended Resources below).

  Get help from the church or the government.

6. Set New Priorities and Parameters

- Do *not* run up any new debt. Leave credit cards for true emergencies only.
- Discuss needs versus wants (see Phil. 4:11).
- Decide on a thirty-day moratorium on any purchases over a certain amount of money. You may find you don't want it so much after thirty days.

7. Be Patient

- Your crisis is not a permanent condition. It's a turning point. It will get better.
- Don't be ashamed. Hold your head high, trust God for guidance, follow that guidance, and remember that somehow God is going to work all these things together for your good (Rom. 8:28; see also Matt. 6:25–26).
- Where is God guiding? What is God teaching? Read Matthew 6:19–21.

- Don't let the crisis turn you from God. Draw nearer. Study His Word. Pray for wisdom, protection, and provision.

BIBLICAL INSIGHTS **6**

The sleep of a laboring man *is* sweet,
Whether he eats little or much;
But the abundance of the rich will not permit him to sleep.

Ecclesiastes 5:12

> 73% of Americans rank their finances as the No. 1 stress in life.[5]

"You have sown much, and bring in little. . . .
And he who earns wages,
Earns wages *to put* into a bag with holes."

Thus says the LORD of hosts: "Consider your ways!"

Haggai 1:6–7

"Bring all the tithes into the storehouse,
That there may be food in My house,
And try Me now in this,"
Says the LORD of hosts,
"If I will not open for you the windows of heaven
And pour out for you *such* blessing
That *there will* not *be room* enough to *receive it.*"

Malachi 3:10

Be anxious for nothing, but in everything by prayer and supplication, with thanksgiving, let your requests be made known to God; and the peace of God, which surpasses all understanding, will guard your hearts and minds through Christ Jesus.

Philippians 4:6–7

For the love of money is a root of all *kinds of* evil, for which some have strayed from the faith in their greediness, and pierced themselves through with many sorrows.

1 Timothy 6:10

PRAYER STARTER **7**

Lord, _____ has come today with a difficult situation. We know, Lord, that nothing is too hard for You. We humbly ask that You help him [her] to be wise as he [she] prepares a budget, seeks new income, and tries to pay off these debts, because we know this honors You. Show him [her] what You would have him [her] do, and we ask for provision and protection . . .

8 | RECOMMENDED RESOURCES

Blue, Ron. *God Owns It All—Bible Study Book: Finding Contentment and Confidence in Your Finances.* Lifeway, 2016.

Blue, Ron, and Karen Guess. *Never Enough? 3 Keys to Financial Contentment.* B&H, 2017.

Cruze, Rachel. *Know Yourself, Know Your Money: Discover WHY You Handle Money the Way You Do, and WHAT to Do About It!* Ramsey Press, 2021.

Ramsey, Dave. *The Total Money Makeover Classic Edition: A Proven Plan for Financial Fitness.* Thomas Nelson, 2013.

Organization

Christian Credit Counselors (ChristianCC.org)

Websites

American Association of Christian Counselors (AACC.net)

Christian Care Connect (Connect.AACC.net)

Crown Financial Ministries (Crown.org)

Pain and Chronic Pain

- Sally has deteriorating arthritis. The pain has become so bad that she can no longer help in the nursery with the toddlers as she loved to do for the past twenty years. "What use am I if I can't even do the simplest thing to serve the Lord?" she asks dejectedly.

- Ben, a construction worker, was in a car accident that left him with several crushed discs and constant pain. "Why me?" he asks. "What did I do to deserve this? I can't work and we can barely get by on my disability check. I feel like I'm hitting a closed door when I try to get answers from God. He doesn't seem to care."

- Kristy was diagnosed with lupus a year ago. "Every day I feel like I have the flu," she says wearily. "The fatigue is debilitating. I can't make any plans with the kids because the day we plan to go to the beach or to a movie I always end up too sick to go. I'm so tired of this stupid disease!"

- Josh's leg was amputated below the knee due to bone cancer. Now after months of painful chemotherapy, he has learned the cancer is in the thigh bone and he will have to begin another round of chemo with the chance of losing the rest of his leg. *I don't know what's worse, the pain or the fear*, he wonders. *How much more can I stand? I'm so afraid.*

- Kevin hurt his back playing football in high school, and it has been a nagging problem for ten years. He went to his doctor to try to get relief, and he got a prescription for an opioid painkiller. It helped a lot, and in fact, it made him forget some emotional pain he had been suffering. Soon, he is hooked, but the doctor won't prescribe any more. Kevin finds another doctor and lies to him to get another prescription. Before long he moves to heroin, and a few months later he is arrested for selling. Initially, the drugs helped with his pain, but the consequences for Kevin—relationally, emotionally, physically, and with law enforcement—prove to be devastating.

DEFINITIONS AND KEY THOUGHTS **2**

Pain hurts, and chronic pain hurts all the time. Pain refers to unpleasant and unwanted sensory/emotional experience that is associated with body or tissue damage or injury. Acute pain is usually attached to bodily injury, and by its intensity—the level of felt pain—reveals the seriousness of the injury. Chronic pain refers to these unpleasant feelings occurring over a longer time span.

- *God is present* and always working, even in a person's pain. The *physical, emotional, and spiritual are all connected.* When people are in pain, they may feel God is not there. Nothing could be further from the truth. Their brain is not sending the right signals; their feelings are not to be trusted. They must put their faith in God's Word, not their feelings.

- Pain tends to blind the eyes. When a person says, "I'm knocking at God's door, but *He doesn't answer*," his or her feelings contradict Matthew 7:7 where Jesus says, "Knock, and it will be opened to you." When a person says, "I pray, but *God is not listening*," his or her feelings contradict Isaiah 65:24 where God says, "Before they call, I will answer; and while they are still speaking, I will hear." People need to be challenged with the truth that God's words in the Bible trump their feelings.

- *Illness or chronic pain is not due to a lack of faith.* On the contrary, it is often the suffering itself that drives a person to God, motivates him or her to grow spiritually, and helps a person understand that he or she cannot cope alone. We cannot conclude that the presence of pain (or illness) implies that a person doesn't have a deep and mature faith, hasn't been praying enough, has sinned in some terrible way, or has neglected his or her spiritual growth. We know that a deep religious faith does equip people with a powerful tool to endure and cope with their pain.

- *God allows pain for a reason.* If pain is to have meaning, it must bring us closer to God. We can hear God in our pain. Many who have suffered chronic pain state that if they had to choose between never becoming ill or learning the things they learned through pain, they would choose the pain because of the wisdom it brought.

- *God's grace is sufficient.* Paul's thorn in the flesh gives authority to his claim that God's grace is sufficient (2 Cor. 12:7–10).

- What the world considers blessings—health, family, and riches—can sometimes draw a person away from Christ. *When one has everything, he or she may forget the need for God.* What the world considers curses—tragedy, pain, and heartache—reveal a need for Him. People run to Him because they have nothing left but Him.

- The Center for Spirituality, Theology and Health at Duke University has conducted more than twenty-five research studies exploring the association between religion, mental health, and the need for health services. Hundreds of additional studies around the globe have recently been completed on these issues. This is what was found:

    Many people turn to religious beliefs and practices to *help them cope when they become sick.* When people are anxious, suffering, and at the end of their rope, they turn to God. Often there is no other place to turn.

    Religious beliefs and practices are associated with *better mental and physical well-being.* Physical wellness includes lower blood pressure, better immune system functioning, and a longer life span.

> If you had never known physical pain in your life, how could you appreciate the nail-scarred hands with which Jesus Christ will meet you?
>
> Joni Eareckson Tada

People actively involved in a religious community, who pray regularly, and who keep religion as an instrumental part of their lives often experience *less depression and anxiety and greater hope, meaning, and purpose.*

They also *recover more speedily from hurtful emotions.*

Religious persons are *less likely to engage in addictive behavior,* such as alcohol or drug abuse. They are less likely to participate in *risky sexual practices* outside of marriage.

It seems that it is during the most difficult and trying circumstances that *religion separates those who can cope* from those who cannot.

ASSESSMENT INTERVIEW 3

Rule Outs

1. On a scale of 1 to 10 with 10 being no depression and 1 being extremely depressed, where are you today?
2. Do you abuse alcohol or drugs to escape the pain? (*If you suspect that severe depression or substance abuse is present, you should deal with this problem along with pain management.*)
3. Do you ever have thoughts of suicide? (*If you think the person is suicidal, make out a safety contract in which he or she promises not to hurt him- or herself without first calling you. If he or she calls you, take the person to the safe environment of a hospital for medical help. See the section on Suicide.*)

General Questions

1. What brought you to counseling today?
2. When did the pain first start?
3. How long has it been going on?
4. What are its symptoms?
5. How has this changed your life?
6. How are your family and friends responding to your pain?
7. How would you like them to respond?
8. What things have you tried to help manage the pain?
9. How have these been working?
10. Besides the physical pain, have you had any feelings of anger, doubt, or fear?
11. Tell me about these feelings.
12. Where do you think God is in all this?
13. Why do you think God let this happen to you?
14. What are your feelings toward God right now? Be honest.
15. What do you want God to do?
16. If He chooses not to heal you, how do you feel about that?
17. Has anything good come out of your pain?

Blessed be the God and Father of our Lord Jesus Christ, the Father of mercies and God of all comfort, who comforts us in all our tribulation, that we may be able to comfort those who are in any trouble, with the comfort with which we ourselves are comforted by God. For as the sufferings of Christ abound in us, so our consolation also abounds through Christ.

2 Corinthians 1:3-5

4 | WISE COUNSEL

Empathize with the client about the pain. He or she needs to know that you understand the difficulty of the situation and that you care.

Explain that the client has experienced a loss that may feel similar to losing a loved one. Make clear to the person that *a loss of health needs to be grieved.*

Validate the struggle and the strength the person has already shown. People in chronic pain get down on themselves because they can't do what they used to and what they see others doing. They may see themselves as weak, pathetic, or useless. It is important to identify their strengths and help them see how strong they are just to cope with the pain each day.

Explain that God understands and cares what the client is going through. Even if the person can't feel His presence, He is still there. Share verses that show this truth and talk about how the suffering person needs to trust God's Word.

Share Paul's story of the thorn in his flesh (2 Cor. 12:7–10). Though Paul prayed to God to remove the thorn, God refused, stating that His grace was sufficient. Ask the suffering person what he or she thinks grace looks like and how it could be sufficient for him or her. Ask questions that require the person to think through what God means in these verses.

5 | ACTION STEPS

1. Live within Your Limits

> In 2019, 20.4% of adults had chronic pain and 7.4% of adults had chronic pain that frequently limited life or work activities (referred to as high impact chronic pain) in the past 3 months.[1]

- Part of acknowledging the lordship of Christ is living within the limits *He* gives. If you need pain medication, take it. If you need a nap, take one.
- There is nothing heroic about going beyond your God-given limits to the point where you are grouchy and nasty to everyone around you. Pace your day so you don't get too tired. Ask for help when you need it.
- Good nutrition, exercise that your doctor approves, and sufficient sleep are essential. Make it a priority to get these three.

2. Do Things That Improve Your Attitude

- It will not be the pain that defeats you; it will be your attitude toward it that will lead to despair or hope.
- Identify what helps lift your spirits and do those things. Some suggestions are:
  pray
  read the Bible
  sing and praise
  listen to music that feeds your soul or tickles your fancy
  watch a funny TV show and comedy movies (laughter releases endorphins that improve mood)
  try to see the humor in situations

spend time around cheerful people
write in a journal or write letters to friends
start a hobby or pick up a pastime you enjoy
help someone else
learn something new
cultivate a grateful attitude

3. Get Support

- The only thing worse than pain is bearing pain alone.
- Read books about people who lived with pain and see what helped them.
- Join a support group. Do not isolate yourself. God made us to be in community with others. People in a support group can comfort you with the same comfort God has given them (2 Cor. 1:3–4).

4. Keep Truth before You

- When self-pitying and negative thoughts come into your mind, replace them with truth.
- Write your negative thoughts in a notebook. Divide the page in half and on one side write LIES and on the other side write TRUTH. Under LIES, write the self-defeating thought that came into your head. Under TRUTH, write the truth that contradicts the negative thought. For example, when you think: *God isn't here for me*, replace it with: *How can you say the Lord does not see your troubles? No one can measure the depths of His understanding* (see Isa. 40:27–28).

5. Comfort Others

- Redeem the pain by comforting others with the same comfort God gave you (2 Cor. 1:3–4).

BIBLICAL INSIGHTS 6

For we do not have a High Priest who cannot sympathize with our weaknesses, but was in all *points* tempted as *we are, yet* without sin. Let us therefore come boldly to the throne of grace, that we may obtain mercy and find grace to help in time of need.

Hebrews 4:15–16

When Jesus saw him lying there, and knew that he already had been *in that condition* a long time, He said to him, "Do you want to be made well?"

John 5:6

And lest I should be exalted above measure by the abundance of the revelations, a thorn in the flesh was given to me, a messenger of Satan to buffet me, lest I be exalted

It is estimated that 126.1 million adults reported some pain in the previous 3 months, with 25.3 million adults (11.2%) suffering from daily (chronic) pain and 23.4 million (10.3%) reporting a lot of pain.[2]

In 2016, an estimated 48.5 million persons in the US, or 18.0% of persons aged 12 years and older, reported use of illicit drugs or misuse of prescription drugs in the past year.[3]

above measure. Concerning this thing I pleaded with the Lord three times that it might depart from me. And He said to me, "My grace is sufficient for you, for My strength is made perfect in weakness." Therefore most gladly I will rather boast in my infirmities, that the power of Christ may rest upon me. Therefore I take pleasure in infirmities, in reproaches, in needs, in persecutions, in distresses, for Christ's sake. For when I am weak, then I am strong.

2 Corinthians 12:7–10

7 | PRAYER STARTER

The pain Your child is facing today is acute, dear Lord. He [she] is suffering and doesn't understand why. He [she] wants to feel better, wants to function better, wants to serve You better, but the pain constantly gets in the way. What are You seeking to teach him [her] through this pain, Lord? What wisdom and comfort can You give Your child today? . . .

8 | RECOMMENDED RESOURCES

> Chronic pain and high-impact chronic pain both increased with age and were highest among adults aged 65 and over.[4]

Clinton, Tim, Archibald D. Hart, and George Ohlschlager. *Caring for People God's Way: Personal and Emotional Issues, Addictions, Grief, and Trauma.* Thomas Nelson, 2006.

Elliott, Elisabeth. *Suffering Is Never for Nothing.* B&H, 2019.

Koenig, Harold G. *Chronic Pain: Biomedical and Spiritual Approaches.* Routledge, 2003.

Mintle, Linda, and James Kribs. *Living beyond Pain: A Holistic Approach to Manage Pain and Get Your Life Back.* Baker Books, 2019.

Tada, Joni Eareckson. *Place of Healing: Wrestling with the Mysteries of Suffering, Pain, and God's Sovereignty.* David C Cook, 2015.

Websites

American Association of Christian Counselors (AACC.net)

Christian Care Connect (Connect.AA.net)

Parenting

PORTRAITS | 1

- "If the principal calls me one more time, I think I'll scream. Why can't that boy just listen?" Martha yells with exasperation.
- Randy and Casey, just one year apart, are constantly fighting with each other. Randy hits Casey in the face with a soccer ball, which sends Casey running to his mother in tears.
- Rob was a very compliant child, but when he hit puberty, it seemed a switch was flipped, and he became defiant and demanding. His parents try pleading, reasoning, and punishing him, but nothing seems to work. They're afraid he'll do something really foolish and hurt himself or others. They are even worried he may leave home and never come back.
- Sandy and Ron always felt important in their children's lives, but now that their children are married and have children of their own, they are feeling left out. Sandy has commented to her daughter-in-law about her parenting style and Ron has confronted his son-in-law on his choice of career. Sandy and Ron's children are starting not to call as much, and they don't understand why this is happening.

DEFINITIONS AND KEY THOUGHTS | 2

- God placed certain people in leadership roles over children and named them parents. *God has ordained parents to be the leaders* in the home.
- *Children need both a mother and a father.* Unfortunately, fathers are often physically or emotionally absent. According to the US Census Bureau, 18.4 million children, 1 in 4, live without a biological, step, or adoptive father in the home.[1] These children have more physical, emotional, and behavioral problems than children whose father is present, and it is more likely that they will be incarcerated.
- Raising children is a *high calling* that God has given to parents. We must not take this position lightly.
- We must recognize that as a parent, *we have been given authority* over our children. In other words, we have been handpicked by God Himself to assume the leadership role in the raising of our children.
- Dr. James Dobson says that our role as a parent is to *work ourselves out of a job.* While we never really stop being a parent, our role changes as our children grow

> Foolishness *is* bound up in the heart of a child; The rod of correction will drive it far from him.
>
> Proverbs 22:15

and mature. Ultimately our role becomes less and less active and we serve more as an advisor or friend to our adult children.

Ingredients for Good Parenting

Just as bread needs yeast to rise, children need certain ingredients to reach the potential that God has placed in them. Three of these ingredients are love, discipline, and guidance. While the ingredients will be required at all stages of parenting, the actual amount of each required at various stages in the parenting process will depend on the age and maturity level of the child.

Do not withhold correction from a child.

Proverbs 23:13

1. Love

- Children need hugs, physical contact, words of encouragement and affirmation, and quality time—all of these *communicate love*. Love also helps break down barriers and walls that we can't see with our eyes.
- Keep in mind that adolescent children are very *aware of appearances* and may not want to be hugged in front of peers.
- Sometimes, especially in adolescence, our children can feel like our enemies, but in reality they are simply learning how to think and act on their own. *A certain amount of rebellion is normal, but it is important to address it if it becomes a sin issue.*
- As a parent, you are to love your children even when it is undeserved. That doesn't mean you accept everything they do. Love and acceptance are not synonymous. It does mean that you remind them that you *love them even when you disagree* with or are heartbroken by their actions.

2. Discipline

84% of parents agreed that family meals were important, but only 50% of family dinners were eaten together.[2]

- The Bible cautions fathers *not to discourage* their children (Col. 3:21), but it also says that those who love their children are careful to discipline them (Prov. 13:24). *Discipline, unlike punishment, always envisions a better future* for the child.
- *Balance is the key.* As a parent, you must discipline and train your children, but you should not discipline as though you are running a boot camp.
- Too many parents try to reason with their children instead of simply delivering on the consequences that were threatened. If you say the child must go to his room if he "does that one more time," and he does it again, *you must follow through* with exactly what you said.
- *Consistency is king.* The actual consequence is less important than the consistency of having consequences when children misbehave.
- There are *three rules* that may help to serve as guides in disciplining your children.
  The KFC Rule: KFC stands for *kind, firm,* and *consistent.*
  Granny's Rule: This simply means that, first, the child does what the parent wants and then the child gets to do what he or she wants. For instance, the parent might say, "If you want to go swimming, then first you must do these chores."

The Millennial Rule: This simply means that if you allow your child to get away with something, it may take a thousand times of correction to retrain him or her.

3. Guidance

- As a parent, it is in your job description to *teach your children about life*, guiding them in all areas, especially in God's Word (Deut. 6:4–9).

- Guiding your children may also mean *allowing them to make mistakes.* When a mistake is made and the principal or police officer calls to inform you of the situation, understand that as the parent you are about to walk through a crisis with your child. Be prepared to be disappointed with some of your child's choices and behaviors. Do not make the mistake of too readily helping your child get out of difficulties he or she is experiencing because of his or her choices and behaviors. More growth takes place through a crisis than at any other time.

- Let your child see what you do when you make a mistake. They will follow your example more than they will follow your words. If you did something wrong, say you are sorry and make it right.

- Let your child see your relationship with God. When you are struggling with something, let them see you pray about it. When you are excited about something, let them see you praise God.

ASSESSMENT INTERVIEW 3

Parents often *feel that they have failed* if their child needs help. Being a parent is not easy.

Reassure parents that seeking counseling is proof that they are, in fact, good parents. Having a family problem does not mean that the child is a "problem child." Avoid labeling anyone with such a title.

If the family is seeking help because the child is unruly or uncontrollable, you may want to consider having them *see their family physician* to rule out a physical problem. Problems like Attention Deficit Hyperactivity Disorder (ADHD) and Autism Spectrum Disorder (ASD) seem to be more and more prevalent, and a professional evaluation may be warranted.

> The goal of parenting is not control of behavior, but rather heart and life change.
> Paul David Tripp

General Questions

1. What would you consider problem behavior?
2. When did the problem first begin to surface?
3. How often do you struggle with this issue?
4. How have you addressed the problem in the past?
5. Can you describe a typical scenario in which everything seemed to fall apart?
6. What can you tell me about your child's early development?
7. When your child misbehaves, what do you do? How is that similar or different from your spouse?
8. How do you and your spouse work together with the discipline of your child?

9. How consistent are you with consequences?
10. What is each member of the family doing when the problem arises?
11. What does each member of the family do after the problem occurs?
12. What had changed in the family when this problem started happening?
13. What can you tell me about the other children in the family?
14. What would the perfect family look like?
15. What would you want your family to be like?

4 | WISE COUNSEL

Again, convey to the family that *God has placed them together*. God will help them and show them how to journey together as a family.

Changes may need to be made and, while the *changes may be difficult* at first, the parents will be able to accomplish these changes with the Lord's help.

Encourage the parents of *tough or strong-willed children* not to panic when considering their child's future. Some of the most successful adults were the most difficult children.

Encourage parents to *envision through faith a positive future* for the child and share that vision lovingly with the child.

Talk about the importance of *spending time together*. In this day and age it can be quite difficult to get the whole family together unless there is a crisis.

5 | ACTION STEPS

Your goal is to help this family develop a plan. This may be a plan regarding the rules to be followed:

Train up a child in the way he should go,
  And when he is old he will not depart from it.
Proverbs 22:6

- how discipline will be handled for infractions of the rules
- what the rules are
- what the consequences are for breaking the rules
- what is negotiable and what is not (for example, curfews are nonnegotiable)
- setting aside family times (a particular night of the week or breakfast or dinner together)
- chores (who does what, what is required, when the chores must be completed)

1. Develop the Plan

- What needs to be in the plan (*this varies depending on the ages of the children and the issues involved*).
- Have the whole family talk together and share ideas to be incorporated into the plan.
- Try to incorporate everyone's ideas into the plan. Even the youngest members can have input, but you as parents are responsible for the final plan.

2. Adjust the Plan as Needed

- If you sense that the parents are immature enough that they won't even be able to develop a good plan (or that their kids will run over them), follow up after they have had their family meeting to look over the plan they developed. You may need to help them take on the parental role or be more realistic.
- If the parents are capable of making the changes and following through, tell them to work through the plan for a couple weeks and make tweaks as needed—always with a family meeting. (For example, if chores are still not getting done, you may need to add consequences that will bring results.)
- The plan should reward desired behavior and specify consequences for undesired behavior.

3. Review the Plan on a Regular Basis

- Lifestyles change and children grow up, so the plan should be evaluated occasionally for fit. The basics are still the same (certain behaviors are still expected), but consequences will be different for older children.
- Review the plan as part of a family meeting.

4. Be Consistent

- Post the plan where everyone can see it.
- Mom and Dad must be 100 percent together on this. The kids must not think that they can get one to overrule the other or that they can pit their parents against each other.

5. Pray Together

- Ask for God's leading in your family as you raise your children to be responsible adults.

6. Spend Time Together

- Try to get at least one meal a day together as a family. Eating breakfast together may be more feasible than eating dinner together, depending on your family's commitments.
- Direct the conversation into positive learning experiences. Do a Bible study or simply talk about the mistakes that others made that day. Take the focus off your family and learn by discussing other situations.
- Use a family meeting time to discuss a family vacation or even a fun weekend activity. Try to choose varied activities so everyone has fun.

Today, 69% of children younger than 18 are living with two parents, down from 87% in 1960. A record-low 62% of children live with two married parents, while 7% live with two cohabiting parents. Meanwhile, the share of children living in single-parent households has increased threefold, from 9% in 1960 to 26% in 2014.[3]

6 | BIBLICAL INSIGHTS

"For this child I prayed, and the Lord has granted me my petition which I asked of Him. Therefore I also have lent him to the Lord; as long as he lives he shall be lent to the Lord." So they worshiped the Lord there.

1 Samuel 1:27–28

For I have told him that I will judge his house forever for the iniquity which he knows, because his sons made themselves vile, and he did not restrain them.

1 Samuel 3:13

Then Adonijah the son of Haggith exalted himself, saying, "I will be king"; and he prepared for himself chariots and horsemen, and fifty men to run before him. (And his father had not rebuked him at any time by saying, "Why have you done so?" He *was* also very good-looking. His *mother* had borne him after Absalom.)

1 Kings 1:5–6

But the mercy of the Lord *is* from everlasting to everlasting
On those who fear Him,
And His righteousness to children's children,
To such as keep His covenant,
And to those who remember His commandments to do them.

Psalm 103:17–18

But you must continue in the things which you have learned and been assured of, knowing from whom you have learned *them*, and that from childhood you have known the Holy Scriptures, which are able to make you wise for salvation through faith which is in Christ Jesus.

2 Timothy 3:14–15

> And you, fathers, do not provoke your children to wrath, but bring them up in the training and admonition of the Lord.
>
> Ephesians 6:4

7 | PRAYER STARTER

Thank You for these parents who have come today, Lord. They want to raise their children well; they want to be good parents. Right now, they feel as if things are going awry at home, and they don't quite know which way to turn . . .

8 | RECOMMENDED RESOURCES

Clinton, Tim, and Gary Sibcy. *Loving Your Child Too Much*. Integrity, 2006.
Dobson, James C. *Bringing Up Boys*. Tyndale, 2018.
Dobson, James C. *Bringing Up Girls*. Tyndale, 2018.
Dobson, James C. *The NEW Strong-Willed Child: Birth Through Adolescence*. Tyndale Momentum, 2017.
Early, Justin Whitmel. *Habits of the Household: Practicing the Story of God in Everyday Family Rhythms*. Zondervan, 2021.

Siegel, Dan, and Tina Payne Bryson. *The Power of Showing Up: How Parental Presence Shapes Who Our Kids Become and How Their Brains Get Wired*. Ballantine Books, 2021.

Thomas, Gary. *Sacred Parenting: How Raising Children Shapes Our Souls*. Zondervan, 2017.

Tripp, Paul David. *Parenting: 14 Gospel Principles That Can Radically Change Your Family*. Crossway, 2016.

Websites

American Association of Christian Counselors (AACC.net)

Christian Care Connect (Connect.AACC.net)

Perfectionism

1 | PORTRAITS

- Genevieve, a young wife, is constantly complaining to her new husband about the way he hangs his clothes in the closet, parks the car in the driveway, and sets his shoes by the bed. Everything has to be perfect for her, and Randall can't seem to do anything right. He is always on pins and needles.
- Matt, the teenage perfectionist, always feels his schoolwork and efforts on the hockey rink are never good enough. He studies for hours and practices his hockey in the driveway until dark. When he gets anything less than a 95 on a test, he is crushed and ends up with a migraine.
- Danny and his new boss, William, are constantly butting heads. Danny has worked in the same accounting firm for ten years and is fairly set in his ways and how he does things around the office. William has come in with some very perfectionistic and demanding requests.

2 | DEFINITIONS AND KEY THOUGHTS

- Perfectionism is a disposition to feel that *anything less than perfect is unacceptable*. It is rooted in the need for control and affirmation.
- An unhealthy form of perfectionism has been linked to obsessive-compulsive disorder (OCD). People who struggle with this disorder are consumed by anxious thoughts and repetitive habits. They have inordinate worries about being hurt, doing tasks perfectly, or being exposed as crazy. They may focus on keeping things clean, hoarding, not stepping on cracks, turning off lights, repeatedly checking locked doors, and many other behaviors that are attempts to control their environment.[1]
- Perfectionistic people *think* they should *know everything* and so beat themselves up for mistakes. They think they should be *totally powerful* and they become upset when things are out of their control. They believe they should *accomplish the work of ten people* in a given day and they become depressed and discouraged over what "little" they can accomplish.[2]
- Perfectionistic people *are idealistic* in that they frequently think about how things "should" be, not how they really are. They are always *setting impossibly high goals*, which lead to discouragement, failure, and ultimately quitting. They are *afraid of failure*, equating failure to achieve their goals with a lack of personal

worth. They are *tied up in the "shoulds"* of life and require rigid rules. With such an overemphasis on "shoulds," perfectionists rarely take into account their own wants and desires. They are *product-minded*, believing that contentment, happiness, and a sense of accomplishment are not permissible until their current project or activity has been completed. The "process" is overlooked because the end result has not been reached, thus there is no "joy in the journey."

- Perfectionistic people *feel* that they *have to be the best* at what they do. To simply do one's best is not good enough. They believe their *worth is determined by their performance*. Since day-to-day performance in various areas of life fluctuates, a perfectionist's sense of worth fluctuates as well.

- Christians can be especially susceptible to the problem of perfectionism because the Bible teaches that the standard of holiness is very high and the punishment for falling short is severe. Perfectionists feel trapped between what should be and what is, and they feel both defeated and desperate. In the Bible, God's law was given for three purposes: to demonstrate the holiness of God, to reveal our sinfulness and our need for a Savior, and to serve as a guide for believers as God's grace motivates us to obey Him. Sadly, perfectionists see the commands in the Bible as necessary but unreachable, leaving them deeply confused and discouraged. The remedy is a deeper, richer grasp of the wonderful grace and limitless love of God.

Personality Types

- *Type A people* are usually very *strict and rigid* and are often called perfectionists. They have a certain way for things to be done, and *flexibility is not an option*. They need to be *on time* and have problems with people who are more relaxed with time. They are often described as *workaholics* and are driven. They were probably given *conditional love* at some time in their lives; that is, only if a standard was met were they rewarded and accepted. They are more likely to *suffer heart attacks* at an earlier age than other personality types.

- *Type B people* are usually more *laid back*, more carefree with their time. They are not so rigid and are considered *more flexible* in their relationships. They tend to *cope with daily stress* in a more positive way than type A people.

- Many references in the Bible use the word *perfect*; for example, "Therefore you shall be perfect, just as your Father in heaven is perfect" (Matt. 5:48). We need to help people understand that *perfection is not something God demands* from them. God knows we cannot do it or He would not have had to send His Son.

- As Christians, we need to be *more concerned with our relationship with God—* allowing Him to make us perfect—than with being perfectionists. A perfect heart will do more to ensure a life of healthy relationships and a good self-worth than any perfectionist's rigid schedule or ways will.

3 | ASSESSMENT INTERVIEW

1. How would you describe yourself?
2. How do you feel when something doesn't go the way you thought it would?
3. What happens when someone does something that is not the way you would do it?
4. What kinds of goals do you set for yourself?
5. Are those goals pretty much across the board in every area of life; that is, are your expectations as high at home as they are at work?
6. Do you see life as "all or nothing," "black or white"?
7. How would your friends and family describe you?
8. Tell me about your growing-up years. When did you feel most loved by your friends and family?
9. Did you ever feel that you were loved based on your performance?
10. Have you always felt this way?
11. Would you define yourself as a type A or type B personality?
12. Do you think one personality type is better than the other?
13. What does God's love look like to you?

4 | WISE COUNSEL

Your job is *not to overhaul totally an individual's personality or makeup*. Wouldn't you prefer to have a perfectionist performing heart surgery on you than someone who is willing to be just "good enough"? We need to celebrate what perfectionists bring to their work while helping them manage their personality in a manner that minimizes damage to themselves and others.

Perfectionism is a problem if it is *adversely affecting the person's health or self-esteem* or if it is *dripping over onto others* at work or at home and causing stress. Remind the person that *God is all-powerful*; He can help the perfectionist relax with who he or she is.

If your counselee is *struggling with someone* who is a perfectionist, there is a good chance that the counselee is a type B personality dealing with a type A. He or she needs to understand how the type A individual thinks, that a type A person is more likely harder on himself [herself] than he or she is on the counselee.

5 | ACTION STEPS

1. Identify Your Personality

- Do some self-exploration by taking a personality inventory, such as the Myers-Briggs or other similar test that is available online. This is a great way to discover what makes you tick. Seeing yourself on paper and realizing that you have personality tendencies that are similar to those of others can be part of your life journey in discovering the *you* God made.

2. Open Your Heart to God's Grace

- The gospel of Christ contains the dual message that we're so flawed that it took the death of the Son of God to pay for our sins but that He loves us so much He was glad to do it. The cross completely satisfied God's requirement for the penalty of sin to be paid, and Christ's perfect life satisfied God's requirement for perfect holiness.

- Again and again in the New Testament, the writers tell us we are "in Christ." That means we are identified with Him in His death, so we're forgiven, identified in His resurrection so we have new life, and identified in Him in the ascension where He has authority over everything. The Father loves us as much as He loves Jesus. As His love melts our hearts, the obsession to be perfect and the compulsion to blame ourselves mercilessly gradually subside. We learn to give ourselves grace like God has given us grace.

3. Learn Flexibility and Acceptance

- Realizing, for example, that "I am more rigid with my time and you are more flexible" is okay and doesn't mean that I am better than you.

- Ask, "What's the worst that can happen?" The answer (for example, that the report goes through with one typographical error) probably isn't worth losing sleep over.

- God's love is unconditional. You don't have to earn His love by being a perfectionist or by setting unrealistic standards for yourself or others.

- God sets no conditions that we have to meet to be His children. We, in turn, need to be unconditional in how we accept and love others.

4. Laugh a Little

- Don't be so judgmental of yourself and others. Find humor in who you are.

- Laugh at yourself when you do something foolish or funny. Be prepared to laugh with others who are laughing with/at you.

5. Be Realistic

- You're not going to be God, so stop trying.

- Look at life as it *is*, not as you think it *should be*.

- Meet people halfway.

- Don't expect the impossible—of yourself or others. Set attainable goals and reasonable time limits.

- In your life, determine when perfectionism is appropriate and when it is not. Learn to accept "good enough" on certain tasks.

- Realize that many positive things can be learned from making mistakes.

6 | BIBLICAL INSIGHTS

Therefore you shall be perfect, just as your Father in heaven is perfect.

Matthew 5:48

I am indeed a Jew, born in Tarsus of Cilicia, but brought up in this city at the feet of Gamaliel, taught according to the strictness of our fathers' law, and was zealous toward God as you all are today.

Acts 22:3

For by grace you have been saved through faith, and that not of yourselves; *it is* the gift of God, not of works, lest anyone should boast.

Ephesians 2:8–9

For by one offering He has perfected forever those who are being sanctified.

Hebrews 10:14

7 | PRAYER STARTER

Lord, we know that You call us to be perfect, but Your child needs to understand better what that means. He [She] wants to do well at everything he [she] does, and that's a good quality. Unfortunately, his [her] drive for perfection is ruining his [her] life and his [her] relationships . . .

8 | RECOMMENDED RESOURCES

Antony, Martin, and Richard Swinson. *When Perfect Isn't Good Enough: Strategies for Coping with Perfectionism.* New Harbinger Publications, 2009.

Brown, Brené. *The Gifts of Imperfection: Let Go of Who You Think You're Supposed to Be and Embrace Who You Are.* Hazelden Publishing, 2010.

Jaynes, Sharon. *Enough: Silencing the Lies That Steal Your Confidence.* Harvest House, 2018.

Kolber, Petra. *The Perfection Detox: Tame Your Inner Critic, Live Bravely, and Unleash Your Joy.* Da Capo Lifelong Books, 2018.

Niequist, Shauna. *Present Over Perfect: Leaving Behind Frantic for a Simpler, More Soulful Way of Living.* Zondervan, 2016.

Norris, Emma. *Progress Over Perfection: A Guide to Mindful Productivity.* Rock Point, 2020.

Winter, Richard. *Perfecting Ourselves to Death: The Pursuit of Excellence and the Perils of Perfectionism.* InterVarsity, 2005.

Websites

American Association of Christian Counselors (AACC.net)

Christian Care Connect (Connect.AACC.net)

Pornography

- Sharon can't shake the nagging feeling she has. Finally she asks Paul if he has been looking at pornography again. He replies in a defensive manner: "I have but I have it under control now. You have nothing to worry about." Sharon weeps as she describes her horror at seeing the obscene websites he frequently visits on their web history. "I trusted him," she says.

- Fifteen-year-old Andrew remembers the first time he viewed sexually arousing material. He was at his friend's house and was checking his email. He got a message from someone he didn't recognize with a file attachment. He opened the file and saw a photo of a man and woman engaged in sexual activity. Andrew felt flush with excitement and guilt. Now he goes online when no one is home to view similar images because he likes the feeling they give him.

- Ryan is living a secret life. Several nights each week, he tells his wife he is staying up late to work on projects related to his job, but he is on his computer looking at porn. When he travels on business, he watches X-rated movies. When someone in the accounting office tells Ryan's boss about charges to his room for these movies, his boss hits the roof. Within hours, Ryan is out of a job. He tries to keep his secret from his wife, but she has already guessed the problem.

- Steven begins looking at porn with his friends in junior high. By the time they are in high school, they compete with each other to find the most salacious images and movies. In college, he gravitates to new friends who share his interests, and they find girls who are more than happy to have sex with them. A campus Christian organization holds an event on campus, and Steven attends. His heart is moved by the promise of forgiveness and a new life, but he doesn't think he can abandon his addiction and his friends.

DEFINITIONS AND KEY THOUGHTS | 2

- Pornography is sexually explicit material that dehumanizes, objectifies, and degrades men and women for the purpose of sexual arousal. Often it is photos, videos, or live action; sometimes it takes the form of stories or comic book drawings and stories.

- Pornography *promotes "sex without consequences"* and serves as an aid to self-gratification.

183

- Like some addictive substances, pornography changes the brain. Dopamine is responsible for reward-driven learning. Dopamine surges when a person is exposed to sexual stimuli, just as it surges from stimulants such as cocaine and methamphetamine. Erotic imagery triggers more dopamine than sex with a familiar partner, producing "arousal addiction," creating a drive for more visual stimulation and less drive for actual sexual partners.[1]

- Although it is believed that only men watch porn, women also are susceptible to pornography.

- A man or woman will come to counseling when they have been found out by someone, or sometimes they will seek counseling because they are weary of their feelings of guilt and shame.

- A spouse may come to counseling because they either suspect or have found evidence that their spouse has been involved in viewing pornography, and they do not know what to do.

- A *teenager may come* in for counseling at the insistence of *his or her parents*.

- Many *rationalize their behavior as "harmless"* because they think they are not actually committing adultery or sexual sin.

- Eventually, use of pornography *loses its power to stimulate*, and the user is enticed to involve others (usually strangers).

  - Pornography is used by many as a *stress reliever* that gives *escape* from life's perceived hardships.

  - Pornography use may be a *symptom of a deeper issue* (low self-esteem, loneliness, past sexual abuse).

  - Many use pornography to avoid emotional or sexual intimacy with their spouse.

  - Consistent use of pornography promotes the notion that *women are to be viewed as objects* and that *sex is unrelated to love*, commitment, and marriage.

  - Viewing pornography *increases the likelihood of sexual addiction* and sexual pathology.

  - Use of pornography can create *unrealistic sexual expectations* of one's spouse.

  - The user of pornography will *struggle consistently* with anger, guilt, shame, increasing anxiety, and oppressive memories.

  - It is not uncommon for many people to have their *first exposure* to pornographic material during the *junior high school years*.

- Many adolescents begin viewing pornography because of *curiosity* and as a release for hormonal tension.

> Approximately two-thirds (64%) of US men view pornography at least monthly. Three out of ten men (29%) between the ages of 18 and 30 view pornography daily. 65% viewed porn at work in the last 90 days.[2]

3 ASSESSMENT INTERVIEW

Interviewing the Person Viewing Pornography

Recognize that the person who is struggling with this issue will feel a *great deal of shame* and will be reluctant to speak about it.

It is important to *communicate acceptance* and a willingness to understand the struggle that has been occurring.

Approach the person with grace rather than judgment. Cite Romans 3:23: "For all have sinned and fall short of the glory of God."

Be patient in encouraging the person to relate how the struggle began, how it progressed, and what is currently happening.

In the assessment process you need *to evaluate the length of time* the person has been involved in this activity and *the extent of the involvement.* (Is it daily or sporadic? Is it reaching an addiction? Is it affecting his or her work or home life?) In addition, it is important to evaluate the degree to which the person feels *sorrow and regret* and to test his *willingness to change.*

1. When did you start looking at porn?
2. How long has this pattern been going on? If there are times when you have not looked at porn, how long have those been?
3. What prompted you to start with this current bout of wanting to look at porn?
4. When do you find you most often engage in viewing pornography (at night; when stressed; when you are on the computer and no one is around)?
5. What is it like to admit to this? (*Listen for the degree of defensiveness.*)
6. How do you think this is affecting your relationship with your spouse/friends/family?
7. When do you find yourself most tempted?
8. When you have been tempted to look at pornography before, has there been a time when you chose not to? What helped you make that choice?
9. Have you made any attempts to stop? If so, how?
10. What are you willing to do about this?
11. How do you see God in your life right now?

> One in ten boys under the age of 9 have viewed pornography. Nearly three in ten (27%) boys view pornography before turning 12 years old. Before 16 years old, more than three-fourths (78%) of boys have viewed pornography. Only 3% of men did not see pornography before turning 21 years old. The age that Christian men first began viewing pornography is virtually the same as national averages (78% viewed porn before turning 16 years old).[3]

Interviewing the Spouse Seeking Counsel

If the counselee is a spouse or parent of someone suspected of using pornography, she will probably be *expressing a variety of emotions* from anger to shame to guilt (feeling as if she is somehow at fault).

In the initial interview you will need to show a willingness to *listen and provide hope* that God will show a way through this difficult experience.

It will be important to *evaluate what specifically she wants to do.* She may be dealing with fear of confronting her husband. She may be struggling with thinking clearly about this situation and needs to talk it through with you.

1. When did you find out about this?
2. How did you discover this information?
3. Have you made any attempts to talk with your spouse or child about this?
4. If not, why not? Are you afraid of their reaction?
5. If so, what happened? How did you approach it and what did you say?

6. How did they respond?
7. Have you seen any unusual changes in their behavior lately?
8. How are you feeling in regard to finding this out?
9. How specifically can I help you?
10. Would you like me to talk to your spouse or child? Do you think they will be willing to talk to me?

4 | WISE COUNSEL

For the Person Viewing Pornography

Evaluate how *honest* the person is being with himself/herself and you. *Repenting is a crucial spiritual component* in the healing of sexual sin. You may wish to investigate with the person David's confession of sin in Psalm 51.

Determine how *willing the person is to take steps to change*. Honest confession and repentance are pivotal to begin the process of change.

It is important to *identify the triggers* that are involved in tempting the person. Alcoholics Anonymous narrowed down most of the moods associated with triggers to a simple acrostic: HALT, standing for:

Hungry
Angry
Lonely
Tired

Provide hope that the counselee will be able to realize victory over this. Let the person know that there will be times of temptation and possible setbacks, yet God is faithful to forgive and restore.

Assure the person of your continued support through this process. Instruct the person to structure a system of accountability through the help of a trusted friend.

5 | ACTION STEPS

For the Person Viewing Pornography

1. Flee Temptation

Help the person identify all the locations and activities that provide temptation.

- Avoid websites, social media, or bookstores that sell pornographic magazines.
- Use accountability software like Covenant Eyes on all devices.

2. Identify Emotional Triggers

- Are there work associates, times of the day, or particular stressful situations that trigger the temptation?

- Which part of HALT (hungry, angry, lonely, tired) is the strongest trigger for you?
- *Encourage the person to take specific steps to minimize the triggers.*

3. See It as Sin

- It is important to see the behavior as sin and no longer to justify it.
- *Discuss how God views the sin, the nature of forgiveness, and God's unconditional love. Evaluate with the counselee how he sees himself in relationship to how God sees him.*

4. Refocus on Christ

- You will need to develop a plan to strengthen and deepen your relationship with Jesus Christ.
- You will be accountable for daily Scripture reading and prayer.
- Memorize Scripture so that you can bring "every thought into captivity to the obedience of Christ" (2 Cor. 10:5).

5. Get Support and Accountability

- Get involved in a local Christian ministry that supports men or women who are experiencing this struggle.

6. Check In on the Marriage

- Evaluate their relationship with their spouse (if married) and provide an invitation to meet with both to explore the effects of this behavior on their relationship and to find healing for wounds.
- Work with the spouse on forgiveness and repairing the relationship.

7. Seek Further Help

- Pornography use can cause long-term problems.
- If this has been a *long-standing pattern* with a high degree of involvement, it is important to *enlist the support of a professional* trained in the arena of sexual addiction and/or a local 12-step group.

For the Spouse or Parent Seeking Counsel

If the spouse or child will not come in and talk with you, or if the person doesn't want them to know about their conversation with you, then you will need simply to offer encouragement to the counselee.

1. Watch for Patterns or Triggers

- Identify the locations and activities that provide temptation.
- You can help your spouse avoid these temptation areas by avoiding movies that have nudity or by using a software that prohibits graphic content.

> 15% of Christian women say they watch porn at least once a month.[4]

- Move the computer out of isolation.
- Enable parental controls on children's TVs, mobile devices, and computers.
- Have a standing rule that you are able to look at your child's or spouse's phone or computer at any point in time.

2. Notice Your Own Triggers

- Do you sense that there are work associates, times of the day, or particular stressful situations that trigger the temptation? What can you do to help?
- Which part of HALT (hungry, angry, lonely, tired) is the strongest trigger for your spouse? What can you do to offset this?
- If your spouse is willing to be helped, you can talk to them about these triggers and how you can be their ally in minimizing them.

3. Continue to Love Him/Her

- Nagging, anger, or humiliation will not work. Continue to love your spouse. It will be difficult because you will feel "cheated on," but ask God to help you choose to love them through this.
- Let your spouse know that you want them back from the darkness and you want your marriage unhindered by anything or anyone else.
- Tell them how you feel when they view pornography.
- Explain to them that eventually pornography cannot satisfy the intimacy or connection that God has created them for.

4. Pray for Him/Her

- Your spouse is making bad choices; fortunately, God gives us the ability to make good choices.
- Pray that your spouse will be sickened by what he or she sees and will choose to turn away.
- Let God go to work in your spouse's life.

5. Encourage Support

- Encourage your spouse to join a support group or Bible study that will provide accountability.
- Do whatever it takes to free them up to attend such a group.

6 BIBLICAL INSIGHTS

Now Israel remained in Acacia Grove, and the people began to commit harlotry with the women of Moab.

Numbers 25:1

90% of teens and 96% of young adults are either encouraging, accepting, or neutral when they talk about porn with their friends.[5]

For this is the will of God, your sanctification: that you should abstain from sexual immorality; that each of you should know how to possess his own vessel in sanctification and honor, not in passion of lust.

1 Thessalonians 4:3–5

I am He who searches the minds and hearts. And I will give to each one of you according to your works.

Revelation 2:23

Create in me a clean heart, O God, And renew a steadfast spirit within me.
Psalm 51:10

PRAYER STARTER 7

Oh, Lord, this family is being devastated by Satan's abomination of something You created to be good and wholesome. Help this family deal with the pain that pornography is causing. We ask that You strengthen Your child to stand firm in his [her] commitment to be free from the addictive power of pornography . . .

RECOMMENDED RESOURCES 8

Arterburn, Stephen, Fred Stoeker, and Mike Yorkey. *Every Man's Battle, Revised and Updated 20th Anniversary Edition: Winning the War on Sexual Temptation One Victory at a Time*. WaterBrook, 2020.

Arterburn, Stephen, and Jason Martinkus. *Worthy of Her Trust: What You Need to Do to Rebuild Sexual Integrity and Win Her Back*. WaterBrook, 2014.

Dallas, Joe. *5 Steps to Breaking Free from Porn*. Harvest House, 2013.

Ethridge, Shannon, and Stephen Arterburn. *Every Woman's Battle: Discovering God's Plan for Sexual and Emotional Fulfillment*. WaterBrook, 2003.

Feree, Marnie. *No Stones: Women Redeemed from Sexual Addiction*. IVP Books, 2010.

Laaser, Mark. *Healing the Wounds of Sexual Addiction*. Zondervan, 2004.

Makinney, Rosie. *Fight for Love: How to Take Your Marriage Back from Porn*. B&H, 2020.

Struthers, William. *Wired for Intimacy: How Pornography Hijacks the Male Brain*. InterVarsity, 2010.

Websites

American Association of Christian Counselors (AACC.net)

Christian Care Connect (Connect.AACC.net)

Covenant Eyes (CovenantEyes.com)

Is Porn Wrong? Video (TrueLife.org/Answers/Is-Porn-Wrong)

Proven Men (ProvenMen.org)

Prejudice

1 PORTRAITS

- Michelle and her family just moved into a suburban area in the South. She is nervous about her first day at school and having to make new friends again. When she walks into her new class, she feels the stares from all over the room and realizes she is the only person of color in the class. She instantly feels judged and uneasy about her new school.

- Janna is a young adult who is serious about her career in human resources. She has risen to a position where she is hiring personnel. Janna struggles with prejudices she has against people of different races.

- Rick grew up in a small town where there were "two sides of the tracks," and his family always told him that he lived on the "right" side of the tracks and to avoid going to the "wrong" side. The summer after his high school graduation, he becomes a Christian. When he moves to a large university in a diverse city, he encounters teammates on his football team who are from what his parents would call "the wrong side of the tracks." He struggles with how to "love his neighbor" and how doing so fits with the worldview he has known since he was as child.

2 DEFINITIONS AND KEY THOUGHTS

There is neither Jew nor Greek, there is neither slave nor free, there is neither male nor female; for you are all one in Christ Jesus.

Galatians 3:28

- Prejudice is an emotional response based on fear, mistrust, and ignorance. It is usually directed at a racial, religious, national, or other cultural group, although it can also focus on financial or other perceived differences.

- Racial trauma, or race-based traumatic stress (RBTS), refers to the mental and emotional injury caused by encounters with racial bias and ethnic discrimination, racism, and hate crimes.[1]

- Prejudice is also a superiority mindset that often is passed on from one generation to the next. Children who live in an environment where one or both parents have shown prejudice toward other religions or ethnicities, for example, will often become adults with those same prejudices.

- The prejudiced person will refuse involvement in situations and with groups of people simply because of who is involved. The fellowship that God intends for His children to share is therefore short-circuited.[2]

- Prejudice causes the whole body of Christ to suffer: "For as the body is one and has many members, but all the members of that one body, being many, are one body, so also is Christ" (1 Cor. 12:12).[3]

- Some argue that prejudice is a matter of personal opinion, and say, "I can't help the way I feel." However, Christians are instructed to exercise personal choices based on what they see in the character of God. (See Acts 10:9–48.) Furthermore, becoming a Christian means that you put away the former things and "be renewed in the spirit of your mind," according to Ephesians 4:22–23.

- Second Chronicles 19:7 states: "Now therefore, let the fear of the LORD be upon you . . . for *there is* no iniquity with the LORD our God, no partiality." Romans 2:11 says that God does not show favoritism: "There is no partiality with God."

- God's unbiased disposition toward the world is the basis for John 3:16: "For God so loved the world that He gave His only begotten Son, that whoever believes in Him should not perish but have everlasting life."

- The prejudiced person:
  » needs to address deep issues of anger and/or attitude
  » has issues that can stem from group, societal, cultural, or family history or from an event in his or her past
  » has a false view of self—seeing self as uniquely separate and better than others
  » has an incorrect understanding of God and His creation of and love for all people

- Prejudice can lead to discrimination—putting prejudicial attitudes, thoughts, and opinions into action.

- Any discriminating thoughts, feelings, or behaviors violate the substantial rights, privileges, and equal protections granted to others by the laws of the land and mandated by Scripture.

- The person experiencing prejudice or racial trauma:
  » may be reexposed to the trauma by distressing or current events
  » can experience hypervigilance or increased stress during political seasons and/or current events
  » may have difficulty coping and need to learn proper self-care during times of stress
  » should connect with their friends, family, community, and church to find support and express feelings and concerns
  » should build an awareness of things that may be a trigger of the previous trauma and limit exposure

> Darkness cannot drive out darkness; only light can do that. Hate cannot drive out hate; only love can do that.
> Martin Luther King Jr.

191

3 | ASSESSMENT INTERVIEW

For Those Who Struggle with Prejudice

1. What are your thoughts about people who are different from you?
2. What is your earliest memory of becoming aware that someone looked different from you?
3. What is your earliest memory of becoming aware of racism?
4. How would your parents, grandparents, or aunts and uncles respond to or talk about someone who looked different from you? Explain what your parents and/or family taught you about different cultures or people groups.
5. Did you ever have a negative experience with a person from another culture? What happened?
6. How do you feel around different cultures or people groups?
7. How have you expressed your ideas about these cultures or groups of people? Have you been discriminatory?
8. What makes you think that people from different cultures deserve this kind of treatment?
9. Have you ever been misunderstood or treated differently because of the way you look?
10. How did that make you feel?
11. When you feel prejudice toward someone, how does that make you feel?
12. What does it mean to you when you hear: "Walk a mile in someone's shoes"?
13. How did Jesus treat those who were different from Him?
14. What does your relationship with God look like?
15. How do you understand unconditional love?

For Those Who Have Experienced Prejudice

1. Tell me about your experience with discrimination.
2. What does a typical day look like for you at your job, school, or in your community?
3. What is your earliest memory of becoming aware that someone looked different from you?
4. How old were you when you first experienced racism? How did you feel? Did you speak to anyone about it?
5. How did your parents, grandparents, or aunts and uncles talk about or respond to people of other races?
6. What do you do when there is a traumatic or distressing event involving racism in the national news?
7. What self-care practices do you use when you may become triggered by an event?
8. Do you have family, friends, community, church, or a support group around you?
9. What does your relationship with God look like?

WISE COUNSEL | 4

Don't assume that the client has any knowledge of life outside his or her own cultural boundaries. As a society, we are becoming more globally minded, but some remain very narrow-minded in their understanding of differences in cultures.

Share some examples of how other cultures live or think. Help the person understand that he or she must learn to celebrate the differences instead of judging the differences. There are good documentaries or docu-series that talk about different cultures.

As the love of God flows through Christians, we are drawn together as one body; our relationships with one another are rooted in biblical teachings like:

> *Be* kindly affectionate to one another" (Rom. 12:10).

> "Be of the same mind toward one another" (Rom. 12:16).

> "Love one another" (Rom. 13:8).

> "Pursue the things *which make* for peace and the things by which one may edify another" (Rom. 14:19).

> "The members should have the same care for one another" (1 Cor. 12:25).

> "Through love serve one another" (Gal. 5:13).

> "Be kind to one another, tenderhearted, forgiving one another" (Eph. 4:32).

> "Bearing with one another, and forgiving one another" (Col. 3:13).

> The US population is continuing to become more diverse. By 2044, more than half of all Americans are projected to belong to a minority group (any group other than non-Hispanic White alone).[4]

ACTION STEPS | 5

1. Grow in Multicultural Appreciation

- Examine your own cultural roots and become more personally aware of who you are and where your ancestors came from (we are a nation of immigrants—everyone came from somewhere else, unless you're Native American).

- Look up information about the culture in question—the one causing the prejudice. (*Give one specific item to look up, for example, meals or special celebrations. The client may find something like brides wear white in the United States, but in India they prefer red or yellow.*) This item of information should be brought to the next session.

2. Get Personal

- Think of a time when you were made fun of (perhaps for your curly hair or your "Irish temper"). Remember how it made you feel.

- How is that any different from the prejudice you are showing someone? (*Encourage the individual to answer this—it may really stretch his or her thinking and bring the client to a point of realization.*)

Lack of cultural understanding by health care providers may contribute to underdiagnosis and/or misdiagnosis of mental illness in people from racially/ethnically diverse populations. Factors that contribute to these kinds of misdiagnoses include language differences between patient and provider, stigma of mental illness among minority groups, and cultural presentation of symptoms.[5]

3. Avoid Stereotypes

- Would you want to be generalized as a "dumb blonde" or a "tough German" or a "loud Italian"? Then don't do that to others.
- Generalizations are made about people without regard to their uniqueness. *Lead the client through an experience where he or she was not allowed to show their uniqueness and had to be like "everyone else."*
- Usually when you make generalizations, it is a way of *avoiding* the need to deal with the person as an individual.

4. Practice Empathy

- Walk a mile in someone else's shoes *before you make* a judgment about that person. Get into his or her head, think about what life must be like for this individual. This is called empathy.
- Consider how you would feel landing in another country where you don't know the customs or the language.

5. Do What Jesus Would Do

- Remember your common bond in Christ with fellow believers. This common bond tears down any walls of prejudice (see Col. 3:11).
- For those who aren't believers (or you don't know if they are), develop sensitivity with God's help. This along with empathy will help you begin living outside the box.
- Changing your deeply rooted attitudes and beliefs will not come overnight. This is a process that will take time. As you continue to examine your own beliefs and talk to others about them, change will occur.
- People who wish to overcome prejudice need to have renewed minds (Eph. 4:23). By studying God's Word, we can acquire the mind of Christ (Phil. 2:5). Christ will then empower you through the Holy Spirit to remove the prejudice that can do harm to your ability to relate to all persons and fellow image-bearers.

6 BIBLICAL INSIGHTS

Gilead's wife bore sons; and when his wife's sons grew up, they drove Jephthah out, and said to him, "You shall have no inheritance in our father's house, for you *are* the son of another woman."

Judges 11:2

But he disdained to lay hands on Mordecai alone, for they had told him of the people of Mordecai. Instead, Haman sought to destroy all the Jews who *were* throughout the whole kingdom of Ahasuerus—the people of Mordecai.

Esther 3:6

Then he said to them, "You know how unlawful it is for a Jewish man to keep company with or go to one of another nation. But God has shown me that I should not call any man common or unclean."

Acts 10:28

There is neither Jew nor Greek, there is neither slave nor free, there is neither male nor female; for you are all one in Christ Jesus.

Galatians 3:28

If you really fulfill *the* royal law according to the Scripture, "You shall love your neighbor as yourself," you do well; but if you show partiality, you commit sin, and are convicted by the law as transgressors.

James 2:8–9

> People from racial/ethnic minority groups are less likely to receive mental health care. For example, in 2015, among adults with any mental illness, 48% of Caucasians received mental health services, compared with 31% of African Americans and Hispanics, and 22% of Asians.[6]

PRAYER STARTER 7

Thank You, Lord, that Your child has come today to deal with this issue of prejudice. The reasons run deep, but not so deep that You cannot heal, Lord. Help him [her] see that You created all people in Your image and because of that all people have dignity and value . . .

RECOMMENDED RESOURCES 8

Crear, Mark. *Peace Be Still: How to Promote Racial Reconciliation and Healing.* Book Writing Inc., 2020.

McPherson, Miles. *The Third Option: Hope for a Racially Divided Nation.* Howard Books, 2018.

Morrison, Latasha. *Be the Bridge: Pursuing God's Heart for Racial Reconciliation.* WaterBrook, 2019.

Websites

American Association of Christian Counselors (AACC.net)

Christian Care Connect (Connect.AACC.net)

> Among all racial/ethnic groups, except American Indian/Alaska Native, women are much more likely to receive mental health services than men.[7]

Premarital Sex

1 PORTRAITS

- Stan has been divorced for three years. For a while, he assumed he'd never love anyone again, but then he met Marie. She, too, is divorced. They faithfully attend different churches, so they decide to go together to his church one weekend and hers the next. After a few months, she invites him to her apartment, and there, kissing soon leads to touching, caressing, and sex. They know it's wrong, but they don't care. It feels right.

- Phyllis and Robert suspect their daughter Rachel is having sex with her boyfriend, but she denies it every time they bring it up. One night at about 2:00 in the morning, they hear a strange noise in the house. They walk down the hall and open Rachel's door. Rachel's boyfriend is in the bed with her. She had opened her window to let him in. Her parents are furious. The young couple quickly gets dressed, Rachel throws some clothes in a suitcase, and she storms out of the house with her boyfriend. After a week, her parents still haven't heard from her.

- Laurie is in high school and is devastated when she breaks up with her boyfriend. Only her best friend knows that her emotional pain is heightened by the fact that she lost her virginity to him.

- Kim is twenty years old, in college, and has a one-night stand with Jordan after a party. A few weeks later she discovers that she's pregnant. Upon hearing the news of her pregnancy, Jordan wants nothing to do with the baby.

- Dave has always had the mentality to "test drive before you buy" and has been having sex with every girl he has been in a relationship with since middle school. He really doesn't understand what all the fuss is about from his parents.

> I say then: Walk in the Spirit, and you shall not fulfill the lust of the flesh.
>
> Galatians 5:16

2 DEFINITIONS AND KEY THOUGHTS

- The desire for sex is a *God-given appetite* that needs to be controlled.
- According to the whole counsel of the Bible, sex outside of marriage is wrong—no matter how old you are or how much you love your partner.
- Sex typically refers to intercourse between a man and a woman.
- A common misconception of teens is that "it's not really sex" if it's oral sex. The Bible teaches that any sexual engagement with another outside of the covenant of marriage is sin. (See Exod. 20:14; Prov. 5:1–6, 15–20; 1 Cor. 6:12–20.) Ad-

ditionally, most teens do not understand that STDs (sexually transmitted diseases) can be transferred during oral sex.

- Our society has been sexualized by media that uses sex to sell and to entertain.
- Teens whose parents speak to them openly about biblical sexual ethics will be more informed and more thoughtful about their behavior than those whose parents don't talk with them about sex. Ignorance can lead to recklessness.
- More than anything else, drugs and alcohol contribute to risky sexual behavior and impulsive decision-making.
- Often, teen girls who mature early struggle to accept their sexuality. They are frequently treated as sex objects by boys whose sexuality is just awakening, and they may be rejected by other girls who are envious of the attention they get.
- Girls who strive for acceptance and rarely assert themselves may be susceptible to boys who tell them they must have sex or they will no longer date them.
- Whether true or not, the statement "everybody is doing it" is frequently cited by teens to justify sexual acting out.
- Rape and date rape may be far more common than we think, especially on college campuses where reporting a rape may carry a stigma.

> When it comes to living together, the majority of adults (65%) either strongly or somewhat agree it's a good idea to live with one's significant other before marriage, compared to one-third (35%) who either strongly or somewhat disagree.[1]

ASSESSMENT INTERVIEW 3

Teens may seek counseling for an unrelated problem and then slowly—if trust develops—admit to premarital sex, pregnancy, or abortion.

Most people who seek counseling for a sexual indiscretion will be hyper-attuned to criticism. Remember they may be coming to you because a family member or friend has suggested it.

The following questions will help you assess the situation once it becomes clear that sexual misbehavior has occurred.

Rule Outs

1. Were you pressured or forced to have sex? If so, when did this take place? (*If it has just occurred, the rape should be reported to the police so that evidence can be gathered. This may not be what the individual wants to do, but your state laws may require you to do so as a mandated reporter.*)
2. Is there any possibility that you are pregnant? If so, what are your thoughts? (*If she is considering abortion, see the section on Abortion.*)
3. Sexually transmitted diseases can be caught through oral sex as well as intercourse. Have you engaged in unprotected oral sex or intercourse? (*If so, the person needs a medical exam immediately. If infected, the counselee should*

contact every person he or she has been with, at least within a particular window of time, so those people can be tested.)

4. Has your sexual experience caused you to feel stressed, anxious, or depressed? Have you considered harming yourself? (*If yes, see the section on Suicide.*)

General Questions

1. Describe your relationship with your boyfriend/girlfriend to me.
2. What does your physical relationship look like?
3. Are you comfortable with your physical relationship?
4. What are your sexual boundaries between you and your partner?
5. Have you violated them? If so, how?
6. What brings you enjoyment in your physical relationship?
7. With how many partners have you had sex?
8. Do you use protection when you have sex?
9. Do you plan your sexual activity ahead of time, or does it just happen?
10. How do you feel about having sex as far as your health goes?
11. Do you want to continue having sex?
12. If you want to change, what strategies have you tried? How well have they worked?
13. Have you ever been pressured into having sex? What would you do if it happened again?
14. What does love mean to you?
15. Are you feeling guilty? What do you plan to do with your feelings?
16. What does your relationship with God look like?
17. What does unconditional love look like to you?
18. What do you think you should do now?

Keep your heart with all diligence, For out of it *spring* the issues of life.

Proverbs 4:23

4 WISE COUNSEL

Christian counselors do not condone or advocate for the pursuit of or active involvement in premarital and/or extramarital sexual behavior by clients, acknowledging that sex is part of God's good creation and a gift when confined to one man and one woman within the boundaries of marriage. Counselors may agree to and support the client's desire to work through issues related to sexual behavior, identity, and attractions, but will encourage sexual celibacy or biblically prescribed sexual behavior while such issues are being addressed.

Counselors acknowledge the client's fundamental right to self-determination and further understand that deeply held religious values and beliefs may conflict with sex outside of marriage, or same-sex attraction and/or behavior, resulting in anxiety, depression, stress, and inner turmoil.

ACTION STEPS | 5

1. Talk It Out

- If the client is a young person, help him or her feel comfortable. Simply listen and encourage the person to talk.
- The client may not have come in with issues about premarital sex, but you may discover that it underlies presenting issues such as self-esteem, depression, and so on.

2. See a Pregnancy Resource Counselor If Needed

- If you discover that the counselee is pregnant or has gotten a female pregnant, encourage her or him to reveal this information to family members.
- Refer the person to a pregnancy resource center to discuss the options for raising the child or giving the baby up for adoption.

3. Confess Sin

- If the client is a Christian, they need to be willing to admit and confess the sin. Confession, repentance, and forgiveness are crucial elements in the healing process.

4. Accept God's Forgiveness

- The person may be suffering from intense feelings of guilt. Help him or her process these feelings, confess the sin(s), and experience forgiveness.
- Sometimes using a guided visual meditation to teach a biblical truth helps us feel forgiven. Imagine placing all the sins into a trash bag and turning it over to Jesus. He deals with it by destroying it and then covers you with a clean, perfect coat. *It is important to help some people feel God's presence and experience His leading as parts of their healing journey.*
- Focus on God's love and forgiveness. Passages like Psalm 51 remind us that God forgives and heals our pain.
- Even though you have lost your virginity, you can, in a sense, start over with God. You can determine from now until marriage to remain pure.
- *Note: Encourage the client to be honest and open about their past with their future spouse. This topic will most likely come up in premarital counseling.*

5. Discover the Reasons

Help the counselee understand the reasons he or she engages in sex. Is it:

- a search for intimacy?
- a desire to prove manhood or womanhood?

> Practicing Christians (72%) are almost twice as likely as adults of no faith (38%) to say that choosing not to have sex outside marriage is a healthy choice. Women (56%) are more likely than men (43%) to hold this view. Compared to those who have never been married (41%), people who are married (53%) and, somewhat surprisingly, cohabitating adults (49%) are more likely to strongly agree with the statement.[2]

- a need to be accepted or popular with others who are having sex?
- a need to hold on to a particular boyfriend or girlfriend?
- a good physical sensation?
- a desire to feel loved and cherished?
- a feeling that it is expected?

6. Remain Pure

Having sex is like many other life-dominating, impulsive behaviors. Brainstorm ways to avoid having sex outside of the biblical covenantal context in the future. This might include:

- ending the dating relationship if the other person does not share the conviction that sex should stop
- seeking out new friends who believe in preserving sex until covenantal marriage
- searching for activities that will help to refocus sexual drives
- being physically active on a daily basis
- asking every day for God to take over and sanctify your sexual drive
- finding a Bible study and books on the topic

6 | BIBLICAL INSIGHTS

But it happened about this time, when Joseph went into the house to do his work, and none of the men of the house *was* inside, that she caught him by his garment, saying, "Lie with me." But he left his garment in her hand, and fled and ran outside.

Genesis 39:11–12

I am my beloved's,
And his desire *is* toward me.

Song of Solomon 7:10

Do you not know that your bodies are members of Christ? Shall I then take the members of Christ and make *them* members of a harlot? Certainly not!

1 Corinthians 6:15

7 | PRAYER STARTER

Dear Lord, thank You that _____ is seeking help. Please aid _____ to see Your plan for sexuality. Help _____ learn new strategies to handle temptation. We know that once we ask for Your forgiveness, we have it. And once we are forgiven, we are pure. This is a reality. We praise You for this reality and thank You for Your forgiveness. Please be with us every step of the way as we seek to preserve purity in the days to come . . .

RECOMMENDED RESOURCES 8

Evans, Tony. *Sacred Sex: Embracing Your Sexuality as God Designed It*. Moody, 2014.

Rosenau, Doug, and Michael Todd Wilson. *Soul Virgins: Redefining Single Sexuality*. Sexual Wholeness Resources, 2012.

Slattery, Julie. *Rethinking Sexuality: God's Design and Why It Matters*. Multnomah, 2018.

Smalley, Michael, and Amy Smalley. *Don't Date Naked*. Tyndale, 2010.

Websites

American Association of Christian Counselors (AACC.net)

Christian Care Connect (Connect.AACC.net)

Self-Esteem

1 PORTRAITS

- Patrick grew up in a home with alcoholics with a lot of drama and chaos. His sister's way to cope was to seek acceptance in the arms of young men and numb the pain with drugs, but Patrick tried to please, to be conscientious, to earn his parents' approval. But no matter how hard he tried, the best he got was mixed messages. In his thirst for approval, however, all he heard were the negative ones: "You messed up again," "Why can't you do anything right?" "You'll never amount to anything." And he believed them.
- Jennifer believes her marriage has no hope. She feels that apart from her husband and children, she has no purpose in life. Her husband keeps reminding her that without him, she is nothing.
- Henry has lived his entire life trying to please his parents. At forty, he still sees every decision he makes as an opportunity to win the favor of his father. He is sad and discouraged, and he can't seem to hold a job or a long-term relationship.
- From the time she was a young child, Sandy has been told that she is ugly and stupid. At eighteen, she is frightened to enter college for fear of failure in relationships.
- Jill has had multiple boyfriends during her adult life. She feels frustrated and pressured to give in to their sexual advances to escape rejection. She doesn't understand why she can't keep someone's love.
- David grew up in a family that told him he was the "king." He gravitated toward weaker friends who would do anything to please him. His wife has brought him to counseling because she can't take his arrogance and demanding nature. "I don't even know why I'm here," David says. "She's the problem; always has been, always will be. If she would just do what I say, we would be fine!"

2 DEFINITIONS AND KEY THOUGHTS

- Self-esteem refers to an inner sense of worthiness that gives a person resilience and resistance to attack or criticism.
- Generally speaking, each person has a concept of his or her self-worth (which may or may not be accurate), and self-esteem is how the person feels about (or evaluates) that concept.
- Perhaps self-esteem could be referred to as the "attitude of the self to the self."[1]

- A biblical sense of identity isn't based on accomplishments, approval, appearance, wealth, or status. These are the measuring sticks for most people, but no matter how much they get, it's never quite enough, which leaves them empty and desperate for more. Instead, our sense of worth should be based on God's evaluation of us: He knows the worst about us and loves us still. He has paid the price to ransom us from slavery to sin, and He has adopted us as His cherished children. That's the firm foundation of our identity. It provides humility because we know we didn't earn it, and it thrills us because we realize the God of the universe calls us His own.

- Low self-esteem can manifest itself in many ways:
  - » feelings of self-hate, believing that one is unworthy or incompetent
  - » refusal to get close to people, believing one doesn't deserve strong or supportive relationships
  - » refusal to trust others
  - » inability to accept oneself as special and unique
  - » rejection of what God intended the person to be in Him
  - » depression
  - » suicidal thoughts
  - » a need for lots of attention
  - » a competitive spirit
  - » poor decisions that are based on fears and not reality
  - » lack of trust in people who have shown themselves trustworthy
  - » fear of rejection
  - » self-fulfilling prophecies about people not wanting to be connected with them
  - » returning to relationships that the person knows are abusive or painful

- High self-esteem can manifest itself in many ways:
  - » feeling that other people are beneath the individual
  - » demanding that other people change, while not seeing one's own personal faults
  - » an intense temper when feeling wronged or slighted
  - » feeling entitled to be treated in the best ways
  - » enjoying people struggling or trying for their approval
  - » not helping with everyday chores, because "that is someone else's job"

- People's self-esteem is in trouble when *they allow others to assess and convince them of their value or significance* instead of relying on the assessment of the One who created them.

- Poor self-esteem is often the result of prolonged periods of negative feedback in a person's life, resulting in deep wounds and pain. As a counselor, you need to apply active listening skills to determine how far back the negative influence has gone.

- High self-esteem could come from the family of origin or a manifestation of a personality disorder. It will be important to assess for both.

Have I not commanded you? Be strong and of good courage; do not be afraid, nor be dismayed, for the LORD your God *is* with you wherever you go.
Joshua 1:9

203

- Society is constantly assessing our value. At work, we have performance evaluations. We are graded in schools. We are evaluated for loans. Assessment of our value begins early in life and continues even after we are dead.

- Often the imposition of value is a means to an end. A negative example of this is the young lady who finds herself in the back seat of a car with a boy who says: "If you want me to cherish/value/love you, you will have sex with me." This is the worst form of value imposition.

- God has determined our value based on His purpose for creating us in the first place and on the price He has paid to redeem us for all eternity.

- Many Christians feel that self-esteem doesn't even belong in a Christian's vocabulary—that any assessment of our own value is vanity and therefore sinful. This, of course, is true when a person has an overinflated sense of his or her worth, resembling conceit powered by pride. However, as counselors we must deal with those who come with a damaged or painful sense of their worth or an inflated sense of self. Searching for God's perspective on our worth or significance is worthy of our time and spiritual energy.

- Most who struggle with low self-esteem are believing lies about their significance to God. Those who are struggling with high self-esteem are believing lies about themself that do not reflect God's perspective.

- The goals of counseling should be to:
  » correct false or erroneous beliefs about the individual's worth and significance
  » make an accurate, genuine assessment of the person's strengths, gifts, significance, and potential
  » bring healing from deep relationship wounds
  » help the person get over the distortions and be able to admit honestly his or her strengths as well as weaknesses
  » help the person on the journey to adopting God's perspective on his or her worth

3 ASSESSMENT INTERVIEW

Most clients tend to feel bad about themselves *without having ever identified the problem* as being related to self-esteem. They may feel like a failure or have strong feelings of inadequacy that can result in periods of depression and anxiety.

Some people with poor self-image have been *sexually abused and still feel dirty and worthless* as a result. If your counseling session uncovers sexual abuse, you will need to deal with this issue or refer the person to someone else. (See the section on Sexual Abuse in Childhood.)

Many individuals with poor self-esteem have come from families where a *divorce* made them insecure or where they might have even been *blamed* (or just assumed responsibility) for the divorce.

Some may simply have *overly sensitive personalities* that make them vulnerable to slights or criticism.

Use "normalization" to help build rapport and *make it clear that the person's feelings are normal.*

1. How would you describe yourself?
2. How would your best friend or spouse describe you?
3. Have you ever been told that you have low self-esteem? If so, by whom and when? Do you agree?
4. Have you ever been told that you are prideful or arrogant? If so, by whom and when? Do you agree?
5. What standard do you hold yourself to? Would you say that is a biblical standard?
6. How do you feel when things don't work out the way you wanted them to?
7. How do you handle a situation where someone wants you to do something that you don't want to do?
8. Tell me about a situation where you had to take a risk. What was that like for you?
9. When you make a mistake, what do you tell yourself?
10. If I were to ask your family what standard you hold them to, what would they say?
11. What does it look like for you when you get angry with someone? What normally happens? (*Look for if they are able to forgive.*)
12. How do you feel about the way you look?
13. Would you say that you are competitive or just love playing the game?
14. Can you tell me about a time when you wanted to be someone else?
15. What sorts of supportive friendships do you have?
16. In what sorts of situations do you feel most self-conscious? Least self-conscious?
17. Talk to me about how you use social media. Who do you follow? Do you post pictures of yourself? How do you respond when you don't get enough likes or comments?
18. What does it mean to you to be a child of God?
19. Do you believe that God loves you? Can you "feel" God's love or is it more of an intellectual understanding that God loves you?
20. How many siblings do you have? Where are you in the birth order?
21. Tell me about life in your family growing up.
22. How were you treated as a child when you did something wrong or failed at something?
23. Did your parents have high expectations or low expectations of you? Or neither?
24. Who was the favorite in the family and how did that feel?
25. Have you ever experienced abuse (sexual, emotional, spiritual, or physical) of any kind? If so, did you report it? How was it handled and what happened?
26. Describe the people in your life who made you feel good about yourself. Where are they now? Are any still in your life?
27. What makes you feel good about yourself?

> Blessed *is* the man who trusts in the LORD, And whose hope is the LORD. For he shall be like a tree planted by the waters, Which spreads out its roots by the river, And will not fear when heat comes; But its leaf will be green, And will not be anxious in the year of drought, Nor will cease from yielding fruit.
>
> Jeremiah 17:7–8

4 | WISE COUNSEL

Helping a person with low self-esteem *does not mean telling him or her untruths.* Instead, help the person develop a *realistic assessment of his or her unique set of skills, abilities, and character traits.* Further, help this individual develop a *strong sense of God's love and forgiveness.*

Remind your client of the story in John 5 where Jesus heals the crippled man who had lived for thirty-eight years with brokenness and pain. Jesus asked him if he *wanted* to be healed. Why would Jesus ask that? It seems that a person can live for so long with brokenness that he or she may not want to do the work that it takes to receive healing. Is your client willing to *do the work to receive healing?*

5 | ACTION STEPS

1. Recognize Your Value

- There is a difference between having an inflated ego and simply understanding your significance based on your God-given gifts and value to Him.[2]
- Make a list of ten talents, character traits, physical traits, abilities, accomplishments, and so on that set you apart. (*You can give this as homework. The person must come back to another session with the list in hand and be ready to share it with you.*)
- On the list, include five traits that you perceive are negative. Write down some ideas for how you can turn these negatives into positives.
- You mentioned a few people who made you feel good about yourself (*Assessment Interview question 26*). Are these people still in your life? If not, is there a way you can get them back into your life?
- Identify other positive people and spend more time with them.

2. Recognize Harmful Thought Patterns

- Consider some of the thought patterns and other factors that are leading you to believe lies about your worth.
- When do you most often find yourself feeling these thought patterns?
- What provokes these thought patterns? Is it watching movies, going to the mall, or spending hours on social media?

3. Begin New Thought Patterns

- Each negative thought can be countered with God's assessment of your value. For example, if you feel your self-worth sizzle when a coworker with less experience is promoted over you, stop the negative thoughts before they take hold of you. Ask yourself if there might be any good reason this person received the promotion over you. If not, remind yourself that life isn't always fair.

- Remember that God has your life in His hands. Not receiving that promotion may end up being a blessing in disguise.

4. Be Patient

- It has taken years of bad habits to get to where you are with your self-esteem. Healing will not happen overnight and will require replacing the bad thought patterns with good ones.
- It may take a while until your reflex action is quick to respond in a proactive way to negative thinking.

5. Read God's Word

- Study what the Bible says about your worth to God. Explore what God says about His love for you and His purpose for your life. (*Give the client the verses from Biblical Insights below for starters.*)
- Keep a journal to record significant breakthroughs.

BIBLICAL INSIGHTS 6

But Moses said to God, "Who *am* I that I should go to Pharaoh, and that I should bring the children of Israel out of Egypt?"

Exodus 3:11

> What is man that You are mindful of him,
> And the son of man that You visit him?
> For You have made him a little lower than the angels,
> And You have crowned him with glory and honor.

Psalm 8:4–5

> But now, thus says the Lord, who created you, O Jacob,
> And He who formed you, O Israel:
> "Fear not, for I have redeemed you;
> I have called *you* by your name;
> You *are* Mine."

Isaiah 43:1

Are not two sparrows sold for a copper coin? And not one of them falls to the ground apart from your Father's will. But the very hairs of your head are all numbered.

Matthew 10:29–30

Behold what manner of love the Father has bestowed on us, that we should be called children of God!

1 John 3:1

> Are not five sparrows sold for two copper coins? And not one of them is forgotten before God. But the very hairs of your head are all numbered. Do not fear therefore; you are of more value than many sparrows.
> Luke 12:6–7

7 PRAYER STARTER

Thank You that Your precious child is here today, Lord, to talk about how he [she] feels of so little value. Lord, help him [her] see that he [she] is of great value to You. Help him [her] see the gifts You have given him [her] and the special "package" that he [she] is—his [her] background, interests, abilities, and ideas make him [her] Your special creation . . .

8 RECOMMENDED RESOURCES

[Self-esteem] is the most popular way that the fear of other people is expressed. If self-esteem is a recurring theme for you, chances are that your life revolves around what others think. You reverence or fear their opinions. You need them to buttress your sense of well-being and identity. You need them to fill you up.

Ed Welch

Batterson, Mark. *In a Pit with a Lion on a Snowy Day: How to Survive and Thrive When Opportunity Roars*. Multnomah, 2016.

Clinton, Tim, and Gary Sibcy. *Why You Do the Things You Do: The Secret to Healthy Relationships*. Thomas Nelson, 2006.

Cloud, Henry. *The Power of the Other: The Startling Effect Other People Have on You, from the Boardroom to the Bedroom and Beyond—and What to Do About It*. Harper Business, 2016.

Groeschel, Craig. *Winning the War in Your Mind: Change Your Thinking, Change Your Life*. Zondervan, 2021.

Lyons, Rebekah. *You Are Free: Be Who You Already Are*. Zondervan, 2017.

McGee, Robert S. *The Search for Significance*. Thomas Nelson, 2003.

Welch, Ed. *When People Are Big and God Is Small: Overcoming Peer Pressure, Co-dependency, and the Fear of Man*. P&R, 1997.

Websites

American Association of Christian Counselors (AACC.net)

Christian Care Connect (Connect.AACC.net)

Sexual Abuse in Childhood

PORTRAITS | 1

- Jean never told anybody what had happened when she was growing up. She hoped if she never talked about it, the memory would go away. After all, it had happened only once and it really wasn't that bad. She never told her parents because she doesn't think they would believe her. She had avoided her uncle as often as she could after that. She really doesn't think it makes sense to talk about it now.

- Betty tried to tell him no, but he kept touching her. She had been so excited to have been asked out by an older guy that she had tried to act more sophisticated than she felt. Now she keeps thinking about what had happened and doesn't know what she should do.

- Danielle's father is a belligerent alcoholic. Almost daily, he and her mother fight and scream at each other. One night after a fight, he walks in her room. He takes his clothes off and demands she lie down on her bed. She is only 10, and intercourse hurts terribly. She cries herself to sleep that night. The next morning, she tells her mother what happened, and her mother slaps her. She growls, "I never want to hear another word about this come out of your mouth." Danielle feels crushed by the betrayal of both of her parents.

- Samuel isn't a very good athlete, and he is shy around other boys. They often pick on him, and he takes it without fighting back. One day after school, a boy on the football team grabs him, takes him into an empty room, hits him several times, and then demands oral sex. Samuel is humiliated. He doesn't tell anyone, but he is sure the other boy told all his friends.

> The highest percentages of professionals who report child maltreatment come from education personnel (18.9%), legal and law enforcement personnel (18.4%), and social services personnel (11.2%). Nonprofessionals—including friends, neighbors, and relatives—submitted one-fifth of reports (18.1%).[1]

DEFINITIONS AND KEY THOUGHTS | 2

- Abuse generally is taking *unfair advantage of a difference of power* to take control of someone else.[2]

- Childhood sexual abuse occurs when a *person exploits another, aged 17 and younger*, to satisfy the abuser's needs. It consists of any sexual activity—verbal, visual, or physical—engaged in with a minor.

- Sexual abuse is most often perpetrated by an adult who has access to a minor by virtue of *real or imagined authority* or kinship.

- When a child is abused, often *the child knows and even loves the abuser*, and this may cause intense confusion and damage.
- Sexual abuse *violates personal boundaries*. The abuser crosses a person's boundaries to take what he or she wants. A key to helping the abused person is to set up boundaries that cannot be crossed.

Physical Consequences

Long-lasting physical symptoms and illnesses have been associated with sexual victimization, including chronic pelvic pain, premenstrual syndrome, gastrointestinal disorders, and a variety of chronic pain disorders, including headache, back pain, and facial pain.

Psychological Consequences

Immediate reactions to sexual abuse include shock, disbelief, denial, fear, confusion, anxiety, and withdrawal.

Victims may experience emotional detachment, sleep disturbances, and flashbacks. Approximately one-third of sexual abuse victims have symptoms that become chronic.

Sexual abuse victims often experience anxiety, guilt, nervousness, phobias, substance abuse, sleep disturbances, depression, alienation, suicidal behavior, and sexual dysfunction. Often they distrust others, replay the assault in their minds, and are at increased risk of revictimization.

> One in 9 girls and 1 in 53 boys under the age of 18 experience sexual abuse or assault at the hands of an adult.[3]

Social Consequences

Sexual abuse can strain relationships because of its negative effect on the victim's family, friends, and intimate partners.

Victims of sexual violence are more likely than nonvictims to engage in risky sexual behavior, including having unprotected sex, having sex at an early age, having multiple sex partners, and trading sex for food, money, or other items.

Limits of Confidentiality

As you counsel a person who has been sexually abused, you must know the limits of confidentiality.

Sexual abuse is *illegal and must be reported*. You must *report it to the appropriate agencies*, such as local law enforcement, the Department of Social and Health Services, or Child Protective Services.

You must report sexual abuse *within a period of time*, usually between twenty-four hours and seven days.

Usually you can *report by phone, in writing, or in person*.

Even if the counselee does not admit to abuse, but you highly suspect it, you should *report your suspicions*.

If the person is over eighteen at the time of disclosure, reporting abuse may not be mandatory. However, *if the abuser still has access to children*, you may have an ethical obligation to report the abuse to protect the children.

ASSESSMENT INTERVIEW 3

Rule out any *suicidal risk, depression, or medical concerns* (especially if the abuse was recent).

Assess for the *type of abuse* perpetrated—its degree and its history. Sometimes the person is *seeking help for other problems* that actually stem from sexual abuse. You need to get him or her to talk about the core issue. Be careful, however, not to re-traumatize the person with your questions. Trust and safety are of vital importance.

Assume Three Things in the Process of Treatment

1. The problem is treatable and your client will be a survivor.
2. The client is not responsible for the abuse; he or she is only responsible for recovery.
3. To heal, your client needs to express, accept, and be prepared to deal with his or her feelings.

General Questions

1. What has happened that has brought you here today?
2. Is this the first time you've sought help?
3. Tell me about your family. How are things going at home?
4. Tell me about your past. Have you had any painful or unusual things happen—even a long time ago?
5. How long did that go on?
6. Can you tell me who was doing this to you? (*If the person seems reticent, explain that you need to know to help him or her, others who might be abused, and the abuser. In addition, if your client is a minor and still in contact with the abuser so that the abuse might recur, immediate action must be taken.*)
7. Do you know if others are being abused?
8. What problems are you currently having as a result of what has happened? (*Listen to how the abuse affected the person. No two people are alike in their experiences or the consequences of the abuse. Be aware that victims tend to minimize the impact of the abuse.*)
9. How do you feel about what has happened to you? (*The client needs to have permission to feel his or her true emotions.*)
10. Do you feel responsible for the abuse? (*Reassure the client that he or she is not alone and that he or she is not responsible for the abuse.*)
11. What do you believe about yourself? (*Dig down for unhealthy beliefs that have developed as a result of abuse. For example, what does the person think about him- or herself since this abuse occurred?*)

> The experience of chronic abuse carries within it the gross mislabeling of things. Perpetrators are really "nice daddies." Victims are "evil and seductive" (at the age of three!). Nonprotecting parents are "tired and busy." The survivor makes a giant leap forward when [he or] she can call abuse by its right name and grasp the concept that what was done was a manifestation of the heart of the perpetrator, not the heart of the victim.
>
> Diane Langberg

12. What do you believe about the person who is abusing you? (*Listen for rationalizations. "He couldn't help it; he was drunk." These defenses have helped the client cope, but have also made him or her less capable of seeing him- or herself as a true victim of abuse.*)
13. Have you ever tried to stop the abuse? What happened?
14. What would you like to have happen as a result of our meeting today?
15. What kinds of boundaries do you think need to be set up to protect you?
16. Who else have you told about this?
17. How did that person respond?
18. Who can help you maintain the boundaries that you set? Who will be your ally?
19. Where do you think God has been in all of this?
20. To heal from this, what do you need?

4 WISE COUNSEL

People who have been abused have had their boundaries violated in a horrible way. Healing from abuse involves *restoration of healthy boundaries and of trust*. The counseling process must be gentle and not contribute to an unintentional re-wounding or shaming of the person.

Follow the client's lead in the telling of his or her story. Reassure the person that the abuse was not his or her fault.

One of the questions often asked by someone who has been sexually abused is "Why me?" Sometimes feelings of lack of value and worthlessness result from sexual abuse. As counselor, you need to keep your own anger in check to provide a safe environment so the client is able to talk freely.

5 ACTION STEPS

1. Be Patient

- Healing from sexual abuse is a process and people will vary in the amount of time required for their healing.
- It takes courage to seek help for healing, to talk about your experience, and to bring what was once in darkness into the light.

2. Grieve Your Loss

- Much has been taken from you, so you are allowed to feel the pain and grieve the loss.
- Allowing yourself to feel the feelings will help you regain some of the power you need.

3. Regain Control

- Being believed and being able to say what happened has been the first step.
- You have permission to stand strong, to say no, to be empowered over the one who has exerted power over you.

4. Find Support

- Attending a group for survivors of sexual abuse can be an excellent next step.

5. Establish Boundaries

- Now you need to learn how to take care of yourself and reestablish healthy boundaries. What are the healthy boundaries you need to establish?
- Be sure trusted people are aware of these boundaries. That's the reason others will need to be let in on what is happening—no matter how painful. You may need their help in dealing with the abuser.
- Establishing boundaries may take the form of (1) speaking the truth to the abuser, (2) having the support of others in the Christian community, and/or (3) informed withdrawal from the abuser.
- *If the abuser has access to the victim, it is important to get people involved to make sure that the victim is not around the abuser and that the abuser cannot get to the victim. This may have to result in drastic measures, but the family must know the importance of the victim not being revictimized even by the individual talking to them.*

6. Know That You Will Heal

- You do have a bright future. You're not a victim but a survivor.
- You may have lost a lot, but you are not "ruined" for the future. God can heal you.

7. Trust God

- Know that God did not leave you and was not working against you as this abuse occurred.
- Plan on several more counseling sessions to discuss the spiritual concept of God's love even in the midst of such painful circumstances.

8. Seek Professional Help

- *As much as you can help with the spiritual aspect, the person may need some professional guidance to truly deal with the depth of the pain that sexual abuse causes.*
- *Refer to a Christian licensed mental health counselor with expertise in this area.*

The effects of child sexual abuse can be long-lasting and affect the victim's mental health. Victims are more likely than non-victims to experience the following mental health challenges. About 4 times more likely to develop symptoms of drug abuse. About 4 times more likely to experience PTSD as adults. About 3 times more likely to experience a major depressive episode as adults.[4]

To be abused is to be touched by evil. Chronic childhood abuse does damage to the body, the mind, the emotions, and the ability to relate to another person.
Diane Langberg

6 | BIBLICAL INSIGHTS

When Shechem the son of Hamor the Hivite, prince of the country, saw [Dinah], he took her and lay with her, and violated her.

Genesis 34:2

But as for you, you meant evil against me; *but* God meant it for good, in order to bring it about as *it is* this day, to save many people alive.

Genesis 50:20

Beloved, do not avenge yourselves, but *rather* give place to wrath; for it is written, "Vengeance *is* Mine, I will repay," says the Lord. . . . Do not be overcome by evil, but overcome evil with good.

Romans 12:19, 21

All the churches shall know that I am He who searches the minds and hearts. And I will give to each one of you according to your works.

Revelation 2:23

7 | PRAYER STARTER

We are facing an extremely difficult situation here today, Lord, a situation that You know about but is now just coming into the light for people whom we know and love. Give them wisdom to handle this situation correctly. Bring healing to this child of Yours who has been used so wrongly . . .

8 | RECOMMENDED RESOURCES

Allender, Dan. *Wounded Heart: Hope for Adult Victims of Childhood Sexual Abuse.* NavPress, 2008.

Jantz, Gregory L., and Ann McMurray. *Healing the Scars of Childhood Abuse: Moving beyond the Past into a Healthy Future.* Revell, 2017.

Langberg, Diane. *On the Threshold of Hope: Opening the Door to Healing for Survivors of Sexual Abuse.* Tyndale, 1999.

Langberg, Diane. *Suffering and the Heart of God: How Trauma Destroys and Christ Restores.* New Growth Press, 2015.

Websites

American Association of Christian Counselors (AACC.net)

Christian Care Connect (Connect.AACC.net)

Singleness

PORTRAITS 1

- Janelle uses dating apps and online sites yet rarely finds anyone who both interests her and is interested in her. It's just hard to meet people these days, and Janelle feels lonely.
- Bart was divorced within a year of a disastrous marriage. Now he can't seem to succeed in any relationship.
- Single after fifteen years of marriage, Ana struggles to figure out who she is as a single woman.
- Ricardo lives with his mother and rarely dates. He is painfully shy and feels that he will probably never marry.

DEFINITIONS AND KEY THOUGHTS 2

- Singleness means *being without a spouse*. People can be single because they *never married* or because they have *lost a spouse* through death or divorce.
- Some people remain *single by choice*, while others *have not met anyone* who attracts them and who is attracted to them.
- Since *women have not been encouraged to be the initiators* in romantic relationships, singleness may feel like something that is out of their control.
- Those with *mental, emotional, or physical disabilities face particular challenges* in finding a spouse.
- *Widowers often remarry* soon after the wife's death, while *widows often remain single*.
- *Being single and being alone and lonely are two different things.* Many single people would not characterize themselves as lonely at all.[1]
- It is very helpful when churches *make single people feel welcome*. Not every activity should be for families. Seek to use the gifts of the single people in your congregation.

3 | ASSESSMENT INTERVIEW

Some churches provide a welcoming atmosphere for singles, while other churches are so family oriented that singles feel out of place. If your church is one of the former, you may have singles to counsel. If they are seeking aid, they may be uncomfortable with their singleness.

1. In your opinion, what is the reason that you are single?
2. Is your singleness your choice?
3. What is your parents' attitude toward those who aren't married? (*Some parents make children without dates feel inadequate.*)
4. Are family members pressuring you to get married?
5. Have you ever been in a close relationship—something that might have led to marriage? What happened?
6. Describe your support system—friends and family members who are "there for you." Does your support come primarily from other singles or from married people as well?
7. Do you have many opportunities to meet other singles? (*There's a wide range in singles' groups—from the dismal support group for the socially inept to the lively social group for well-adjusted singles.*)
8. What does it mean to be a "well-adjusted single"?
9. Do you think you fit that category?
10. Do you have any leisure pursuits, such as sports, hobbies, or volunteer work?
11. What is your first thought when people tell you they want to "set you up" with a friend or acquaintance of theirs?
12. What, if anything, makes marriage preferable to singleness?
13. What advantages do you think married people have?
14. What, if anything, makes singleness preferable to marriage?
15. What advantages do you think single people have?
16. Choose four terms that best describe what singleness means to you, then explain your choices:
     loneliness
     independence
     self-focus
     freedom
     poverty
     spontaneity
     burden
     outward focus
     isolation
     deprivation
     wealth
     inward focus
17. Does our culture view singleness (especially celibate singleness) as a positive or a negative state?

18. How many TV shows can you name that feature a mature single person who is celibate and happy?
19. Why are so many Christian singles made to feel "incomplete"?
20. What does the Bible teach?

WISE COUNSEL 4

Encourage the person to closely *examine his or her own beliefs about singleness.* Investigate the messages that the person received from his or her family of origin. (Some parents communicated to their children destructive messages, which can leave an adult bereft of feelings of self-worth and independence.)

Our culture pictures those who marry as "victors" who have won "conquests" and "prizes." So what does that mean for the single person? Help the person understand the *unbiblical values exhibited by those who put down singles.*

Paul made it clear that *singleness is a high calling* that allows the single person to *focus more intensely on God.*

The single person must *come to terms with being single*—knowing that he or she is *complete and whole* as an individual in his or her relationship with Christ.

Single parents may be particularly in need of encouragement, as parenting keeps them from pursuing many social engagements. They may also worry—rightly—about the effect of dating relationships on their children.

ACTION STEPS 5

1. Know Your Worth[2]

- Live life to its fullest as you seek God's purpose and direction. Accept your singleness as a high calling with the ability, like Paul, to do things for Christ that you might not have the opportunity to do if you were married.
- Seek God in all you do. Never rush to get married.
- Realize that you are a complete and whole person in your relationship with Christ.

2. Flee Sexual Temptation

- You may be frustrated by your singleness because you are not sexually fulfilled.
- *Discuss reasons for remaining celibate (if needed, see the section on Premarital Sex).* To be celibate is the spiritual ability to have complete control over your sexual desires. This doesn't necessarily mean you have the *gift* of celibacy—just that you have a biblical mandate to live a pure life.[3]
- *Discuss sexual temptations and drives. Help the person discover methods for coping with these in positive ways.* Remaining chaste involves more than refraining from sexual activity; it also means bringing all sexual desires under submission to God.

- This is not easy, but if you wish to honor God with your life, you must allow God to be at the center, helping you handle your fears, desires, hopes, and dreams.

3. Get Involved

- Pursue hobbies, sports, or volunteer work so you can meet new people.
- Find a church that has a strong singles program. Lacking that, find a church that provides opportunities for all church members to mix and have fun together. The same activities will both encourage fellowship and sharing and help you get to know new people, including other singles.[4]
- You need a community of friends whom you can trust and with whom you can share activities and interests.
- You need a balance of male and female friends.

4. Learn to Love the Quiet

- Practicing contemplation and solitude may help you feel more comfortable with being alone. This teaches that *alone* is not a synonym for *lonely*.
- Learn to listen to God in the undistracted quiet.

6 BIBLICAL INSIGHTS

But I say to the unmarried and to the widows: It is good for them if they remain [single] even as I am.

1 Corinthians 7:8

Every good gift and every perfect gift is from above, and comes down from the Father of lights, with whom there is no variation or shadow of turning.

James 1:17

Now there was one, Anna, a prophetess, the daughter of Phanuel, of the tribe of Asher. She was of a great age, and had lived with a husband seven years from her virginity; and this woman *was* a widow of about eighty-four years, who did not depart from the temple, but served *God* with fastings and prayers night and day.

Luke 2:36–37

But I say to the unmarried and to the widows: It is good for them if they remain even as I am.

1 Corinthians 7:8

PRAYER STARTER | 7

Dear Lord, _____ is feeling uncomfortable with being single. Please reveal to him [her] Your special purpose for his [her] life as a single person. Encourage him [her]; bring friends and family around him [her] who can help him [her] achieve a new appreciation for his [her] singleness. Give him [her] the wisdom to see his [her] opportunities for service and enable him [her] to serve You with joy . . .

RECOMMENDED RESOURCES | 8

Chapman, Gary. *The 5 Love Languages Singles Edition: The Secret That Will Revolutionize Your Relationships*. Northfield Publishing, 2017.

Evans, Tony. *Living Single*. Moody, 2013.

Smith, Joy Beth. *Party of One: Truth, Longing, and the Subtle Art of Singleness*. Thomas Nelson, 2018.

Stuart, Ben. *Single, Dating, Engaged, Married: Navigating Life and Love in the Modern Age*. Thomas Nelson, 2017.

Thomas, Gary. *The Sacred Search: What If It's Not about Who You Marry, But Why?* David C Cook, 2013.

Websites

American Association of Christian Counselors (AACC.net)

Christian Care Connect (Connect.AACC.net)

Spiritual Warfare

1 PORTRAITS

- Randy confesses and repents dozens—maybe hundreds—of times, but he can't get the images of pornography out of his mind. They seem to reemerge at almost any time of the day: at work, in the car, when he is with friends, and when he is at home with his wife and children. He hasn't viewed porn in over a year, but it still has a powerful grip on him.

- Bethany was beaten many times by her father, and her mother never lifted a finger to stop him. She internalized all that anger, hurt, and fear. As a teenager, the only relief she experiences is when she cuts her arms and burns her legs.

- Larry is a good student and a gifted athlete in high school. He is a good kid, never getting into trouble. When he goes off to university, he decides to live it up. He becomes a Christian in college, but after he had sex with multiple partners and used marijuana and then heroin with his new friends. He joins a Christian group on campus, but when he goes to their meetings, he is haunted by vicious internal name-calling. *How can I call myself a Christian after all I've done? I'm a phony, a loser, and if anybody knew what I've done, they'd never speak to me again.* He responds to these thoughts by trying very hard to do everything the Bible commands, but he fails often and blames himself even more. Forgiveness seems like a foreign concept to Larry.

2 DEFINITIONS AND KEY THOUGHTS

- The term *spiritual warfare* can conjure up all sorts of images and thoughts of demonic possession and exorcisms. Others may think of speaking in an unknown voice or having convulsions or not having control of their own actions. For the purposes of this guide, we must understand *the definition* to be much *broader and simpler* than those images may imply.

- Spiritual warfare, simply put, is a struggle between light and darkness. God has secured the victory, but Satan still attempts to wage war against God and His people. *Light* is sourced in God and infuses all that is good; *darkness* is sourced in Satan and permeates all that is evil.

  Psalm 18:28—For You will light my lamp; the LORD my God will enlighten my darkness.

  Isaiah 9:2—The people who walked in darkness have seen a great light.

John 1:5—The light shines in the darkness, and the darkness did not comprehend it.

John 3:19—This is the condemnation, that the light has come into the world, and men loved darkness rather than light, because their deeds were evil.

John 8:12—Then Jesus spoke to them again, saying, "I am the light of the world. He who follows Me shall not walk in darkness, but have the light of life."

John 12:46—I have come *as* a light into the world, that whoever believes in Me should not abide in darkness.

Acts 26:18—To open their eyes, *in order* to turn *them* from darkness to light, and *from* the power of Satan to God, that they may receive forgiveness of sins and an inheritance among those who are sanctified by faith in Me.

2 Corinthians 4:6—For it is the God who commanded light to shine out of darkness, who has shone in our hearts to *give* the light of the knowledge of the glory of God in the face of Jesus Christ.

2 Corinthians 6:14—Do not be unequally yoked together with unbelievers. For what fellowship has righteousness with lawlessness? And what communion has light with darkness?

Ephesians 5:11—Have no fellowship with the unfruitful works of darkness, but rather expose *them*.

Colossians 1:13—He has delivered us from the power of darkness and conveyed *us* into the kingdom of the Son of His love.

- The enemy's primary ways to get people off track are *temptation, deception*, and *accusation*. Temptation is a seemingly uncontrollable urge, especially to sin but also to overindulge in something good. Deception consists of lies about the character of God and His good plans for us. An accusation is a condemning, degrading thought that often is crafted in the first person (e.g., "I'm such a fool!") so we don't realize its true source.

- All believers face spiritual warfare. If you belong to Jesus, then you will engage in a war against the darkness. Sometimes it is very *clear and evident* and at other times it is more *subtle and elusive*. But regardless of our awareness, we all engage in the battle.[1]

- The victory is in direct proportion to our willingness to surrender to Jesus Christ. We don't win by our own strength or by our own intelligence or strategies. *We win by submitting to Jesus and resting in His authority over Satan.*

- Romans 6:16 says, "Do you not know that to whom you present yourselves slaves to obey, you are that one's slaves whom you obey, whether of sin *leading* to death, or of obedience *leading* to righteousness?" We will submit to something. Submitting to darkness leads to death and submitting to the Lord leads to righteousness.

- Putting on the full armor of God is key in battling against evil.

    Ephesians 6:11–17—Put on the whole armor of God, that you may be able to stand against the wiles of the devil. For we do not wrestle against flesh and blood, but against principalities, against powers, against the rulers of the darkness of this age, against spiritual *hosts* of wickedness

> For though we walk in the flesh, we do not war according to the flesh. For the weapons of our warfare *are* not carnal but mighty in God for pulling down strongholds, casting down arguments and every high thing that exalts itself against the knowledge of God, bringing every thought into captivity to the obedience of Christ.
>
> 2 Corinthians 10:3-5

221

in the heavenly *places*. Therefore take up the whole armor of God, that you may be able to withstand in the evil day, and having done all, to stand. Stand therefore, having girded your waist with truth, having put on the breastplate of righteousness, and having shod your feet with the preparation of the gospel of peace; above all, taking the shield of faith with which you will be able to quench all the fiery darts of the wicked one. And take the helmet of salvation, and the sword of the Spirit, which is the word of God.

- These verses found in Ephesians are *not a magical formula* that defeats the enemy when recited like a mantra. It is a biblical truth conveyed in a word picture. For example, putting on the belt of truth simply means that we are to know and to adhere to the truth as spelled out for us in God's Word.

- It is important *not to overemphasize* demonic influences in our lives; at the same time, it is important *not to underemphasize* the fact that we do have an enemy who leads an army of demons. Their job description is to steal, kill, and destroy (see John 10:10).

- The enemy wants to harm us, yet God promises to protect us. When we step *outside of God's will*, we automatically open up the door for the enemy to sow seeds of destruction. This doesn't mean that all struggles involve demons, but consistently opening ourselves up to evil will bring us into contact with the evil one and his messengers. Discernment becomes important when determining demonic involvement in a person's life. When demonic oppression or possession is suspected, the biblical pattern for deliverance should be engaged with those who have experience with it.

- Sometimes spiritual warfare occurs because a person is right *in the middle of God's will*. Bible giants such as Daniel, David, Paul, and even Jesus Himself fought against the schemes of the devil.

3 | ASSESSMENT INTERVIEW

People don't often come in for counseling complaining about the struggles of spiritual warfare. It takes *discernment* to be able to ascertain when and why people are engaging in spiritual warfare.

What the counselor should look for are:

Doors that were opened or places in the person's life that were repeatedly exposed to sin. (For example, pornography opens the door for sexual problems and dissatisfaction, which if left untreated can lead to sexual abuse.) The person has stepped outside of God's will and needs to get back in by way of repentance.

Projects, persons, or victories in the person's life that could shed light on why Satan is after him or her. The person may be in God's will and needs to put on all the armor, stay strong, and continue to resist the devil.

You are not fighting for victory—you are fighting from victory. This battle has already been won!
Tony Evans

1. Tell me what brings you here today.
2. When did you first begin to experience these problems?
3. Can you tell me about your life when these problems first began?
4. What was your relationship with the Lord like during that time period?
5. Was anything happening in your life that brought conviction from the Lord?
6. Is there anything in your life that has an addictive quality about it? If so, explain.
7. Do you ever feel like you do things that you shouldn't?
8. Are there thoughts that seem to plague you?
9. What temptations have you faced recently?
10. Do you feel that there is anything you don't have control over?
11. What solutions have you tried?

WISE COUNSEL 4

"Therefore submit to God. *Resist the devil* and he will flee from you" (James 4:7). *This is the promise* that we can lean on.

The issue may be *the length of time one has to resist*. Too often *people don't resist long enough*. Many times we short-circuit our own efforts by giving up too quickly. Meditate on the promise and resist until you see victory; be assured that victory will come.

ACTION STEPS 5

Exposure to Sin

If it is determined that resisting the devil is needed because of sin that has come into the counselee's life, then a vital issue within the counseling process is *how the person should go about resisting*. Dean Sherman writes in his book *Spiritual Warfare* that there are three battlefields that need to be fortified against an attack. These battlefields are the mind, the heart, and the mouth. If the person fortifies his life in these three areas, he or she will be waging war from a point of strength. The person will be closing any of those "open doors" that began the battle in the first place. The enemy will not have a way into his or her life and therefore will not be able to influence the person. God will have free access.

Be sober, be vigilant; because your adversary the devil walks about like a roaring lion, seeking whom he may devour.
1 Peter 5:8

1. Confess Any Known Sin

- The only way to get free from Satan's grip is to know where he's holding on.
- Honestly determine the source, then confess and willingly give up your sin.

2. Fortify Your Mind

- How do you fortify the mind? Take every thought captive (see 2 Cor. 10:5).
- Think about pure and godly things (see Phil. 4:8).

- A person cannot think of two things simultaneously. He or she can have two different thoughts in rapid succession, but not at exactly the same time. So you can combat impure thoughts by purposely thinking pure thoughts.

3. Purify Your Heart

- When the Bible uses the word *heart*, it refers to our innermost being. It is more than just thoughts; it is also our emotions and attitudes.
- Stand guard against any bitterness (see Heb. 12:15). Too often people open up the door to strife because they have been treated unfairly and think they have a right to retaliate. Let God retaliate for you (Rom. 12:19).
- If you hold on to bitterness, that root will blossom into pain for both you and the other person. Remember that your own emotions must be filtered through God's Word. If you are not careful, unchecked emotions may lead to sin (see James 1:14–27).

4. Guard Your Mouth

- Proverbs 18:21 says, "Death and life are in the power of the tongue." The tongue is small but can do great damage (James 3:2–12).
- Be careful to speak godly things.

Victories in the Christian Life

If it is determined that resisting the devil is needed because of victories in the faith—big projects that Satan wants to hinder, ministries Satan doesn't want to happen, and so on—encourage the person to put on daily the whole armor of God.

1. Pray for Insight

- Be sensitive to God's leading if indeed there is sin in your life. Never assume there isn't!
- Be sensitive to what might be happening in the spiritual realm regarding the situation at hand. Ask God for discernment.

2. Put on the Armor of God!

- *Gird your waist with truth.* The belt was the foundation for the Roman soldier's armor. The truth of the gospel is the foundation of the Christian life, the standard by which we measure everything else. When Satan speaks lies, you must counter with the truth from God's Word.
- *Put on the breastplate of righteousness.* The breastplate protected a soldier's vital organs, covering his body from neck to thighs. The righteousness you put on is not your own, but Christ's, bought for you by His precious blood. Because you are God's child, when Satan attacks with doubts and strikes at the vital parts of your faith and life, counter with the righteousness you have because of Jesus. You are protected because you are His child.

As counselors, it's tempting for us to trust our theories of motivation and causality, and our knowledge of how people tend to react to certain struggles. It's easy to feel so confident in what we know that we don't depend on our good Shepherd for wisdom, help, and the power to change. But if you realize that there are forces at work bigger than you, it makes you really pray and really mean it.

David Powlison

- *Put on shoes of the preparation of the gospel of peace.* You have peace with God because of what Christ has done, and peace to carry you through life because of Christ's promise: "Peace I leave with you, My peace I give to you; not as the world gives do I give to you. Let not your heart be troubled, neither let it be afraid" (John 14:27). When Satan wants to make you worry or keep you up at night, remember your shoes.

- *Take the shield of faith.* A soldier's shield protected him in hand-to-hand combat and against "fiery darts" being shot from a city's walls. Your faith is your total dependence on God. When you hold your shield of faith, nothing Satan sends your way can hurt you.

- *Take the helmet of salvation.* Every soldier must protect his head. You were saved when you trusted Christ as Savior and were rescued from sin's bondage. The helmet of salvation can protect your mind from the doubts that creep in. When you know, beyond a doubt, that you are saved, Satan can do nothing to affect you.

- *Take the sword of the Spirit, which is the Word of God.* Your offensive weapon is your knowledge of God's Word. With it, you will be prepared to answer all of Satan's attacks.

BIBLICAL INSIGHTS 6

> How you are fallen from heaven,
> O Lucifer, son of the morning! . . .
> For you have said in your heart:
> "I will ascend into heaven,
> I will exalt my throne above the stars of God." . . .
> Yet you shall be brought down to Sheol,
> To the lowest depths of the Pit.
>
> Isaiah 14:13, 15

And He said to them, "I saw Satan fall like lightning from heaven. Behold, I give you the authority to trample on serpents and scorpions, and over all the power of the enemy, and nothing shall by any means hurt you."

Luke 10:18–19

For we do not wrestle against flesh and blood, but against principalities, against powers, against the rulers of the darkness of this age, against spiritual *hosts* of wickedness in the heavenly *places.*

Ephesians 6:12

Be sober, be vigilant; because your adversary the devil walks about like a roaring lion, seeking whom he may devour.

1 Peter 5:8

7 | PRAYER STARTER

Lord, we pray about the spiritual battle being faced today. The enemy wants to defeat our friend, and we want to claim the promises that You make in Your Word of victory over Satan and all of his schemes . . .

8 | RECOMMENDED RESOURCES

Anderson, Neil. *The Bondage Breaker: Overcoming Negative Thoughts, Irrational Feelings, and Habitual Sins*. Harvest House, 2019.

Evans, Tony. *Victory in Spiritual Warfare: Outfitting Yourself for the Battle*. Harvest House, 2011.

Ingram, Chip. *The Invisible War: What Every Believer Needs to Know about Satan, Demons, and Spiritual Warfare*. Baker Books, 2015.

Jeremiah, David. *The Spiritual Warfare Answer Book*. Thomas Nelson, 2016.

Powlison, David. *Safe and Sound: Standing Firm in Spiritual Battles*. New Growth Press, 2019.

Websites

American Association of Christian Counselors (AACC.net)

Christian Care Connect (Connect.AACC.net)

Stress

PORTRAITS 1

- John sits on the side of the hospital bed and buttons his shirt. Yesterday he had been sure he was having a heart attack. His chest had been tight, and he had struggled to breathe. But today, after many tests, his doctor told him that his heart is fine. Nothing is physically wrong. "I think you're under a lot of stress," his doctor had told him and had recommended seeing a counselor.
- Cindy isn't sure she can make it one more day. In only two months, her father died, her mother had to be put in a senior living facility, her daughter failed two of her courses in college, and the family finances took a huge hit with college and funeral expenses. Cindy's mood alternates between gloom and rage. Her friends have tried to help, but she whines, explodes, and pushes them away.
- Kailey has been through a lot lately. Her husband lost his job, and the bill collectors are beginning to call. In addition, her mom is sick, her kids are having difficulty in school, and the water heater just died. Kailey doesn't think she can handle one more crisis.
- Micah is trying to be a good student, but lately things have been tough. His mom and dad are getting a divorce, his grades are slipping, he lost his place on the basketball team for missing too many practices, and he has finals next week. Micah feels completely overwhelmed.

DEFINITIONS AND KEY THOUGHTS 2

- Stress is defined as "how the brain and body respond to any demand."
- Stress is a normal part of life and can be positive, alerting us to a problem area needing attention and helping us to respond to it.
- There are different types of stress, "*all of which carry physical and mental health risks. A stressor may be a one-time or short-term occurrence, or it can happen repeatedly over a long time.*"[1]
- Not all stress is bad. For example, "*in a dangerous situation, stress signals the body to prepare to face a threat or flee to safety. In these situations, your pulse quickens, you breathe faster, your muscles tense, and your brain uses more oxygen and increases activity—all functions aimed at survival and in response to stress. In non-life-threatening situations, stress can motivate people, such as when they need to take a test or interview for a new job.*"[2]

Therefore do not worry about tomorrow, for tomorrow will worry about its own things. Sufficient for the day *is* its own trouble.

Matthew 6:34

227

- Sometimes stress comes from a *difficult life situation*, but sometimes stress results from *perceptions* about life situations, such as worries about failure and perfectionistic tendencies.
- Stress without relief can lead to *physical symptoms*, such as headaches, upset stomach, elevated blood pressure, chest pain, and problems sleeping.
- *Some personalities cause stress* in themselves and in others. Some people may have extremely driven or perfectionistic personalities or may live or work with someone who does, thereby feeling the stress of the other person's drivenness.
- Stress can be harmful if it *affects a person's relationships adversely*.
- Stress can *affect the body, mind, and spirit*. Pay attention to each area to reduce the effects of stress on overall well-being.
- If we do not learn to control stress, it will eventually *control us*. We need not be overwhelmed by stress. Philippians 4:6–7 says, "Be anxious for nothing, but in everything by prayer and supplication, with thanksgiving, let your requests be made known to God; and the peace of God, which surpasses all understanding, will guard your hearts and minds through Christ Jesus."

3 | ASSESSMENT INTERVIEW

When considering the physical and emotional toll of increased stress, nearly half of adults (49%) report their behavior has been negatively affected. Most commonly, they report increased tension in their bodies (21%), "snapping" or getting angry very quickly (20%), unexpected mood swings (20%), or screaming or yelling at a loved one (17%).[3]

1. What brings you here today?
2. What would you say are the stressors in your life right now?
3. Are you being caused stress by someone else (for example, a stressful spouse or boss)?
4. Are you causing your own stress by being a perfectionist or trying to control situations over which you have no control?
5. What percentage of your total stress is being caused by each of these stressors?
6. How long has each of these stressors been present?
7. Tell me about each stressor. (*Get as many details as you can so you can begin to assess how the person views these stressors.*)
8. How realistic is it that the things you're worried about will happen? (*For example, if the person is experiencing persistent fears of job loss, is this fear based in current reality?*)
9. With whom do you talk about your stressors? (*The impact of stress is greater if an individual feels that he or she is alone in handling it.*)
10. Are those people helpful to you?
11. What things are you doing to reduce your stress? (*For example, sports, drugs—either over-the-counter or prescription—alcohol, excessive television or computer use.*)
12. What is helpful and what is not in reducing your stress?
13. Where do you experience the least stress in your life?
14. Is there any place where you do not experience stress?
15. What do you think you can change to help reduce your stress levels?
16. What are some healthy ways you can think of to handle the stress you're currently under?

WISE COUNSEL | 4

If the person is experiencing physical effects of the stress and hasn't seen a physician, encourage him or her to *schedule a physical.*

Are there *immediate situational stressors* that need attention, such as resolving a concern in the workplace or finding help for a problem with a child?

Assess ways to *provide a break* from the stress. Suggest exercise, frequent breaks throughout the day to pray and meditate on a Bible verse, sharing burdens with a trusted friend, taking a vacation.

Because stress affects the mind, body, and spirit, the person needs to protect all three:

To protect the mind, think truthfully, refuse to make mountains out of molehills, and set priorities.

To protect the body, get enough sleep, eat well, and learn to breathe deeply.

To protect the spirit, meditate on God and His Word, learn to trust God, and pray without ceasing.[4]

ACTION STEPS | 5

1. Examine the Causes of Stress

- Examine the causes of stress and gain some perspective on what is causing the stress.
- "Break apart" the stress overload into manageable pieces.
- Begin to address each component.

2. Consider What God Is Doing

- One of the best antidotes to stress is seeing God's purposes in the difficulties.[5]
- God may use certain situations to develop one of the fruits of the Spirit in you. Knowing that God uses every situation, even the petty, irritating situations of life, to teach you to become more like Jesus can help you feel less stressed by things you cannot control.

3. Get Alone with God

- Planned times of quiet and solitude are a good balance to a busy life. Cultivating a heart of prayer helps you see God's perspective and to more fully experience His presence throughout the day (Ps. 16:8–11).[7]
- Many use prayer as a way to change a stressful situation. Although this is not a bad idea, prayer often does not change the situation as much as it changes you.
- As you purposely quiet your heart each day, the Holy Spirit has a chance to change the way you see your stressful situation.

Work is a significant source of stress for many. 76% of people said workplace stress "had a negative impact on their personal relationships," 66% have lost sleep due to work-related stress, and 16% have quit jobs because stress became too overwhelming.[6]

4. Share Your Burden with Others

- This can be done literally or figuratively. In other words, talking about your stressors can bring relief and prayer support.
- Perhaps some of the stress is because you're doing too much. Even Moses had to delegate when he got overwhelmed (Exod. 18:13–26). Maybe you can do the same.

5. Guard Your Heart

Casting all your care upon Him, for He cares for you.

1 Peter 5:7

- Stress has a way of orienting us toward the things that are wrong in our lives.[8]
- Guard your heart and mind against negativity and pessimism. Take time each day to check your thinking and take every thought captive to the obedience of Christ (2 Cor. 10:5).

6. Live Intentionally

- Stop majoring in minor things. At the end of life, many will realize that they spent most of their time on what mattered least, and the least time on what mattered most.[9]
- Decide what is really important, choose your priorities, and live for them. Become more intentional about the way you spend your time and energy. Learn to say no to things that are just not that important.

7. Remember Your Limits

- Often our lives become filled with stress because we refuse to accept our limits.[10]
- Feeling overwhelmed may be a reminder that you are not living within the limits and boundaries that God has created for you. It may be time to reevaluate, cut back, say no, or slow down.

8. Find Things That Help You Relax

- Try to remove the stressful events in your life by finding outlets such as exercise, sports, hobbies, an activity without your phone, or coffee with friends.
- Allow for some levity in your life.
- Make sure you are getting enough sleep and have a healthy diet.

6 BIBLICAL INSIGHTS

You will keep *him* in perfect peace,
Whose mind *is* stayed on *You*,
Because he trusts in You.

Isaiah 26:3

Let not your heart be troubled; you believe in God, believe also in Me.

John 14:1

Persecuted, but not forsaken; struck down, but not destroyed.

2 Corinthians 4:9

Be anxious for nothing, but in everything by prayer and supplication, with thanksgiving, let your requests be made known to God; and the peace of God, which surpasses all understanding, will guard your hearts and minds through Christ Jesus.

Philippians 4:6–7

My brethren, count it all joy when you fall into various trials, knowing that the testing of your faith produces patience.

James 1:2–3

> Somewhere between 75 to 90 percent of all physician office visits are for stress-related ailments and complaints. Stress is linked to the six leading causes of death: heart disease, cancer, lung ailments, accidents, cirrhosis of the liver, and suicide.[11]

PRAYER STARTER | 7

Thank You, Lord, that _____ has come today for help in relieving this burden of stress. You never intended for Your children to live overwhelmed and unhealthy lives by carrying undue amounts of stress all by themselves. Give him [her] wisdom to handle what he [she] can, Lord, and we ask for Your hand in the situations that are beyond their control . . .

RECOMMENDED RESOURCES | 8

Amen, Daniel. *Feel Better Fast and Make It Last: Unlock Your Brain's Healing Potential to Overcome Negativity, Anxiety, Anger, Stress, and Trauma.* Tyndale Momentum, 2018.

Clinton, Tim. *The Care and Counsel Bible.* Thomas Nelson, 2019.

Jantz, Gregory L., and Ann McMurray. *Six Steps to Reduce Stress.* Rose Publishing, 2016.

Leaf, Caroline. *Cleaning Up Your Mental Mess: 5 Simple, Scientifically Proven Steps to Reduce Anxiety, Stress, and Toxic Thinking.* Baker Books, 2021.

Weaver, Joanna. *Having a Mary Heart in a Martha World: Finding Intimacy with God in the Busyness of Life.* WaterBrook, 2000.

Websites

American Association of Christian Counselors (AACC.net)

Christian Care Connect (Connect.AACC.net)

> Stress not only dampens our spirits and frazzles our nerves, but the constant rush of adrenaline overstimulates the heart and can weaken the immune system, leaving us prone to more illnesses and stress related problems.
> Leslie Vernick

Suffering

1 | PORTRAITS

For I consider
that the suf-
ferings of
this present
time are not
worthy *to be
compared*
with the glory
which shall
be revealed
in us.

Romans 8:18

- Brittany and her husband sit on the floor and weep. They have just returned from an appointment with her doctor, who told them Brittany's cancer, which had been in remission, has returned in a more virulent form. The doctor gave her three to five months. They know they have to begin talking about the heartache that is coming, but they can hardly face the heartache of the present.
- Janet bites the inside of her cheek to fight back tears. Her friend chats blithely on about her family going to the church picnic next week, and Janet nods woodenly and smiles. Inside she is in such pain. She knows her family won't be going to the picnic. No one can understand what it is like for her to continue to live in the marriage that she had committed to ten years ago. Her husband isn't a believer, and the day-to-day pain of loving and respecting her husband when he does not return her love and commitment is so very difficult.
- Bob just can't get through the pain. The death of his eldest son in a car accident has caused a hole in his heart that no one can fill. He can't even seem to function with his other children or his wife because the pain is so fresh every morning and the suffering so intense. If only their last conversation had not been an argument.
- Mark and Jill lost everything in the recent flooding on the Mississippi River. Their house was destroyed, and few of the objects inside were even salvageable. They have the clothes on their backs, a few books, a family Bible, and two cots at the local Salvation Army.

2 | DEFINITIONS AND KEY THOUGHTS

- Suffering comes for *many reasons*:
  Suffering may come as a result of *personal sin and failure.* For example, some people may suffer financially by not carefully budgeting their money or by being wasteful. Some people may suffer the loss of friendship through their hurtful words or gossip.
  Suffering may also arise due *to other people's sin and failur*e, such as the drunk driver who causes an accident and creates suffering for others.
  Suffering can arise from *forces outside of our control.* For example, a tornado or hurricane can create great suffering for many people.

Suffering can come as a *result of a person's faith*—standing for Jesus in some parts of the world is an invitation to persecution.

- The Bible is filled with passages that describe why suffering is a part of life:
  1 Peter 4:15—Deserved suffering occurs when we sin or act foolishly.
  1 Peter 2:21—Undeserved suffering is part of following in Jesus's footsteps.
  2 Corinthians 12:9–10—Suffering encourages growth.
  John 9:1–3—Suffering may be for testing and to demonstrate God's glory.
  2 Corinthians 1:3–5—We may suffer to help others.

- Helping others in pain requires a *"theology" of suffering.* How do you see God using suffering in the lives of those with whom you work? How do you see God using suffering in your own life?

- Suffering is common to all people and is not removed by the presence of the Holy Spirit. Being a Christian is not a "get out of suffering free" card. *Christians experience suffering* like everyone else.[1]

- Sometimes *God allows suffering* in our lives and we do not know why. His promise to us is not to make our suffering understandable but to be present with us in it.

- Needless suffering, such as refusing to take medication, is not taught in Scripture. There is *no merit to simply enduring pain for suffering's sake.*

- Suffering is easier to deal with when it is *purposeful* (2 Tim. 4:6–8) and when there is an *end in sight.* Romans 8:22–23 says, "For we know that the whole creation groans and labors with birth pangs together until now. Not only *that*, but we also who have the firstfruits of the Spirit, even we ourselves groan within ourselves, eagerly waiting for the adoption, the redemption of our body."

- Suffering *produces character* in us. By contrast, our culture views suffering as evidence that we are failing in some way or that we are doing something wrong.

- Guard against wanting to "fix things" or give answers too quickly. It is much more important to *listen.*

> God had one son on earth without sin, but never one without suffering.
>
> Augustine

ASSESSMENT INTERVIEW 3

Rule Outs

1. Are you suffering physically? Is there pain that needs to be handled? (*If the person is suffering physically, be sure that he or she has gotten adequate medical treatment and if not, encourage him or her to do so. Assess for whether they think they "deserve" this suffering or if it helps them deal with some emotional pain to have the suffering.*)

2. On a scale of 1 to 10, with 1 being "feeling terrific" and 10 being "feeling suicidal," where would you place yourself on most days? (*If you sense that the person is suicidal, deal with that issue first. See the section on Suicide and get outside help.*)

General Questions

1. What is going on in your life right now? (*When someone is in pain, it is important not to move too quickly to answers. Begin by trying to understand the situation and empathize with the person in it.*)
2. How can I be of the most help to you?
3. How do you understand your situation?
4. How long have you been facing this pain?
5. Can you give it a definite starting point (a certain event) or is it more vague?
6. Who is walking with you through the pain?
7. What is your support system?
8. With whom are you the most honest?
9. How is this suffering affecting the other parts of your life?
10. Do you see an end to the suffering or of the intensity you're currently experiencing?
11. How is your relationship with God right now?
12. Do you see God's hand at work in any way in your suffering?
13. Do you feel like you deserve this suffering? Why or why not?

4 WISE COUNSEL

God promises that "a bruised reed He will not break" (Isa. 42:3). As a Christian counselor, you should endeavor to model your caring after His and *not burden a person who is already suffering.*

If the person is suffering for the *consequences of his or her own sin*, he or she may also be dealing with guilt and shame. You will need to help the individual confess sin, assess the lessons learned, and come up with an action plan to move forward.

If the person's suffering is because *of someone else's sin or failure*, listen to the story and gently guide the person to ways that he or she can walk through the pain and get to the other side.

If the person's suffering is due to *circumstances beyond his or her control* (an illness, a natural disaster such as a fire or tornado), begin to assess steps to take that will help him or her handle the situation. Taken in one big chunk, the situation is way too big to handle, but taken one step at a time, the person can get through it.

Remind the individual that suffering can do three things in his or her life, if the person lets it:

Despite its painfulness, suffering can be very valuable. Suffering *clarifies what the heart truly worships*, especially when the pain is unexplained and unabated. Does the client worship the idea of deliverance or the Deliverer?

Suffering also *purifies the heart* by deepening the desire for the day when all tears will be wiped away. The client's growing discontent with the sin and evil in this world increases his or her hopefulness for heaven.

Suffering not only clarifies and purifies, but it also *motivates the heart to action*. If we see a child cry, we offer tenderness. If we see the wounds of a victim, we offer solace. Human suffering arouses anger, invigorates action, and as a result, enables us to push back some of the darkness of the fall. Suffering humanizes the heart and increases hunger for God.

Offer *comfort* and *encouragement. Name any strengths* that you see in the one who is suffering. Silently *pray for the discernment* to understand what God is doing in this person's life.

ACTION STEPS 5

1. Trust God

- Sometimes God allows suffering to come into believers' lives to strengthen their faith.
- Rejoice because of what God will do in your life and what He promises for your future.
- Cast your cares on Christ because His faithfulness never changes (Ps. 46; 2 Cor. 12:7–10; Heb. 13:8).
- Allow God to help you endure (Rom. 8:18; 2 Cor. 4:7–10; 2 Tim. 2:12; 1 Pet. 4:12–13).

> One sees great things from the valley; only small things from the peak.
>
> G. K. Chesterton

2. Seek His Lessons

- What do you think God is teaching you in this situation?
- What would you like to learn? How would you like to come out of it at the other end?
- What may God be trying to teach someone else who is watching you handle this situation?

3. Seek His Actions

- What could God possibly be doing in your situation? Where do you see His hand at work?
- Which of the lessons above (how suffering clarifies, purifies, and motivates the heart) do you think God is teaching you right now?
- Tell me about another time when you were suffering and leaned on God. What happened? What did God do? How can this situation help you think about what God might be doing now?

4. Take Small Steps Forward

- What small step can you take today to move through the pain?
- What do you need to do to function effectively at home, at work, and other places?
- What small step can you take today to begin the process of rebuilding your life?

5. Get Support

- You should be in a small group that will help you walk through the pain, follow up with you, and help you take some of the needed action steps.
- In addition, find a support group of people who have faced similar pain. This can be a huge help as they will have advice that has been tested "in the trenches."

6. Make a Memorial

- When the client gets through a difficult situation, suffering, or trial, remind them to make a memorial that will help them remember how God got them through or taught them something about Him. This is very important since it will help the client the next time he or she experiences suffering to remember that God has already been with him or her in one trial and He will be in this one as well. Memorials can be journals, letters, pictures, or jewelry from the time that reminds the individual of what God is capable of doing in the tough times.

6 BIBLICAL INSIGHTS

And not only *that*, but we also glory in tribulations, knowing that tribulation produces perseverance; and perseverance, character; and character, hope. Now hope does not disappoint, because the love of God has been poured out in our hearts by the Holy Spirit who was given to us.

Romans 5:3–5

Then Job arose, tore his robe, and shaved his head; and he fell to the ground and worshiped. And he said:

> "Naked I came from my mother's womb,
> And naked shall I return there.
> The LORD gave, and the LORD has taken away;
> Blessed be the name of the LORD."

Job 1:20–21

Now when Job's three friends heard of all this adversity that had come upon him, each one came from his own place.

Job 2:11

> For You, O God, have tested us;
> You have refined us as silver is refined.

Psalm 66:10

Beloved, do not think it strange concerning the fiery trial which is to try you, as though some strange thing happened to you; but rejoice to the extent that you partake of Christ's sufferings, that when His glory is revealed, you may also be glad with exceeding joy. . . . Therefore let those who suffer according to the will of God commit their souls to *Him* in doing good, as to a faithful Creator.

1 Peter 4:12–13, 19

PRAYER STARTER | 7

Lord, _____ has come in today feeling overwhelmed with suffering. The pain is intense and is affecting his [her] daily life. He [she] needs Your strengthening presence in a powerful and personal way today. Put Your arms around him [her] and be a God of comfort and encouragement. Give them wisdom, Father, as we seek the best path forward. Our hope is in You, Lord, and the knowledge that You are always with us and always at work in our lives . . .

RECOMMENDED RESOURCES | 8

Elliot, Elisabeth. *Suffering Is Never for Nothing*. B&H, 2019.

Graham, Billy. *Who's in Charge of a World That Suffers? Trusting God in Difficult Circumstances*. Thomas Nelson, 2021.

Tada, Joni Eareckson. *Heaven: Your Real Home . . . From a Higher Perspective*. Zondervan, 2018.

Tada, Joni Eareckson. *Place of Healing: Wrestling with the Mysteries of Suffering, Pain, and God's Sovereignty*. David C Cook, 2015.

Tripp, Paul David. *Suffering: Gospel Hope When Life Doesn't Make Sense*. Crossway, 2018.

Websites

American Association of Christian Counselors (AACC.net)

Christian Care Connect (Connect.AACC.net)

Suicide

1 | PORTRAITS

- Ida has diabetes and is facing amputation of her foot. The day before surgery, she writes notes to her grandkids and overdoses on her pain medications.
- Aaron has been unable to work due to complications from the hazardous chemicals he uses at his job. He is now running out of money. He's been turned down for Medicaid, Medicare, and disability payments, despite his chronic illness. He does not want to be a burden to his family, so the month that he runs out of money, he gives away his valuables and cleans up his apartment. He finds a home for his cat and puts a gun to his head.
- Victor drives off a bridge the night before his graduation from college. Afterward his parents find out that he had been failing all his classes—because he wasn't attending them—and had been told that he would not be allowed to graduate.
- Raysha gets very drunk at a high school drinking party and makes a fool of herself. Humiliated, she leaves the party, focusing on all the other stupid things she's done lately. When she comes to the railroad tracks, she decides to wait for a train.

2 | DEFINITIONS AND KEY THOUGHTS

Come to Me, all *you* who labor and are heavy laden, and I will give you rest.
Matthew 11:28

- Suicide is the tragic and lethal culmination of a psychological process that could result from unresolved events that create depression and hopelessness.[1]
- Suicide is the result of a death caused by self-injury with intent to end one's own life.
- Someone who is considering suicide cannot see any hope that the future will be different from the painful past or present.[2]
- Males tend to use more violent means for suicide (guns, suffocation) and are more often successful in their suicide attempts than women.
- Females tend to attempt suicide more often than men but are less successful at the attempt because they use less lethal means (pills, cutting).

Risk Factors for Suicide

Individual:

- previous suicide attempt[3]
- mental illness, such as depression
- social isolation
- criminal problems
- financial problems
- impulsive or aggressive tendencies
- job problems or loss
- legal problems
- serious illness
- substance use disorder

> Suicide is often one of the top 10 leading causes of death among US adults.[4]

Relationship:

- adverse childhood experiences such as child abuse and neglect
- bullying
- family history of suicide
- relationship problems such as a breakup, violence, or loss
- sexual violence

Community:

- barriers to health care
- cultural and religious beliefs such as a belief that suicide is a noble resolution of a personal problem
- suicide cluster in the community

Societal:

- stigma associated with mental illness or help-seeking
- easy access to lethal means, such as firearms or medications
- unsafe media portrayals of suicide
- remember, always *take seriously the threat* of suicide.

ASSESSMENT INTERVIEW 3

If you think that the person you are interviewing is suicidal, *do not panic*. Stay calm and know that by coming to you this person has already taken a step away from the decision to harm himself or herself.

Don't contradict the suicidal person. Empathy is more helpful. You won't argue him or her out of the way he or she feels.

Rule Outs

Questions for the Suicidal Person

1. Do you ever wish you were dead or think that people would be better off without you?
2. Are you feeling as if you want to harm yourself now? If no, have you ever wanted to kill yourself?
3. When was the last time you felt that way?
4. Have you thought about how you would try to kill yourself?
5. Do you have access to the way you just described to me?
6. Are there weapons at home?
7. If so, are they locked up? Who can get to them?
8. When do you plan on killing yourself?
9. Have you ever attempted to hurt yourself in the past? If so, when? (*A recent, nearly lethal attempt may indicate that this person is very serious in his or her desire to die. Numerous unsuccessful suicide attempts could indicate that the individual uses suicide attempts to gain attention. However, either way, you must take the suicide talk seriously.*)

General Questions for the Suicidal Person

1. How old are you?
2. Have you recently had a baby? (*This checks for postpartum depression.*)
3. Have you suffered a recent loss?
4. What has happened recently to make you feel so hopeless?
5. Do you ever abuse drugs or alcohol?
6. If so, when did you last use?
7. How often and how much do you use?
8. Has anyone in your family committed suicide?
9. If so, who was it?
10. How old were you when it happened?
11. What happened?
12. Do you know why it occurred?
13. How did it make you feel?
14. Is there someone you'd like to get revenge on? Is there anyone you are very angry at? Have you ever thought of death as the ultimate revenge?
15. What is most distressing to you when you think about the future?
16. Can you think of any reasons to go on living?
17. What would make life worth living for you? See if you can list ten things. Are any of them within reach?
18. Where are you spiritually?
19. Do you think that God cares if you live or die?

General Questions for the Friend or Family Member

1. How old is your loved one?
2. Does he [she] suffer from any painful or debilitating medical conditions?
3. Has this person suffered a recent loss or recently had a baby?

4. If not, are there any other recent distressing circumstances?
5. Is there a family history of suicide?
6. Does this person abuse alcohol or drugs?
7. If so, has he [she] ever tried to stop?
8. Has your loved one's behavior changed recently? If so, in what ways?
9. Has this person been taking care of himself [herself] physically?
10. Is he [she] sleeping regularly (that is, not sleeping too much or too little)?
11. Has your loved one been giving away prized possessions?
12. Has he [she] seemed uninterested in plans for the future?
13. Has he [she] made jokes about death or disappearing?
14. Is this person extremely angry?
15. Would he [she] like to get revenge on someone?
16. Could suicide be a form of revenge for him [her]?
17. How does your culture view suicide?

> Suicide was responsible for 48,183 deaths in 2021, which is about one death every 11 minutes.[5]

WISE COUNSEL 4

Protecting the suicidal person must take priority. Don't worry about embarrassing the person or making them angry by calling emergency services or a loved one. Also, check your state laws or workplace reporting guidelines. Safety of the individual is always the top priority.

Pay attention to warning signs. Most people who attempt to kill themselves have given signals of their intentions, often verbally by saying something like, "Someday I won't be here to bother you." Some of those who commit suicide have serious mental disorders; however, most are people who don't have a mental illness—but they have lost hope in the future.

The impulse to die often doesn't last. If we can help them in the moment and then get them professional help, the urge may pass.

It's a false assumption that talking to depressed people about their thoughts of suicide pushes them toward that decision. Quite often, an honest talk and a sympathetic ear release the pressure and bring more hope to the person.

ACTION STEPS 5

1. Get Help Immediately

- Call police or emergency services if this person has a plan and the means to commit suicide. He or she must be protected.
- Inpatient psychiatric units are locked because of the need to protect people from their desire to harm themselves. Every attempt is made to remove from the unit the means of causing harm.
- Do not try to transport a suicidal person to the hospital by yourself. It is too dangerous.

- If a person leaves your office that you know has suicidal ideation, follow them at a safe distance while you are on the phone with emergency personnel.
- If the suicidal person is under the influence of drugs or alcohol, arrange for him or her to be supervised constantly while detoxing or becoming sober. Then the suicidal ideation should be reassessed. If no longer suicidal, this person should be strongly encouraged to seek treatment for substance abuse.

2. Follow Up

Suicide affects people of all ages. In 2021, suicide was among the top 9 leading causes of death for people ages 10 to 64. Suicide was the second leading cause of death for people ages 10 to 14 and 20 to 34.[6]

- See if the suicidal person will sign a contract stating that he or she will not attempt suicide for twenty-four hours. Of course, this contract is only as good as the suicidal person's word. It is not a legal document.
- If willing to sign a contract, send the person home with supervision.
- Reconnect with the suicidal person the next day. (Don't forget!) See if the suicidal thoughts have decreased.
- If the person is still suicidal, seek help immediately.

3. Investigate the Tunnel Vision

- Sometimes the problem can actually be solved rather simply.
- Ask a person with tunnel vision to sign a contract not to harm himself or herself while you investigate the circumstances for three days. In that time, work to find the beginning of some solutions.
- During those three days, the person should be supervised. If you cannot make substantive progress in three days, then refer the counselee to a professional therapist or a hospital.

6 BIBLICAL INSIGHTS

The good news is that more than 90% of people who attempt suicide and survive never go on to die by suicide.[7]

Then Saul said to his armorbearer, "Draw your sword, and thrust me through with it, lest these uncircumcised men come and thrust me through and abuse me." But his armorbearer would not, for he was greatly afraid. Therefore Saul took a sword and fell on it.

1 Samuel 31:4

Then [Judas] threw down the pieces of silver in the temple and departed, and went and hanged himself.

Matthew 27:5

7 PRAYER STARTER

Dear Lord, _____ is feeling right now as if there is no reason to live. And even though he [she] feels that way, we know that is not the case. Please take away these feelings.

Please protect _____ from himself [herself]. Help him [her] to know and to feel how much You love him [her]. Show him [her] hope for the future . . .

RECOMMENDED RESOURCES 8

Anderson, Neil. *Victory Over the Darkness: Realize the Power of Your Identity in Christ*. Bethany House, 2020.

Biebel, David, and Suzanne Foster. *Finding Your Way after the Suicide of Someone You Love*. Zondervan, 2005.

Clinton, Tim. *The Care and Counsel Bible*. Thomas Nelson, 2019.

Joiner, Thomas. *Why People Die by Suicide*. First Harvard University Press, 2007.

Stoecklein, Kayla. *Fear Gone Wild: A Story of Mental Illness, Suicide, and Hope Through Loss*. Thomas Nelson, 2020.

Websites

American Association of Christian Counselors (AACC.net)

Christian Care Connect (Connect.AACC.net)

In 2021, an estimated 12.3 million American adults seriously thought about suicide, 3.5 million planned a suicide attempt, and 1.7 million attempted suicide.[8]

Trauma

1 PORTRAITS

- Franklin has been on three tours of duty in Iraq and Afghanistan. He saw fierce fighting, and several of his closest friends were killed or maimed. Now, back home, he is having trouble adjusting to "a normal life." He can't get the images of his friends out of his mind, but he doesn't talk about them to anyone. His marriage is falling apart. Finally, he agrees to go with his wife to see a counselor. The diagnosis isn't difficult to make: Franklin has the classic symptoms of post-traumatic stress disorder.

- Lauri wonders why everyone else seems to be happy, while she wears a smile as a mask to hide her intense pain, shame, and doubt. She prays that all this will go away, but it doesn't. In fact, it gets worse. She had been sexually abused by her older cousin several times when she was 12. He threatened to kill her if she ever told anyone . . . and she believed him. Lauri feels like she's going to implode, but she's terrified of anyone finding out the truth.

- Janet startles awake. Her heart is pounding, and the sheets are tangled around her. For a few moments she wonders where she is. The nightmare had been so vivid and the screams had been real. *What is happening to me?* she wonders. The tornado that ripped through her town was three years ago, but lately the dreams are more frequent.

- Mindy has been in a cycle of bad relationships over the course of her college years—often with older men. Only now is she beginning to understand that her desperate need comes from the time when her father walked out on her mom. That moment is forever etched in her brain and the pain is as fresh as ever.

2 DEFINITIONS AND KEY THOUGHTS

- Trauma is an emotional response to a terrible event like an accident, rape, or natural disaster.[1]

- Immediately after the event, shock and denial are typical. Longer-term reactions include unpredictable emotions, flashbacks, strained relationships, and even physical symptoms like headaches or nausea.

- While these feelings are normal, some people have difficulty moving on with their lives.

Warning Signs of Trauma

- Each person's response to trauma may be different and "*can be immediate or delayed, brief or prolonged.*"[2] For most people, they will have "*intense responses immediately following, and often for several weeks or months after a traumatic event.*" Responses to a trauma can include:
  - » feeling anxious, sad, or angry
  - » trouble concentrating and sleeping
  - » continually thinking about what happened
- For most, these responses are normal and expected and will generally lessen with time.
- For some individuals, their response to a traumatic event can continue for a longer period of time, which interferes with everyday life and functioning. When responses to trauma begin to interfere with daily life or are not getting better over time, it's necessary to seek professional help from a trained trauma specialist. Some signs that an individual may need help include:
  - » worrying a lot or feeling very anxious, sad, or fearful
  - » crying often
  - » having trouble thinking clearly
  - » having frightening thoughts or flashbacks, reliving the experience
  - » feeling angry, resentful, or irritable
  - » having nightmares or difficulty sleeping
  - » avoiding places or people that bring back disturbing memories and responses
  - » becoming isolated from family and friends

> More than two-thirds of children reported at least one traumatic event by age 16.[3]

Trauma in Children and Teens[4]

- Children and teens will often have different reactions to a trauma than adults. Symptoms sometimes seen in very young children (less than six years old) can include:
  - » wetting the bed after having learned to use the toilet
  - » forgetting how to or being unable to talk
  - » acting out the scary event during playtime
  - » being unusually clingy with a parent or other adult
- Older children and teens are more likely to show symptoms that would be similar to those that are typically seen in adults. They can act out and also develop behaviors that are disruptive, disrespectful, or destructive.

Physical Responses to Trauma

Physical symptoms may include:
- headaches[5]
- stomach pain and digestive issues

- feeling tired
- racing heart and sweating
- being very jumpy and easily startled

Those with an existing mental health condition or who have had traumatic experiences in the past, who face ongoing stress, or who lack support from friends and family may be more likely to develop more severe symptoms.

Some dealing with trauma may turn to alcohol or other drugs to cope with their symptoms. Although substance use or misuse may seem to relieve symptoms temporarily, it can also lead to new problems and get in the way of recovery.

3 | ASSESSMENT INTERVIEW

Rule Outs

1. Are you having physical symptoms? Are you able to eat and sleep? (*If the person is dealing with physical issues as a result of the trauma, encourage a medical checkup.*)
2. On a scale of 1 to 10, with 1 being "feeling terrific" and 10 being "feeling suicidal," where would you place yourself on most days? (*If you sense that the person is suicidal, deal with that issue first. See the section on Suicide and get outside help.*)

General Questions

More than half of US families have been affected by some type of disaster (54%).[6]

1. What brought you to see me today?
2. What is currently causing your distress?
3. Do you recall a particular event in your life that was traumatic?
4. If you don't recall anything in particular, what can you tell me about your childhood, other past relationships, and other situations in your life?
5. How do you feel about that situation? (Help in expressing grief or anger is important to survivors of trauma.)
6. What are some of the things that happen to you when you think about the situation?
7. Have you ever sought help for this problem before?
8. Did you receive help at that time?
9. What is daily life like for you currently?
10. Do you feel safe?
11. Whom do you talk to about this?
12. Do you have a support group or network with whom you feel safe?

WISE COUNSEL | 4

If the person is exhibiting behavior that reveals some past trauma that *cannot be remembered or attached to any event*, you may want to refer the person to a Christian mental health professional who specializes in trauma.

While the traumatic event or events can be horrific and the resultant emotional damage overwhelming to the person who is traumatized, *healing from the effects of trauma is possible.*

Often people who are traumatized wonder if they are losing their mind or even losing their self. It can be very reassuring to encourage the survivor that *what he or she is experiencing is a normal reaction to the trauma.*

From you the person needs *comfort, acceptance, and a nonjudgmental listening ear.* He or she wants to know that *there is hope.*[7]

Losses will need to be grieved and anger experienced to move forward. This can be *long-term work* and may involve individual or group counseling.

ACTION STEPS | 5

1. Understand the Nature of the Trauma[8]

- Discuss what happened—if it can all be remembered. Do this gently, as the memories are probably very painful.
- Encourage objectivity about what happened and validate the feelings associated with the events. Be very patient. Many people can only handle portions of the truth at a time, but for some, the rush of buried memories comes back fast and furiously.
- This can begin with you as the counselor but may be better continued in a support group of survivors of similar trauma.
- Understand that you did not deserve the hurts that happened to you and that you didn't cause them.
- Depending on the nature of the trauma, understand that you may need to erect some boundaries with particular people so that you will not be hurt again.

> Going through trauma is not rare. About 6 of every 10 men (or 60%) and 5 of every 10 women (or 50%) experience at least one trauma in their lives.[9]

2. Express Your Feelings

- Express your real feelings. If you have anger at the perpetrators of your trauma, express it.
- This does not necessarily mean confronting them. There are symbolic ways, such as writing letters to perpetrators that won't necessarily be sent, which can be just as powerful.
- If you're angry with God, express that as well. He can handle it.
- If you have grief over a loss experienced through the trauma, express that grief. (*If the client is experiencing grief, see the section on Grief and Loss.*)

3. Healing and Recovery Is Possible

- Healing will come with God's help.
- It is important that you engage in a process through which this will be possible, either in further individual counseling or in group counseling.

4. Know That You Will Have Victory

- Beyond just healing, you will have victory over the trauma. Begin to consider some of the positive strengths you will have in your life as a result of healing from this trauma.
- Know that you will eventually be able to forgive to set yourself free. This is the ultimate spiritual victory. (*To help the client with forgiveness, see the section on Forgiveness.*)
- Know that you will be able to be of great comfort to others who experience similar traumas.

6 | BIBLICAL INSIGHTS

> *Is it* nothing to you, all you who pass by?
> Behold and see
> If there is any sorrow like my sorrow,
> Which has been brought on me,
> Which the LORD has inflicted
> In the day of His fierce anger.
>
> Lamentations 1:12

And [Jonah] said to them, "Pick me up and throw me into the sea; then the sea will become calm for you. For I know that this great tempest *is* because of me."

Jonah 1:12

> This *is* my comfort in my affliction,
> For Your word has given me life.
>
> Psalm 119:50

7 | PRAYER STARTER

Your child is in a lot of pain today, Lord, remembering a situation of the past that is still looming large across the landscape of his [her] life even today. We don't yet understand why You allowed this to happen—what purpose it could possibly have—but we want to trust that You are forging a stronger person through this difficult time . . .

RECOMMENDED RESOURCES | 8

Gingrich, Heather Davediuk. *Restoring the Shattered Self: A Christian Counselor's Guide to Complex Trauma*. IVP Academic, 2020.

Gingrich, Heather Davediuk, and Fred Gingrich. *Treating Trauma in Christian Counseling*. IVP Academic, 2017.

Langberg, Diane. *Suffering and the Heart of God: How Trauma Destroys and Christ Restores*. New Growth Press, 2015.

Van Der Kolk, Bessel. *The Body Keeps the Score: Brain, Mind, and Body in the Healing of Trauma*. Penguin Books, 2014.

Wright, H. Norman. *The New Guide to Crisis and Trauma Counseling*. Regal Books, 2003.

Websites

American Association of Christian Counselors (AACC.net)

Christian Care Connect (Connect.AACC.net)

Operations Iraqi Freedom (OIF) and Enduring Freedom (OEF): About 11-20 out of every 100 veterans (or between 11-20%) who served in OIF or OEF have PTSD in a given year. Gulf War (Desert Storm): About 12 out of every 100 Gulf War veterans (or 12%) have PTSD in a given year. Vietnam War: About 15 out of every 100 Vietnam veterans (or 15%) were currently diagnosed with PTSD at the time of the most recent study in the late 1980s, the National Vietnam Veterans Readjustment Study (NVVRS). It is estimated that about 30 out of every 100 (or 30%) of Vietnam veterans have had PTSD in their lifetime.[10]

Workaholism

1 | PORTRAITS

- Kim has always been conscientious. Now, in a new job, she wants to make a good impression and prove herself to her employer, especially her supervisor. In previous jobs, she often worked overtime, whether she was paid for it or not. In her new position, it seems the workload will never be reasonable. She arrives early and stays late. She worries that the things that aren't getting done will show up in her review that's coming up next month. She thinks about work long after she walks out the door every day, and she has recently been dreaming about making a huge mistake in one of her responsibilities. She used to enjoy her career, but now her job haunts her.

- "I can't remember the last time I really relaxed," explains Dave. "I think what seems to keep me going is fear, fear that if I do stop, I'll lose everything I have worked so hard to achieve." He continues, "My parents lived through the Depression and instilled in me the notion that what matters most is getting ahead in life. They raised me to never be in a position to depend on anyone for anything. Even when I am with my wife and kids, I can't seem to stop thinking about work. Somehow everything that isn't related to my work seems like a waste of time."

- Pam can't enjoy her home or her children. She is constantly cleaning, picking up after her kids, always attempting to maintain a spotless *Better Homes and Gardens*–type of showplace. The children aren't allowed to play anywhere but in their rooms.

- Bill is climbing the corporate ladder and faces expectations that he feels he must meet to make it to the next rung. The stress is affecting his family.

2 | DEFINITIONS AND KEY THOUGHTS

- A workaholic is uncontrollably *addicted to work* to the detriment of self and others.

- Workaholism has become an *all-consuming obsession* for too many modern workers, a sleep-depriving, health-robbing, greed-festering monster that may be the most rewarded—and least challenged—addiction in America.[1]

- While God created work as a meaningful part of this life, for some, work becomes the primary avenue by which they find *approval, respect, and success.*

- God calls on humankind to work honestly, heartily, happily, and as though we are working for the Lord (Exod. 23:12; Eccles. 5:19; Col. 3:23).
- This issue is *not limited to men and women in the workplace.* It can also include women at home who are striving to have the "perfect" home and family.
- Workaholism is an *addiction* and needs to be treated like one.
- Work life must be *managed* within the context of a healthy relation to God, marriage, and family life, and commitments to church and community. When this *balance* is not held, work can become an idol, a terrible taskmaster known as "workaholism."

> Nearly half of employed Americans (48 percent) consider themselves modern-day "workaholics."[2]

Symptoms of Workaholism

Following are some symptoms of workaholism:

- A *compulsive emphasis on work* because it is perceived as the avenue for achieving control and power over one's life and others.
- Working sixty to seventy hours a week or more.
- Work is viewed as the *primary avenue* by which a person finds approval, respect, and success.
- A *chronic sense of urgency* in every activity.
- An *inability to rest.*
- An addictive *need for acceptance and significance* in the eyes of others as a result of one's work.
- *Ignoring the emotional and spiritual demands of family* with the notion that he or she is providing a better lifestyle.
- A workaholic is seen by his or her children as *inattentive, irritable, lacking humor, and always in a hurry.*
- *Valuing performance* over showing love and grace.
- *Family does not feel "safe."* Aside from financial security, the family members know that their feelings or concerns are generally not accepted. Competition is substituted for playful times.
- Struggles with a *poor self-image, rigidity, and problems with intimacy in relationships.*
- *Viewing the stress that work involves as a challenge* to overcome and a way to find significance.

> More than half of American office workers (58 percent) say they do indeed actually check their work email while still in bed after waking up.[3]

ASSESSMENT INTERVIEW   3

Like all addicts, workaholics must be able to admit their obsessive drivenness and confess its many costs. They must be able to establish and maintain times for rest, play, family, and leisure. Work addicts need to realize that the deeper life with Christ comes only after they are able to be still and know God.[4]

1. How many hours do you work a week?
2. Do you often feel fatigued and stressed?
3. Do you have problems sleeping?
4. Do you have stress-related physical issues, such as back pain, headaches, indigestion, ulcers, or chronic fatigue?
5. Do you take work home daily, on weekends, on vacation, on holidays?
6. Do you feel guilty when you relax or have fun, especially when there is work to be done?
7. Do you sometimes resent others for not working as hard as you do?
8. Do you get impatient with coworkers who have other priorities besides work?
9. Has your family given up expecting you to come home on time?
10. Do you find that it is difficult to schedule time for those you love?
11. Are you able to have fun with your family?
12. Do you feel that the more you work the more pleasing you will be to God?
13. Do you have difficulty saying no?
14. Do you sometimes feel that people who have needs are weak?
15. Do you feel better about yourself when you earn more money or realize achievements in your work?
16. Do you feel that you do things rapidly so as not to waste time?
17. Do you often compare yourself to others?
18. Do you find that free time bores you because you would rather be working?
19. Tell me about your growing-up years. What were your parents like?
20. How did your parents assess your worth? Did you feel that you had to achieve at a certain level to be accepted or loved?

4 | WISE COUNSEL

Generally, people who are addicted to work feel:

- highly self-critical
- a pervading sense of emptiness
- a compulsive need to do things perfectly and be better than others
- pain from the past—their worth can only be found in their achievements
- that unrelenting sacrificial service is honorable before God
- that they must measure up to their own impossible standards
- a constant struggle with pride

Communicate unconditional love and *avoid evaluative remarks*. Initially, affirm the person's inner qualities and the courage to address this issue.

Express empathy about the stress the person is experiencing. Give hope that you will help him or her find a way through the pressure.

The person may be completely unaware as to what is fueling the stress and find little value in self-reflection. You will need to gently encourage him or her to *explore the factors* that are fueling the addictive behavior.

Move the focus from the person and what he or she feels must *be done* to have God's unconditional acceptance. God is more concerned about *who the person is becoming* than what he or she is doing.

God's invitation to the workaholic is to let Him take the burden of his life and give him or her rest in its place (Matt. 11:29).

ACTION STEPS | 5

1. Assess the Problem

- What is causing the stress you feel at work? (*Help the person perceive the problem and own it.*)
- *Help him or her understand that workaholism is an addiction and needs to be treated as such.*

2. Evaluate the Past

- Identify negative messages you received about self-worth from your parents, siblings, and/or peers.
- Your significance is provided through Christ, not through work.

3. Refocus on God

- Take time for daily prayer, Scripture reading, and meditation.
- Seek God's guidance in deciding on the activities for the day.
- Read and meditate on the Scriptures that address God's unconditional love and your identity as a follower of Jesus Christ. (*Be sure to place this activity in the context of a relationship and not just as another job or task.*)

> 28 percent of "workaholic" Americans say they work so hard out of financial necessity.[5]

4. Find Balance

- *Evaluate the activities in his or her weekly schedule and assess which involvements are unnecessary and are contributing to the addiction to activity.*
- There needs to be a balance between time spent at work and time spent in close relationships.
- Work must be maintained in proper relation to God and to family. When this balance is not in place, work can become an idol—a false god that is a terrible taskmaster.
- You will need to "schedule" times for leisure and play. Make sure you treat these times as priorities.
- Remember to honor the Sabbath as a day of rest.

5. Slow Down

- *Help the person establish a slower pace for each day and to seek rest.*
- Be sure to honor the body that God has given you by getting sufficient rest and exercise and by eating a nutritionally balanced diet.
- *Explore ways the counselee can include enjoyable activities in his or her schedule—especially family time.*
- Change takes time, and as you try to slow down, God will take care of the things that concern you (Matt. 6:25–34).

6. Get Support

- Seek help from a counselor, accountability partner, or group where the focus is on coming to terms with the underlying motivations for the addiction to work.

6 | BIBLICAL INSIGHTS

It is vain for you to rise up early, To sit up late, To eat the bread of sorrows; *For so* He gives His beloved sleep.
Psalm 127:2

Then he said to them, "This is *what* the LORD has said: 'Tomorrow *is* a Sabbath rest, a holy Sabbath to the LORD. Bake what you will bake today, and boil what you will boil; and lay up for yourselves all that remains, to be kept until morning.'"

Exodus 16:23

Then King Solomon raised up a labor force out of all Israel; and the labor force was thirty thousand men. And he sent them to Lebanon, ten thousand a month in shifts: they were one month in Lebanon *and* two months at home; Adoniram *was* in charge of the labor force.

1 Kings 5:13–14

Here is what I have seen: *It is* good and fitting *for one* to eat and drink, and to enjoy the good of all his labor in which he toils under the sun all the days of his life which God gives him; for it *is* his heritage.

Ecclesiastes 5:18

7 | PRAYER STARTER

Lord, we know that it is good that we work honestly and diligently, and that work is part of Your plan for us. We know that You are honored through our sincere labor. Lord, as You help us with our tasks and occupations, help us also to honor You with our rest. Give us the wisdom to achieve much needed balance so that we may be still and know that You are God. Free Your precious child here from the destructive pressures of workaholism . . .

RECOMMENDED RESOURCES | 8

Clinton, Tim, and Gary Sibcy. *Why You Do the Things You Do: The Secret to Healthy Relationships*. Thomas Nelson, 2006.

Comer, John Mark. *Garden City: Work, Rest, and the Art of Being Human*. Zondervan, 2017.

Hyatt, Michael, and Megan Hyatt Miller. *Win at Work and Succeed at Life: 5 Principles to Free Yourself from the Cult of Overwork*. Baker Books, 2021.

Keller, Timothy. *Every Good Endeavor: Connecting Your Work to God's Work*. Penguin Books, 2014.

Murray, David. *Reset: Living a Grace-Paced Life in a Burnout Culture*. Crossway, 2017.

Websites

American Association of Christian Counselors (AACC.net)

Christian Care Connect (Connect.AACC.net)

Worry

1 PORTRAITS

- Amy and Don have recently found out they are expecting their first child. As Don lies in bed, he wonders if his income will be enough to support Amy and the child since Amy wants to stay at home, just like her mom did.
- Randy is two hours late getting home from being out with his buddies. His parents are angry with him for not calling, but they are also worried because all they can think is that he must have had car trouble, or worse, an accident.
- Phil joined his department of five employees two years ago. Now they are down to three, and rumor has it that soon they will be down to two.
- Christine is pregnant again. After losing the last baby during the second trimester, she can't help but wonder if this new little miracle will ever have a chance to see this world.

2 DEFINITIONS AND KEY THOUGHTS

- Worry is defined by *Merriam-Webster's* as "mental distress or agitation resulting from concern usually for something impending or anticipated."[1] In other words, worry is about *things that have not happened*. Worry is not an emotion; it is a mental exercise.
- It is natural to be worried or anxious when things are tough or unpredictable or when a solution to a particular problem is not clearly evident. This causes us to worry—*replaying possible outcomes* over and over again in our mind. Sometimes, even when we can see a solution in our mind, we continue to worry, refusing to be satisfied until the solution becomes a reality.
- Being concerned can be positive when it propels us to action—such as seeing a doctor when we are ill or a mechanic when the car sounds strange. But *worry is rarely tied to constructive action and is unproductive*.[2]
- Worry rises to an unhealthy level and *takes its toll* when:[3]
  You're not sleeping.
  You're not productive.
  You're worried about two or more topics more days than not.
  You're focusing on situations of worry more than on the other business of life.
  Your life feels out of control

- Worrying about many things at once can contribute to the development of an *unhealthy level of stress*. Then the stress exhibits itself in an anxiety level that just won't seem to go away.

- Worry is simply a smaller level of fear and *fear is the opposite of faith*. When we operate in fear or worry, then we do not have the faith or trust that God has a plan and is in control.

ASSESSMENT INTERVIEW 3

Sometimes the counselor asks questions not to solicit information but to help the person see things differently. In dealing with worry and anxiety, this might be an appropriate time for such a strategy. The person may be instructed to just think of his or her answers and not necessarily speak them out loud. Of course this depends on what you as the counselor prefer to do based on your expertise or need to delve deeper to help the client process the reasons for worrying.

> Come to me, all you who are weary and burdened, and I will give you rest. Take my yoke upon you and learn from me, for I am gentle and humble in heart, and you will find rest for your souls. For my yoke is easy and my burden is light.
>
> Matthew 11:28-30 NIV

1. What has worried you the most in the past that you no longer worry about?
2. Did these previous situations work out the way you thought they would or did they work out differently than expected?
3. Did the pain of these previous situations help you grow? If so, how?
4. What do you currently worry about the most?
5. Do you think that these problems are too big for God?
6. Do you believe that you are important to God?
7. Will God take care of you in this current situation?
8. There is only one person who can circumvent God's plan for your life. Do you know who that is? (*You.*)
9. Do you have control over whether you worry or not?
10. The Bible says we are not to worry. How can you follow that instruction?
11. What is the worst thing that can happen in this current situation?
12. How has worrying helped you in the past?
13. Do you think that worrying will help you now?
14. What difference will worrying about the situation make one hundred years from now?

WISE COUNSEL 4

The worrier needs to understand that he or she really *does have control* over whether he or she worries or not. Some people are more inclined to worry than others. That isn't a character flaw, it's just a built-in reminder to pray and give it to the Lord.

The counselee *needs a plan* to help keep him or her from unnecessary worry. In the Action Steps, help him or her devise that plan. Pray through a plan; let the counselee allow his or her faith and works to coincide.

While it is easy to simply say, "Don't worry!" it can be difficult to change this pattern of thinking. One approach is to *set limits* so that the worry doesn't continue to rage out of control.

5 | ACTION STEPS

The following plan is designed to help aid the person in changing the way he or she thinks about any issue that seems to bring worry into his or her life.

> An easy life isn't an option; an easy yoke is.
>
> John Mark Comer

1. Start Each Day with God

- Begin each day with time alone with God. Tell Him the concerns of the day (this is your time to pray about your worries—see step 2).
- Anticipate your day. Pray about what's ahead. Ask God to give you peace.

2. Pray about Your Worries

- Set up a specific time period in which you can pray out a plan for your worries.
- Limit worrying to a "worry list," and take that list to the Lord in your daily Bible reading and prayer time.
- During the course of the day, when a worry strikes you, repeat the following sentence: "I will take care of that with God at my prayer time tomorrow morning." If the worry continues, write it down on your "worry list" and continue to remind yourself that it is before God now and it has to stay with Him.
- During prayer time, bring the worrisome situation to God. Ask for guidance and direction.

3. Keep a Journal

- Write down the prayer requests and the worries that you are bringing to God.
- Write down the answers God gives. Go back and read these answers as constant encouragement that any new requests you bring to God will indeed be answered.
- As you talk to God, write down anything you feel He is telling you about your course of action. Keep in mind that the course of action may be purposefully to do nothing until God gives you further direction.

4. Set Boundaries[4]

- Get facts and expert advice to prevent worrying unrealistically about a situation.
- Set deadlines to make decisions, rather than ruminating forever.
- Realize that you will not please everyone all the time.
- Learn to say no.

5. Think Differently[5]

- Delegate chores and other responsibilities.
- Give yourself permission to relax and to make mistakes.
- Eat, sleep, and exercise properly.
- To keep a sense of perspective, try to see the humor in a situation.
- Declutter and organize, using calendars and to-do lists.
- Mentally put your worries in a box with a lid and put them on the top shelf of your closet. No peeking!

6. Seek Balance

- The goal is to walk in peace, in calm, in trust, and in assurance. This is done by finding the balance between prayer and action and, ultimately, this produces freedom from worry.[6]

> Peace I leave with you; my peace I give you. I do not give to you as the world gives. Do not let your hearts be troubled and do not be afraid.
>
> John 14:27 NIV

BIBLICAL INSIGHTS | 6

And when Pharaoh drew near, the children of Israel lifted their eyes, and behold, the Egyptians marched after them. So they were very afraid, and the children of Israel cried out to the Lord.

Exodus 14:10

Therefore do not worry about tomorrow, for tomorrow will worry about its own things. Sufficient for the day *is* its own trouble.

Matthew 6:34

Then He said to His disciples, "Therefore I say to you, do not worry about your life, what you will eat; nor about the body, what you will put on. Life is more than food, and the body *is more* than clothing."

Luke 12:22–23

For God has not given us a spirit of fear, but of power and of love and of a sound mind.

2 Timothy 1:7

> The next time you fear the future, rejoice in the Lord's sovereignty. Rejoice in what he has accomplished. Rejoice that he is able to do what you cannot do. Fill your mind with thoughts of God.
>
> Max Lucado

PRAYER STARTER | 7

Worry is immobilizing Your child today, Lord. We know that we don't know the future, and You do. We know that we need to trust You, so we bring our worries to You today, Lord, like a burden we cannot carry, and we ask that You take him [her] . . .

8 | RECOMMENDED RESOURCES

Burton, Valorie. *Brave Enough to Succeed: 40 Strategies for Getting Unstuck*. Harvest House, 2017.

Jantz, Gregory L., and Ann McMurray. *Overcoming Anxiety, Worry, and Fear*. Revell, 2016.

Simpson, Amy. *Anxious: Choosing Faith in a World of Worry*. IVP Books, 2014.

Thompson, Becky. *Peace: Hope and Healing for the Anxious Momma's Heart*. Water-Brook, 2020.

Welch, Ed. *When I Am Afraid: A Step-by-Step Guide Away from Fear and Anxiety*. New Growth Press, 2008.

Websites

American Association of Christian Counselors (AACC.net)

Christian Care Connect (Connect.AACC.net)

Acknowledgments

Dr. Hawkins and I would like to say a special thank you to all involved in helping build a resource that we pray will be used by Christian leaders and people helpers all over the world to foster hope and healing for those who are hurting.

A note of deep appreciation goes to Robert Hosack at Baker Books for believing in the project, to Brian Vos for making the second edition possible, and to Robin Turici for her time in editing.

Likewise, we extend sincere gratitude to our AACC team who helped in the writing, editing, and research for this project:

Zach Clinton, MA
Mercy Connors, PhD
Jennifer Cisney Ellers, MA
Dina Jones, MA

Our special appreciation to Pat Springle and Kyle Sutton for their leadership and attention to detail on this project. We are grateful for your gifts and participation to contribute to a valuable resource for the entire Christian counseling community.

We would also like to thank our wives, Julie and Peggy, and our families, for their love and support through the years. We could not enter into the work we do without you.

And to the entire AACC team led by CEO Ben Allison and tens of thousands of pastors and Christian counselors who are literally entering into the darkness of the lives of hurting people, may this resource help you bring the light and hope of Jesus in every situation. To you we dedicate this series.

Notes

Introduction

1. T. Clinton and G. Ohlschlager, *Competent Christian Counseling* (Colorado Springs: Water-Brook Press, 2002), 54.

Abortion

1. R. K. Jones and J. Jerman, "Population Group Abortion Rates and Lifetime Incidence of Abortion: United States, 2008–2014," *American Journal of Public Health* 107, no. 12 (December 2017): 1904–9.
2. Y. Florczak-Seeman, *A Time to Speak: A Healing Journal for Post-Abortive Women* (Clarendon Hills, IL: Love From Above, 2005).
3. R. K. Jones, E. Witwer, and J. Jerman, *Abortion Incidence and Service Availability in the United States, 2017* (New York: Guttmacher Institute, 2019), https://www.guttmacher.org/report/abortion-incidence-service-availability-us-2017.
4. Jones, Witwer, and Jerman, *Abortion Incidence.*
5. Jones, Witwer, and Jerman, *Abortion Incidence.*
6. K. L. Moore and T. V. N. Persaud, *The Developing Human: Clinically Oriented Embryology* (Philadelphia: W. B. Saunders Co., 1998), 350–58.
7. Moore and Persaud, *Developing Human.*

Addictions

1. National Drug Intelligence Center, The Economic Impact of Illicit Drug Use on American Society, United States Department of Justice, 2011.
2. "The Science of Drug Use and Addiction: The Basics," NIDA, accessed November 19, 2020, https://www.drugabuse.gov/publications/media-guide/science-drug-use-addiction-basics.
3. "The Science of Drug Use and Addiction."
4. "What Is a Substance Use Disorder?," American Psychiatric Association, December 2020, https://www.psychiatry.org/patients-families/addiction/what-is-addiction.
5. "What Is a Substance Use Disorder?"
6. "What Is a Substance Use Disorder?"
7. "What Is a Substance Use Disorder?"
8. "What Is a Substance Use Disorder?"
9. "U.S. Drug Overdose Deaths Continue to Rise; Increase Fueled by Synthetic Opioids," Centers for Disease Control and Prevention, March 29, 2018, https://www.cdc.gov/media/releases/2018/p0329-drug-overdose-deaths.html.
10. "Drug Misuse and Addiction," NIDA, July 13, 2020, https://www.drugabuse.gov/publications/drugs-brains-behavior-science-addiction/drug-misuse-addiction.
11. "Drug Misuse and Addiction."
12. Substance Abuse and Mental Health Services Administration and Office of the Surgeon General, *Facing Addiction in America: The Surgeon General's Report on Alcohol, Drugs, and Health* (Washington, DC: HHS, November 2016).

13. S. Ross and E. Peselow, "Co-Occurring Psychotic and Addictive Disorders: Neurobiology and Diagnosis," *Clin Neuropharmacol* 35, no. 5 (Sept–Oct 2012): 235–43.

14. "Alcohol Use," Centers for Disease Control and Prevention, January 21, 2021, https://www.cdc.gov/nchs/fastats/alcohol.htm.

15. "Illicit Drug Use," Centers for Disease Control and Prevention, January 21, 2021, https://www.cdc.gov/nchs/fastats/drug-use-illicit.htm.

Adultery

1. D. Carder, "Adultery," in *Soul Care Bible*, ed. T. Clinton (Nashville: Thomas Nelson, 2001), 1128–29.

2. "Infidelity," American Association for Marriage and Family Therapy, updated July 2016, https://www.aamft.org/Consumer_Updates/Infidelity.aspx.

3. Carder, "Adultery."

4. Carder, "Adultery."

5. Carder, "Adultery."

6. Adapted from D. Kessler and E. Kübler-Ross, *On Grief and Grieving: Finding the Meaning of Grief through the Five Stages of Loss* (New York: Scribner, 2007), 7–24.

Aging

1. U.S. Department of Health and Human Services and Administration on Aging, Older Adults and Mental Health: Issues and Opportunities (Washington, DC: HHS, 2001), https://www.cdc.gov/aging/pdf/mental_health.pdf.

2. G. Bergen, M. R. Stevens, and E. R. Burns, "Falls and Fall Injuries Among Adults Aged ≥65 Years—United States," *Morbidity and Mortality Weekly Report* 65 (September 2016): 993–98.

3. "Depression and Older Adults," National Institute on Aging, content reviewed July 7, 2021, https://www.nia.nih.gov/health/depression-and-older-adults.

Anger

1. Gallup, "World Unhappier, More Stressed Out Than Ever," June 28, 2022, https://news.gallup.com/poll/394025/world-unhappier-stressed-ever.aspx.

Burnout

1. H. B. London, "Burnout," in *Soul Care Bible*, ed. T. Clinton (Nashville: Thomas Nelson, 2001), 920–21.

2. "Workplace Stress Continues to Rise," Korn Ferry, accessed November 20, 2023, https://www.kornferry.com/insights/articles/workplace-stress-motivation.

3. London, "Burnout."

4. London, "Burnout."

5. London, "Burnout."

Death

1. Kroll, "Finally Home," in *Soul Care Bible*, ed. T. Clinton (Nashville: Thomas Nelson, 2001), 500–501.

2. Kroll, "Finally Home," 500–501.

3. Kroll, "Finally Home," 500–501.

4. D. Kessler and E. Kübler-Ross, *On Grief and Grieving: Finding the Meaning of Grief through the Five Stages of Loss* (New York: Scribner, 2007), 8.

5. Kessler and Kübler-Ross, *On Grief and Grieving*, 11.

6. Kessler and Kübler-Ross, *On Grief and Grieving*, 17.

7. Kessler and Kübler-Ross, *On Grief and Grieving*, 20.

8. Kessler and Kübler-Ross, *On Grief and Grieving*, 24.

9. T. C. Antonucci, H. Akiyama, and K. Takahashi, "Attachment and Close Relationships across the Life Span," *Attach Hum Dev* 6, no. 4 (December 2004): 353–70, https://pubmed.ncbi.nlm.nih.gov/15764124/.

Decision-Making and the Will of God

1. This section is adapted from C. Swindoll, "Decision Making and the Will of God," in *Soul Care Bible*, ed. T. Clinton (Nashville: Thomas Nelson, 2001), 1484–85.

Depression

1. National Institute of Mental Health, "Major Depression," last updated July 2023, https://www.nimh.nih.gov/health/statistics/major-depression.shtml.
2. National Institute of Mental Health, "Depression" last updated September 2023, https://www.nimh.nih.gov/health/topics/depression/index.shtml.
3. National Institute of Mental Health, "Depression."
4. M. Lyles, "The Valley of Depression" in *Soul Care Bible*, ed. T. Clinton (Nashville: Thomas Nelson, 2001), 780–81.
5. M. Lyles, "Valley of Depression."
6. National Institute of Mental Health, "Major Depression."
7. National Institute of Mental Health, "Major Depression."
8. National Institute of Mental Health, "Major Depression."

Discouragement

1. J. Cheydleur, "Overcoming Discouragement," in *Soul Care Bible*, ed. T. Clinton (Nashville: Thomas Nelson, 2001), 266–77.
2. Cheydleur, "Overcoming Discouragement."

Divorce

1. "50+ Divorce Statistics in the U.S., Including Divorce Rate, Race, & Marriage Length," Divorce.com, updated January 6, 2024, https://divorce.com/blog/divorce-statistics/#:~:text=The%20divorce%20rate%20regarding%20second,once%20compared%20to%20all%20adults.
2. "The Connected Generation," Barna Research, September 26, 2019, https://marriedpeoplechurches.org/author/barna/.
3. "The Connected Generation," Barna Research.
4. "The Trends Redefining Romance Today," The Barna Group, February 9, 2017, https://www.barna.com/research/trends-redefining-romance-today/.

Domestic Violence

1. S. G. Smith et al., *The National Intimate Partner and Sexual Violence Survey (NISVS): 2015 Data Brief—Updated Release* (Atlanta, GA: National Center for Injury Prevention and Control, Centers for Disease Control and Prevention, 2018), 11.
2. "Domestic Violence," United States Department of Justice Office on Violence Against Women, updated December 6, 2023, https://www.justice.gov/ovw/domestic-violence#dv.
3. Smith et al., *Sexual Violence Survey*, 2.
4. "Violence Prevention," Centers for Disease Control and Prevention, reviewed October 11, 2022, https://www.cdc.gov/violenceprevention/intimatepartnerviolence/fastfact.html.
5. Smith et al., *Sexual Violence Survey*, 4.
6. Smith et al., *The National Intimate Partner and Sexual Violence Survey (NISVS): 2010–2012 State Report* (Atlanta, GA: National Center for Injury Prevention and Control, Centers for Disease Control and Prevention, 2017), 1.
7. "Violence Prevention."
8. S. P. Jack, E. Petrosky, and B. H. Lyons, "Surveillance for Violent Deaths—National Violent Death Reporting System, 27 States, 2015," Morbidity and Mortality Weekly Report Surveillance Summaries 67 (September 28, 2018): 1–32.

Eating Disorders

1. "The Social and Economic Cost of Eating Disorders in the United States of America: A Report for the Strategic Training Initiative for the Prevention of Eating Disorders and the Academy for Eating Disorders," Deloitte Access Economics, June 2020, https://www.hsph.harvard.edu/striped/report-economic-costs-of-eating-disorders/.

2. "Eating Disorders: About More Than Food," National Institute of Mental Health, last updated 2021, https://www.nimh.nih.gov/health/publications/eating-disorders/index.shtml.

3. "Social and Economic Cost."

4. "Eating Disorders."

5. "Eating Disorders."

6. "Social and Economic Cost."

7. "Social and Economic Cost."

8. "Social and Economic Cost."

9. "Social and Economic Cost."

10. "Social and Economic Cost."

Envy and Jealousy

1. T. Clinton, "Jealousy: A Consuming Passion," in *Soul Care Bible*, ed. T. Clinton (Nashville: Thomas Nelson, 2001), 1656–57.

2. Clinton, "Jealousy."

3. Clinton, "Jealousy."

4. Clinton, "Jealousy."

5. Clinton, "Jealousy."

6. A. Summerville and N. J. Roese, "Dare to Compare: Fact-Based versus Simulation-Based Comparison in Daily Life," *Journal of Experimental Social Psychology* 44, no. 3 (2008): 664–71.

7. Clinton, "Jealousy."

Fear and Anxiety

1. Harvard Medical School, National Comorbidity Survey (NCS) Table 2, updated July 19, 2007, https://www.hcp.med.harvard.edu/ncs/index.php.

2. A. Hart, "Understanding Anxiety," in *Soul Care Bible*, ed. T. Clinton (Nashville: Thomas Nelson, 2001), 1568–69.

3. H. E. LeWine, "Phobia," Harvard Health Publishing, March 9, 2022, https://www.health.harvard.edu/a_to_z/phobia-a-to-z.

4. LeWine, "Phobia."

5. "Panic Disorders," National Institute of Mental Health, revised 2022, https://www.nimh.nih.gov/health/publications/panic-disorder-when-fear-overwhelms/index.shtml.

6. Harvard Medical School, NCS Table 1, updated July 19, 2007.

Forgiveness

1. E. Worthington, "Forgiveness," in *Soul Care Bible*, ed. T. Clinton (Nashville: Thomas Nelson, 2001), 1520–21.

2. "Fetzer Survey on Love and Forgiveness in American Society," Fetzer Institute, accessed January 3, 2024, https://fetzer.org/resources/fetzer-survey-love-and-forgiveness-american-society.

3. Worthington, "Forgiveness."

4. Worthington, "Forgiveness."

5. Worthington, "Forgiveness."

6. Worthington, "Forgiveness."

Grief and Loss

1. H. Wright, "Dealing with Loss and Grief," in *Soul Care Bible*, ed. T. Clinton (Nashville: Thomas Nelson, 2001), 940–41.

2. E. Kübler-Ross, *On Death and Dying* (New York: Simon & Schuster, 2014).

3. Wright, "Dealing with Loss and Grief."

4. Wright, "Dealing with Loss and Grief."

5. Wright, "Dealing with Loss and Grief."

Guilt

1. L. Parrott, "Dealing with Guilt," in *Soul Care Bible*, ed. T. Clinton (Nashville: Thomas Nelson, 2001), 600–601.

2. Parrott, "Dealing with Guilt."

3. Parrott, "Dealing with Guilt."
4. Parrott, "Dealing with Guilt."
5. Parrott, "Dealing with Guilt."
6. Parrott, "Dealing with Guilt."

Homosexuality

1. J. Dallas, "Understanding and Addressing Homosexuality," in *Soul Care Bible*, ed. T. Clinton (Nashville: Thomas Nelson, 2001), 1466–67.
2. "Answers to Your Questions: For a Better Understanding of Sexual Orientation and Homosexuality," American Psychological Association, https://www.apa.org/topics/lgbtq/orientation.pdf.
3. Dallas, "Understanding and Addressing Homosexuality."
4. Dallas, "Understanding and Addressing Homosexuality."
5. Dallas, "Understanding and Addressing Homosexuality."
6. Dallas, "Understanding and Addressing Homosexuality."
7. Dallas, "Understanding and Addressing Homosexuality."

Loneliness

1. M. S. Parent, "Loneliness and Personal Growth," in *Soul Care Bible*, ed. T. Clinton (Nashville: Thomas Nelson, 2001), 734–35.
2. Parent, "Loneliness and Personal Growth."
3. Parent, "Loneliness and Personal Growth."
4. Parent, "Loneliness and Personal Growth."
5. "Cigna Takes Action to Combat the Rise of Loneliness and Improve Mental Wellness in America," Cigna Healthcare, January 23, 2020, https://www.cigna.com/about-us/newsroom/news-and-views/press-releases/2020/cigna-takes-action-to-combat-the-rise-of-loneliness-and-improve-mental-wellness-in-america.
6. Parent, "Loneliness and Personal Growth."
7. National Academies of Sciences, *Engineering, and Medicine, Social Isolation and Loneliness in Older Adults: Opportunities for the Health Care System* (Washington, DC: The National Academies Press, 2020), https://doi.org/10.17226 /25663.

Mental Illness

1. Substance Abuse and Mental Health Services Administration (SAMHSA), "Key Substance Use and Mental Health Indicators in the United States: Results from the 2019 National Survey on Drug Use and Health" (Rockville, MD: Center for Behavioral Health Statistics and Quality, 2020), https://www.samhsa.gov/data/.
2. National Alliance on Mental Illness, "Mental Health Conditions," https://www.nami.org/learn-more/mental-health-conditions.
3. SAMHSA, "Key Substance Use and Mental Health Indicators."
4. SAMHSA, "Key Substance Use and Mental Health Indicators."
5. "Mental Illness," National Institute of Mental Health, last updated March 2023, https://www.nimh.nih.gov/health/statistics/mental-illness.shtml.
6. "Mental Health," U.S. Centers for Disease Control and Prevention, January 26, 2018, https://www.cdc.gov/mentalhealth/learn/index.htm.
7. "About Mental Health," Centers for Disease Control and Prevention, accessed February 9, 2024, https://www.cdc.gov/mentalhealth/learn/index.htm.
8. The material in this section is adapted from "Warning Signs and Symptoms," National Alliance on Mental Illness, https://www.nami.org/About-Mental-Illness/Warning-Signs-and-Symptoms.
9. T. Clinton, P. Meier, and G. Ohlschlager, "Mental Illness: Reducing Suffering in the Church," in *Soul Care Bible*, ed. T. Clinton (Nashville: Thomas Nelson, 2001), 364–65.
10. Clinton, Meier, and Ohlschlager, "Mental Illness."
11. Clinton, Meier, and Ohlschlager, "Mental Illness."
12. D. G. Whitney and M. D. Peterson, "US National and State-Level Prevalence of Mental Health Disorders and Disparities of Mental Health Care Use in Children," *JAMA Pediatrics* 173, no. 4 (2019): 389–91, doi:10.1001/jamapediatrics.2018.5399.
13. P. S. Wang et al., "Delays in Initial Treatment Contact after First Onset of a Mental Disorder," *Health Services Research* 39, no. 2 (2004): 393–415.

14. "Anxiety Disorders," National Alliance on Mental Illness, December 2017, https://www.nami.org/About-Mental-Illness/Mental-Health-Conditions/Anxiety-Disorders.

15. "About Multiple Causes of Death, 2018–2021, Single Race," CDC Wonder, January 11, 2024, http://wonder.cdc.gov/mcd-icd10-expanded.html.

Money and Financial Hardship

1. R. Blue, "Mastering Your Money," in *Soul Care Bible*, ed. T. Clinton (Nashville: Thomas Nelson, 2001), 480–81.

2. Blue, "Mastering Your Money."

3. L. Knueven, "The Average American Debt by Type, Age, and State," *Business Insider*, August 3, 2020, https://www.businessinsider.com/personal-finance/average-american-debt.

4. Board of Governors of the Federal Reserve System, "Consumer Credit," https://www.federalreserve.gov/releases/g19/current/default.htm.

5. A. White, "73% of Americans Rank Their Finances as the No. 1 Stress in Life, According to New Capital One CreditWise Survey," CNBC Select, February 1, 2021, https://www.cnbc.com/select/73-percent-of-americans-rank-finances-as-the-number-one-stress-in-life/.

Pain and Chronic Pain

1. C. E. Zelaya et al., "Chronic Pain and High-Impact Chronic Pain among U.S. Adults, 2019," NCHS Data Brief, no. 390 (Hyattsville, MD: National Center for Health Statistics, 2020).

2. Richard L. Nahin, "Estimates of Pain Prevalence and Severity in Adults: United States, 2012," *The Journal of Pain* 16, no. 8 (May 28, 2015): 769–80, https://www.jpain.org/article/S1526-5900(15)00679-3/fulltext.

3. Brooke E. Hoots et al., "2018 Annual Surveillance Report," Centers for Disease Control and Prevention, August 31, 2018, 7, https://www.cdc.gov/drugoverdose/pdf/pubs/2018-cdc-drug-surveillance-report.pdf.

4. Zelaya et al., "Chronic Pain."

Parenting

1. U.S. Census Bureau, "America's Families and Living Arrangements: 2020," Table C8, last updated November 22, 2021, https://www.census.gov/data/tables/2020/demo/families/cps-2020.html.

2. U.S. Census Bureau, "America's Families," Table C8.

3. The Hartman Group, "Desires, Barriers and Directions for Shared Meals at Home," June 2017, https://www.fmi.org/docs/default-source/familymeals/fmi-power-of-family-meals-whitepaper-for-web.pdf?sfvrsn=13d87f6e_2.

Perfectionism

1. N. Soreni et al., "Dimensions of Perfectionism in Children and Adolescents with Obsessive-Compulsive Disorder," *Journal of the Canadian Academy of Child and Adolescent Psychiatry* 23, no. 2 (2014): 136–43.

2. C. Thurman, "Perfectionism," in *Soul Care Bible*, ed. T. Clinton (Nashville: Thomas Nelson, 2001), 1630–31.

Pornography

1. Joe Carter, "9 Things You Should Know About Pornography and the Brain," The Gospel Coalition, May 8, 2013, https://www.thegospelcoalition.org/article/9-things-you-should-know-about-pornography-and-the-brain/.

2. Proven Men, "Porn Survey" (2014), https://www.provenmen.org/2014pornsurvey/.

3. Proven Men, "Porn Survey."

4. Covenant Eyes, "Pornography Statistics" (2018), https://www.covenanteyes.com/pornstats/.

5. Covenant Eyes, "Pornography Statistics."

Prejudice

1. J. E. Helms, G. Nicolas, and C. E. Green, "Racism and Ethnoviolence as Trauma: Enhancing Professional Training," *Traumatology* 16 no. 4 (2010): 53–62.

2. Material in this section is adapted from S. Black and P. Finner-Williams, "A Christian Response to Prejudice," in *Soul Care Bible*, ed. T. Clinton (Nashville: Thomas Nelson, 2001), 1646–47.

3. Black and Finner-Williams, "A Christian Response to Prejudice."

4. S. L. Colby and J. M. Ortman, "Projections of the Size and Composition of the U.S. Population: 2014 to 2060," US Census Bureau Current Population Reports, March 2015, https://www.census.gov /content/dam/Census/library/publications/2015/demo/p25-1143.pdf.

5. "Mental Health Disparities: Diverse Populations," American Psychiatric Association, December 19, 2017, https://www.psychiatry.org/File%20Library/Psychiatrists/Cultural-Competency/Mental -Health-Disparities/Mental-Health-Facts-for-Diverse-Populations.pdf.

6. "Mental Health Disparities."

7. "Mental Health Disparities."

Premarital Sex

1. Barna Research, "The Trends Redefining Romance Today," February 9, 2017, https://www .barna.com/research/trends-redefining-romance-today/.

2. Barna Research, "What Americans Believe About Sex," January 14, 2016, https://www.barna .com/research/what-americans-believe-about-sex/.

3. American Association of Christian Counselors, "2023 AACC Code of Ethics," AACC Law and Ethics Committee, https://aacc.net/wp-content/uploads/2023/10/AACC_Code-of-Ethics-2023 _FINAL.pdf.

Self-Esteem

1. A. Hart, "Scripture's View of Self-Esteem," in *Soul Care Bible*, ed. T. Clinton (Nashville: Thomas Nelson, 2001), 960–61.

2. Hart, "Scripture's View of Self-Esteem."

Sexual Abuse in Childhood

1. Children's Bureau, "Child Maltreatment 2016," U.S. Department of Health and Human Services, https://www.acf.hhs.gov/sites/default/files/documents/cb/cm2016.pdf, 9–10.

2. D. Langberg, "Hope for Healing," in *Soul Care Bible*, ed. T. Clinton (Nashville: Thomas Nelson, 2001), 328–29.

3. D. Finkelhor et al., "The Lifetime Prevalence of Child Sexual Abuse and Sexual Assault Assessed in Late Adolescence," *Journal of Adolescent Health* 55 no. 3 (2014): 329–33.

4. H. M. Zinzow et al., "Prevalence and Risk of Psychiatric Disorders as a Function of Variant Rape Histories: Results from a National Survey of Women," *Social Psychiatry and Psychiatric Epidemiology* 47, no. 6 (2012): 893–902.

5. L. A. Greenfeld, "Sex Offenses and Offenders," U.S. Department of Justice Bureau of Justice Statistics, February 1997, 2, https://www.rainn.org/images/get-information/Legal-Information /punishing-rapists/usdoj-sex-offenders-study.pdf.

Singleness

1. A. Corry, "Singleness," in *Soul Care Bible*, ed. T. Clinton (Nashville: Thomas Nelson, 2001), 1262–63.

2. Corry, "Singleness."

3. Corry, "Singleness."

4. Corry, "Singleness."

Spiritual Warfare

1. D. Powlison, "Spiritual Warfare," in *Soul Care Bible*, ed. T. Clinton (Nashville: Thomas Nelson, 2001), 1560–61.

Stress

1. "5 Things You Should Know About Stress," National Institute of Mental Health, https://www .jber.jb.mil/Portals/144/Services-Resources/Resiliency-Resources/PDF/SelfCareTipSheets/5-things -stress.pdf.

2. "5 Things You Should Know About Stress."

3. "Stress in America 2020: A National Mental Health Crisis," American Psychological Association, https://www.apa.org/news/press/releases/stress/2020/sia-mental-health-crisis.pdf, 2.

4. L. Vernick, "Stress Management," in *Soul Care Bible*, ed. T. Clinton (Nashville: Thomas Nelson, 2001), 422–23.

5. "Workplace Stress Continues to Rise," Korn Ferry, accessed January 4, 2024, https://www.kornferry.com/insights/articles/workplace-stress-motivation.

6. Vernick, "Stress Management."

7. Vernick, "Stress Management."

8. Vernick, "Stress Management."

9. Vernick, "Stress Management."

10. Vernick, "Stress Management."

11. M. Ashworth, "How Does Stress Affect Us?," PsychCentral, May 17, 2017, https://psychcentral.com/lib/how-does-stress-affect-us#1.

Suffering

1. D. Allender, "Suffering and Glory," in *Soul Care Bible*, ed. T. Clinton (Nashville: Thomas Nelson, 2001), 646–47.

Suicide

1. G. Stewart, "Choose Life," in *Soul Care Bible*, ed. T. Clinton (Nashville: Thomas Nelson, 2001), 322–23.

2. Stewart, "Choose Life."

3. Material in this section is adapted from "Suicide Prevention: Risk and Protective Factors," Centers for Disease Control and Prevention, last reviewed November 2, 2022, https://www.cdc.gov/suicide/factors/index.html.

4. Center for Disease Control and Prevention, "Facts about Suicide," reviewed May 8, 2023, https://www.cdc.gov/suicide/facts/index.html.

5. "About Multiple Cause of Death, 2018–2021, Single Race," Centers for Disease Control and Prevention, accessed February 9, 2024, https://wonder.cdc.gov/mcd-icd10-expanded.html.

6. "About Multiple Cause of Death, 2018–2021, Single Race."

7. D. Owens, J. Horrocks, and A. House, "Fatal and Non-Fatal Repetition of Self-harm," *British Journal of Psychiatry* 181, no. 3 (September 2002): 193–99.

8. SAMHSA, "2021 NSDUH Annual National Report," National Survey on Drug Use and Health, January 2, 2023, https://www.samhsa.gov/data/report/2021-nsduh-annual-national-report.

Trauma

1. "Trauma," American Psychological Association, last updated October 2023, https://www.apa.org/topics/trauma.

2. "Coping with Traumatic Events," National Institute of Mental Health, last reviewed May 2023, https://www.nimh.nih.gov/health/topics/coping-with-traumatic-events/index.shtml.

3. W. E. Copeland et al., "Traumatic Events and Posttraumatic Stress in Childhood," *Archives of General Psychiatry* 64 no. 5 (2007): 577–84.

4. Material in this section is drawn from "Coping with Traumatic Events."

5. "Coping with Traumatic Events."

6. Save the Children, "What Are You Waiting For? 2014 National Report Card on Protecting Children in Disasters," https://www.savethechildren.org/content/dam/usa/reports/emergency-prep/disaster-report-2014.pdf.

7. M. Laaser, "Healing the Wounds that Bind You," in *Soul Care Bible*, ed. T. Clinton (Nashville: Thomas Nelson, 2001), 690–91.

8. Laaser, "Healing the Wounds."

9. "How Common Is PTSD in Adults?," U.S. Department of Veteran Affairs, last updated February 3, 2023, https://www.ptsd.va.gov/understand/common/common_adults.asp.

10. "How Common Is PTSD in Veterans?," U.S. Department of Veteran Affairs, last updated February 3, 2023, https://www.ptsd.va.gov/understand/common/common_veterans.asp#:~:text=At%20some%20point%20in%20their,of%20100%2C%20or%206%25).

Workaholism

1. The material in this section is adapted from T. Clinton and G. Ohlschlager, "The World of Work," in *Soul Care Bible*, ed. T. Clinton (Nashville: Thomas Nelson, 2001), 1588–89.

2. "Survey: Half of Americans Consider Themselves Modern-Day Workaholics," StudyFinds, February 5, 2019, https://studyfinds.org/survey-half-americans-consider-themselves-modern-day -workaholics/.

3. Tyler Schmall, "Almost Half of Americans Consider Themselves 'Workaholics,'" *New York Post*, February 1, 2019, https://nypost.com/2019/02/01/almost-half-of-americans-consider-themselves -workaholics/.

4. "The World of Work," in *Soul Care Bible*, ed. T. Clinton (Nashville: Thomas Nelson, 2001), 1590–91.

5. Schmall, "Almost Half of Americans."

Worry

1. *Merriam-Webster's*, s.v. "worry (*n.*)," accessed March 8, 2021, https://www.merriam-webster .com/dictionary/worry.

2. R. S. Hughes, "Worry or Pray: You Choose," in *Soul Care Bible*, ed. T. Clinton (Nashville: Thomas Nelson, 2001), 1340–41.

3. Hughes, "Worry or Pray."

4. Hughes, "Worry or Pray."

5. Hughes, "Worry or Pray."

6. Hughes, "Worry or Pray."

DR. TIM CLINTON is president of the American Association of Christian Counselors (AACC), the largest and most diverse Christian counseling association in the world. He also serves as executive director of the Global Center for Mental Health, Addiction, and Recovery and is Professor Emeritus at Liberty University. Licensed as a professional counselor and as a marriage and family therapist, Dr. Clinton is recognized as a world leader in mental health and relationship issues and spends much of his time working with Christian leaders and professional athletes.

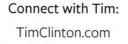

Connect with Tim:

TimClinton.com

   @DrTimClinton

DR. RON HAWKINS is a licensed professional counselor and serves on the executive board of the AACC. He served as Provost and Chief Academic Officer for Liberty University until his recent retirement. He also served as the founding Dean of the School of Behavioral Sciences at Liberty.